Infrastructure as Code with Pulumi

Streamlining Cloud Deployments Using Code

Adora Nwodo

‹packt›

Infrastructure as Code with Pulumi

Portfolio Director: Kartikey Pandey
Relationship Lead: Aaron Tanna
Project Manager: Sonam Pandey
Content Engineer: Sarada Biswas
Technical Editor: Simran Ali
Copy Editor: Safis Editing
Indexer: Rekha Nair
Proofreader: Sarada Biswas
Production Designer: Shankar Kalbhor
Growth Lead: Amit Ramadas

First published: September 2025

Production reference: 1260825

Published by Packt Publishing Ltd.
Grosvenor House
11 St Paul's Square
Birmingham
B3 1RB, UK.

ISBN 978-1-83546-752-7

www.packtpub.com

I dedicate this to my mother, who gave me roots and the courage to grow wings.

— Adora Nwodo

Contributors

About the author

Adora Nwodo is a multi-award-winning Engineering Manager, Author, and Educator advancing cloud-native platforms, developer experience, and AI infrastructure. She has written seven books on cloud technologies and AI, taught widely accessed technical courses, and delivered over 200 talks globally. Her work is used in academic and professional settings worldwide, and she is passionate about creating opportunities for the next generation of technologists. Recognized internationally for her impact, Adora continues to shape the future of technology through engineering, teaching, and storytelling.

About the reviewer

Trenton VanderWert is a Cloud Native Consulting Architect with deep expertise in Kubernetes, DevOps, and Infrastructure as Code (IaC). He has implemented modern IaC solutions to help organizations across fintech, healthcare, manufacturing, and banking modernize and scale their platforms. Skilled in Rust, Go, Python, and automation frameworks, Trenton focuses on accelerating developer productivity, improving security, and building resilient, high-performance cloud environments. Passionate about bridging strategy and execution, he empowers teams to innovate confidently in an ever-evolving cloud landscape.

Table of Contents

Chapter 2: Creating Your First Pulumi IaC

Chapter 10: Managing Multi-Cloud and Hybrid Scenarios   197

Chapter 15: Migrating from Other Tools to Pulumi   305

Chapter 16: Tests and Exercises on Infrastructure Automation with Pulumi   321

Preface

In the past, setting up cloud infrastructure often meant clicking through endless dashboards, running manual scripts, and hoping everything was configured the same way the next time you needed it. Over time, that approach stopped keeping up with the speed and complexity of modern systems. Teams needed something more reliable, more repeatable, and easier to scale.

That is where Infrastructure as Code (IaC) comes in. By defining infrastructure in code, teams can version, review, and automate the environments their applications depend on. Pulumi takes this idea further by letting you write infrastructure in the same programming languages you already use for application development, bringing both worlds together in a way that feels natural and flexible.

This book is here to help you make that shift. We will start with the basics of IaC and Pulumi's core ideas, then move into hands-on deployments across AWS, Azure, Google Cloud, and Kubernetes. You will learn how to integrate Pulumi into CI/CD pipelines, work across multiple regions and providers, and take advantage of the rich provider ecosystem that extends Pulumi far beyond the major clouds.

Later, we will explore advanced features, proven practices for writing clean and maintainable infrastructure code, and ways to enforce governance with Policy as Code. You will also learn how to migrate from other tools and put your skills to the test with real world style exercises.

Each chapter mixes clear explanations with practical examples so you can apply what you learn immediately. The aim is to give you both the knowledge and the confidence to automate infrastructure for anything from a small proof of concept to a complex multi cloud production system.

Who this book is for

This book is for DevOps engineers, cloud engineers, site reliability engineers, infrastructure engineers, and platform engineers who want to explore new ways of managing infrastructure using Pulumi as a modern alternative to traditional infrastructure as code tools. It is also for software engineers at any experience level who want to expand their skills into infrastructure engineering. Basic familiarity with cloud concepts and at least one programming language will help you get the most out of this book.

What this book covers

Chapter 1, Introduction to Infrastructure as Code and Pulumi, provides an understanding of Infrastructure as Code (IaC) and how Pulumi enables managing cloud resources through code, covering core concepts, principles, and essential CLI workflows.

Chapter 2, Creating Your First Pulumi IaC, guides readers through the hands-on process of building their first infrastructure as code project using Pulumi.

Chapter 3, Deploying with Pulumi on AWS, guides readers through using Pulumi to deploy and manage infrastructure on Amazon Web Services.

Chapter 4, Deploying with Pulumi on Azure, introduces readers to deploying and managing infrastructure on Microsoft Azure using Pulumi.

Chapter 5, Deploying with Pulumi on Google Cloud, introduces readers to deploying and managing infrastructure on Google Cloud using Pulumi.

Chapter 6, Deploying with Pulumi on Kubernetes, covers managing Kubernetes clusters and workloads with Pulumi, including environment setup, resource deployment, configuration best practices, scaling, and high availability.

Chapter 7, Integrating Pulumi with CI/CD Pipelines, explains how to integrate Pulumi with CI/CD pipelines to automate infrastructure deployment, covering workflow setup, secrets management, rollback strategies, and pipeline security best practices.

Chapter 8, Exploring Pulumi's Provider Ecosystem, explores Pulumi's support for multiple cloud and service providers, detailing provider setup, resource management, and cross-provider integration for unified infrastructure control.

Chapter 9, Managing your IaC in Multiple Regions and Environments, covers best practices for multi-region and multi-environment infrastructure management with Pulumi, including environment-specific configurations, resource isolation, and staging workflows.

Chapter 10, Managing Multi-Cloud and Hybrid Scenarios, explores multi-cloud and hybrid infrastructure orchestration with Pulumi, covering benefits, challenges, and best practices for networking, data integration, and security across platforms.

Chapter 11, Advanced Pulumi Features, explores the advanced capabilities of Pulumi, including the Pulumi ESC (Environments, Secrets, and Configuration), Pulumi AI and Automation API.

Chapter 12, Writing Maintainable, Testable, and Scalable Code in Pulumi, applies programming paradigms and design principles to Pulumi IaC, emphasizing modularity, reusability, and best practices for project structure, naming, and documentation.

Chapter 13, Testing and Debugging Your Pulumi IaC, talks about the importance of testing your Pulumi Infrastructure as Code (IaC) to ensure that your cloud resources are configured correctly, securely, and efficiently.

Chapter 14, Implementing Policy as Code, focuses on using Pulumi's policy framework to enforce compliance, security, and operational best practices within infrastructure as code.

Chapter 15, Migrating From Other Tools to Pulumi, guides migrating existing IaC projects to Pulumi, covering framework evaluation, configuration translation, multi-language support, state management, and best practices for a smooth, low-downtime transition.

Chapter 16, Tests and Exercises on Infrastructure Automation with Pulumi, provides practical exercises and case studies to reinforce the concepts learned throughout the book.

To get the most out of this book

- Have a basic understanding of cloud computing concepts and services
- Be comfortable with at least one programming language such as Python, TypeScript, or C#

Conventions used

There are a number of text conventions used throughout this book.

CodeInText: Indicates code words in text, database table names, folder names, filenames, file extensions, pathnames, dummy URLs, user input, and Twitter handles. For example: "Run the pb_arista_facts.yml playbook to validate the operational state of our fabric."

A block of code is set as follows:

```
const vnet = new azure.network.VirtualNetwork("myVnet", {
    resourceGroupName: resourceGroup.name,
    location: resourceGroup.location,
    addressSpace: {
        addressPrefixes: ["10.0.0.0/16"],
    },
});
```

Any command-line input or output is written as follows:

```
$ pulumi new azure-typescript
```

Bold: Indicates a new term, an important word, or words that you see on the screen. For instance, words in menus or dialog boxes appear in the text like this. For example: "Begin by navigating to the **Project Settings** page for your specific project. From there, you can manage project environment variables by selecting the **Environment Variables** tab."

Warnings or important notes appear like this.

Tips and tricks appear like this.

Get in touch

Feedback from our readers is always welcome.

General feedback: If you have questions about any aspect of this book or have any general feedback, please email us at customercare@packt.com and mention the book's title in the subject of your message.

Errata: Although we have taken every care to ensure the accuracy of our content, mistakes do happen. If you have found a mistake in this book, we would be grateful if you reported this to us. Please visit http://www.packt.com/submit-errata, click **Submit Errata**, and fill in the form.

Piracy: If you come across any illegal copies of our works in any form on the internet, we would be grateful if you would provide us with the location address or website name. Please contact us at copyright@packt.com with a link to the material.

If you are interested in becoming an author: If there is a topic that you have expertise in and you are interested in either writing or contributing to a book, please visit http://authors.packt.com/.

Your Book Comes with Exclusive Perks - Here's How to Unlock Them

Unlock this book's exclusive benefits now

UNLOCK NOW

Scan this QR code or go to packtpub.com/unlock, then search this book by name. Ensure it's the correct edition.

Note: *Keep your purchase invoice ready before you start.*

Enhanced reading experience with our Next-gen Reader:

- **Multi-device progress sync**: Learn from any device with seamless progress sync.
- **Highlighting and notetaking**: Turn your reading into lasting knowledge.
- **Bookmarking**: Revisit your most important learnings anytime.
- **Dark mode**: Focus with minimal eye strain by switching to dark or sepia mode.

Learn smarter using our AI assistant (Beta):

- **Summarize it**: Summarize key sections or an entire chapter.
- **AI code explainers**: In the next-gen Packt Reader, click the **Explain** button above each code block for AI-powered code explanations.

> *Note: The AI assistant is part of next-gen Packt Reader and is still in beta.*

Learn anytime, anywhere:

Access your content offline with DRM-free PDF and ePub versions—compatible with your favorite e-readers.

Unlock Your Book's Exclusive Benefits

Your copy of this book comes with the following exclusive benefits:

- Next-gen Packt Reader
- AI assistant (beta)
- DRM-free PDF/ePub downloads

Use the following guide to unlock them if you haven't already. The process takes just a few minutes and needs to be done only once.

How to unlock these benefits in three easy steps

Step 1

Keep your purchase invoice for this book ready, as you'll need it in *Step 3*. If you received a physical invoice, scan it on your phone and have it ready as either a PDF, JPG, or PNG.

For more help on finding your invoice, visit https://www.packtpub.com/unlock-benefits/help.

> **Note:** Did you buy this book directly from Packt? You don't need an invoice. After completing Step 2, you can jump straight to your exclusive content.

Step 2

Scan this QR code or go to packtpub.com/unlock.

On the page that opens (which will look similar to Figure 0.1 if you're on desktop), search for this book by name. Make sure you select the correct edition.

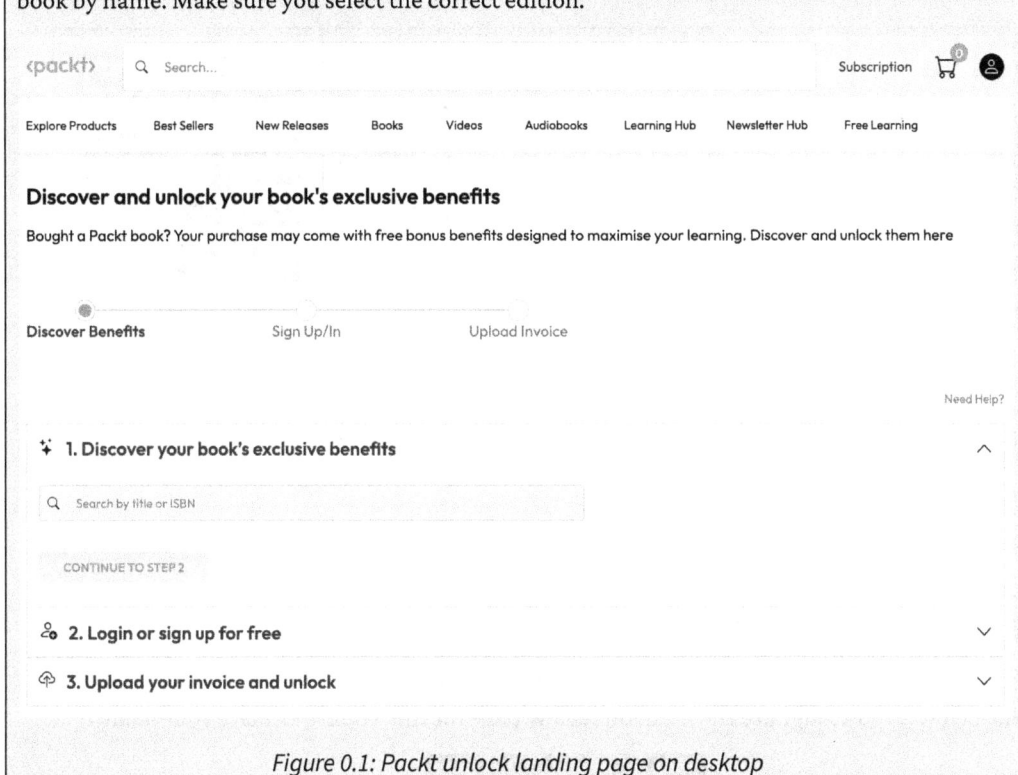

Figure 0.1: Packt unlock landing page on desktop

Step 2

Scan this QR code or go to packtpub.com/unlock.

On the page that opens (which will look similar to *Figure 1* if you're on desktop), search for this book by name. Make sure you select the correct edition.

Step 3

Sign in to your Packt account or create a new one for free. Once you're logged in, upload your invoice. It can be in PDF, PNG, or JPG format and must be no larger than 10 MB. Follow the rest of the instructions on the screen to complete the process.

Need help?

If you get stuck and need help, visit `https://www.packtpub.com/unlock-benefits/help` for a detailed FAQ on how to find your invoices and more. The following QR code will take you to the help page directly:

Note: If you are still facing issues, reach out to `customercare@packt.com`.

Share your thoughts

Once you've read *Infrastructure as Code with Pulumi*, we'd love to hear your thoughts! Scan the QR code below to go straight to the Amazon review page for this book and share your feedback.

`https://packt.link/r/1835467520`

Your review is important to us and the tech community and will help us make sure we're delivering excellent quality content.

Part 1

Introduction to Pulumi and Infrastructure as Code

The first part of the book lays the foundation for everything that follows by introducing Infrastructure as Code (IaC) and Pulumi as a modern, developer-friendly approach to building and managing cloud infrastructure. You will see how Pulumi differs from other IaC tools, how it uses familiar programming languages, and why its flexibility makes it a strong choice for single-cloud, multi-cloud, and hybrid environments.

It begins with the fundamentals of IaC, explaining its benefits, core principles, and role in modern DevOps practices, before moving on to Pulumi's key concepts such as resources, stacks, projects, and state management. You will explore how Pulumi fits into cloud workflows, how it interacts with providers, and the basics of authoring infrastructure code.

From there, you will create your first Pulumi project step by step, starting with installation and configuration and moving to deploying real infrastructure on a cloud provider. Along the way, you will work with Pulumi's CLI, preview and apply changes, and see how Pulumi tracks and manages infrastructure state over time.

This part provides the essential knowledge and practical experience needed to begin building and managing infrastructure with Pulumi, forming a solid base for the advanced scenarios covered later in the book.

This part of the book includes the following chapters:

- *Chapter 1, Introduction to Infrastructure as Code and Pulumi*
- *Chapter 2, Creating Your First Pulumi IaC*

1

Introduction to Infrastructure as Code and Pulumi

With the increasing adoption of cloud technologies and DevOps practices, the ability to define and manage infrastructure through code has become a highly sought-after skill. Developers today are expected not only to build applications but also to *deploy*, *manage*, and *scale* them efficiently in the cloud. Mastering **Infrastructure as Code (IaC)** is key to meeting these demands, and **Pulumi** offers a flexible and powerful way to do just that. However, with the vast amount of information available, structuring your learning to effectively adopt Pulumi can feel overwhelming. This chapter, and the rest of this book, aim to simplify the process of understanding IaC and Pulumi, setting you up for success from the start.

Beginnings are the seeds of the future, and when it comes to managing cloud infrastructure, understanding the basics is key to long-term success. The cloud may sound like an abstract concept, but it's essentially a collection of highly powerful machines housed in data centers around the world. With tools such as Pulumi, you can interact with these machines programmatically, defining and managing resources through code rather than manual configurations.

In this chapter, we'll introduce the core concepts behind IaC and dive into how Pulumi makes it easier to manage your cloud infrastructure. By the end, you'll have a solid foundation to build upon as we explore more advanced topics in later chapters.

In this chapter, we're going to cover the following main topics:

- Introduction to IaC
- Installing Pulumi and dependencies
- Understanding resources and stacks
- Pulumi state and state management
- The Pulumi programming model
- Pulumi CLI: key commands and operations
- Input, output, and configuration

Technical requirements

If you would like to follow along with the examples in this chapter, you will require the following:

- The **Pulumi CLI** is required for executing commands. You can download it from `https://www.pulumi.com/docs/iac/download-install/`.
- Pulumi supports multiple programming languages, but for this chapter, we'll be using **JavaScript/TypeScript**, which requires **Node.js**. You can download and install it from the Node.js official site here: `https://nodejs.org/`.

Introduction to IaC

One of the main problems IaC solves is **configuration drift**. In the early days of managing infrastructure, system administrators would manually configure servers, networks, and storage. Over time, as systems were updated and maintained, the configuration of one server might start to differ from another. This inconsistency, known as configuration drift, could lead to *unpredictable behavior*, *bugs*, or *failures* because different servers no longer worked the same way.

Before IaC, the process of managing infrastructure was also slow and prone to human error. If you needed to set up new servers, you'd do it manually, often following a checklist. But if that checklist wasn't followed exactly or someone made a mistake, the new server might not work properly. Reproducing the exact environment became difficult, and scaling was even harder. If you needed to deploy 10 or 100 servers, you'd have to configure each one individually, which took a lot of time and effort.

Then came IaC. IaC allows you to manage and provision your infrastructure using code, just like you would manage an application. Instead of manually configuring servers, you write code that specifies what you want your infrastructure to look like. This code can be saved, shared, reviewed, and updated just like any other code in a software project.

With IaC, setting up a server becomes as simple as running a script. The true power of IaC lies in its automation—automating infrastructure management was the driving force behind the need for a solution such as IaC, enabling organizations to scale quickly, reduce human error, and ensure that environments are consistently and accurately configured every time.

IaC is important because it has multiple benefits over the alternative (manual infrastructure configuration). These benefits are listed here:

- **Consistency**: Since the infrastructure configuration is defined in code, you can ensure that every server, network, or service is set up the same way every time. If you need to deploy multiple environments, such as development, testing, and production, the same code can be used for all of them. This eliminates the risk of configuration drift and reduces the chances of errors caused by manual setup.

- **Simplifies scaling**: In traditional infrastructure management, scaling up would mean repeating the manual configuration process for each new server. With IaC, you simply modify the code to add more resources, and the system takes care of provisioning them in the cloud. This makes it incredibly easy to add new servers or services when needed, without worrying about configuration errors.

- **Automation**: Since everything is defined in code, you can automate the deployment process, which saves time and reduces the risk of human error. This also allows for **continuous delivery and continuous integration** (**CI/CD**) practices, where infrastructure changes are automatically applied as part of the development pipeline, ensuring that environments are always up to date.

- **Documentation**: In traditional setups, the documentation of infrastructure was often separate from the configuration itself, which meant that documentation could easily become outdated. With IaC, the code itself acts as the documentation, making it easy to see exactly what your infrastructure looks like at any given time.

- **Version control**: Just like with application code, you can track changes to your infrastructure code over time. If something goes wrong after a change, you can easily roll back to the previous version. This makes infrastructure management safer and more reliable, as any mistakes can be quickly corrected.

- **Collaboration**: In traditional setups, only a few people, usually system administrators, knew how the infrastructure was configured. With IaC, the infrastructure is defined in code that can be reviewed, shared, and improved upon by different team members. This leads to better communication and understanding across teams, making it easier to manage complex systems.

Installing Pulumi and dependencies

Pulumi is an IaC tool that takes a different approach by treating infrastructure like software. This means that instead of using configuration files in a **domain-specific language (DSL)** like other IaC tools, you can define and manage your infrastructure using *general-purpose programming languages* such as JavaScript, **Python**, TypeScript, **Go**, or **C#**. With Pulumi, developers can use familiar coding practices, making it easier to integrate infrastructure management into the software development workflow.

The concept of infrastructure as software means that you can manage cloud resources in the same way you manage software code. Just like you write code to build applications, you write code to define your infrastructure. This code can be versioned, tested, reused, and shared, just like application code. This approach brings together the worlds of software development and cloud infrastructure, allowing for more flexible and powerful management.

Pulumi has several key benefits. One of the biggest advantages is the ability to use familiar programming languages. This makes it easier for developers who are already skilled in these languages to adopt Pulumi without needing to learn a new syntax. Another benefit is Pulumi's support for advanced coding features such as loops, conditionals, and functions, which allow for more complex infrastructure configurations. You can also use existing tools and libraries from the language ecosystem, which makes Pulumi highly extensible and adaptable to different needs.

Now that you know about Pulumi, let's get it set up on your local machine. This step-by-step guide will walk you through installing Pulumi and its dependencies on different operating systems, so you can start using it to manage your cloud infrastructure. Follow the instructions based on your operating system.

Installing Pulumi on Windows

To install Pulumi on Windows, you have multiple options depending on your preferred method: Chocolatey, installation script, or manual installation. The following subsections contain step-by-step instructions for each approach.

Installing using Chocolatey

Chocolatey is a package manager for Windows that simplifies the installation of software. It allows you to easily *install*, *update*, and *manage* applications via the command line. You can download Chocolatey from its website: `https://chocolatey.org/install`.

Once you have it installed, you can install Pulumi by running the following command:

```
> choco install pulumi
```

This will install the Pulumi CLI to `$($env:ChocolateyInstall)\lib\pulumi` and cre-ate the **shims**, which are small wrapper executables that point to the actual application, `$($env:ChocolateyInstall)\bin`, to add Pulumi to your path. To verify that Pulumi was suc-cessfully installed, you can run the following command:

```
> pulumi version
```

This command will return the current version of the Pulumi CLI that is installed on your machine. However, if Pulumi does not exist on your machine because the installation wasn't successful, it will return an error message such as `'pulumi' is not recognized as an internal or external command, operable program or batch file`, or something similar. This indicates that either Pulumi was not installed correctly or it is not in your system's PATH. If you encounter this error, double-check the installation steps and ensure that the Pulumi binary is added to the PATH environment variable.

Installing using the installation script

You can run this **installation script** in your terminal. Open a new Command Prompt window (*WIN + R*: cmd.exe). In the window, run the following command to download and install Pulumi:

```
> @"%SystemRoot%\System32\WindowsPowerShell\v1.0\powershell.
exe" -NoProfile -InputFormat None -ExecutionPolicy Bypass
-Command "[Net.ServicePointManager]::SecurityProtocol = [Net.
SecurityProtocolType]::Tls12; iex ((New-Object System.Net.WebClient).
DownloadString('https://get.pulumi.com/install.ps1'))" && SET
"PATH=%PATH%;%USERPROFILE%\.pulumi\bin"
```

If successful, the `pulumi.exe` CLI will be installed to `%USERPROFILE%\.pulumi\bin` and added to your path. To verify that Pulumi was successfully installed, you can run the following command:

```
> pulumi version
```

This command will return the current version of the Pulumi CLI that is installed on your machine. However, if Pulumi does not exist on your machine because the installation wasn't successful, it will return an error message such as `'pulumi' is not recognized as an internal or external command, operable program or batch file`, or something similar.

This indicates that either Pulumi was not installed correctly or it is not in your system's PATH. If you encounter this error, double-check the installation steps and ensure that the Pulumi binary is added to the PATH environment variable.

Installing manually

You can also **manually install** Pulumi by downloading the **Windows x64 binaries**. First, download the Pulumi binaries for Windows x64: `https://www.pulumi.com/docs/iac/download-install/versions`.

After downloading the zip file, unzip it and extract its contents to a folder, such as `C:\pulumi`.

Finally, add `C:\pulumi\bin` to your system's PATH. You can do this by going to **System Properties > Advanced > Environment Variables**, then under **User Variables**, find the **Path** variable and click **Edit** to add the path to the Pulumi folder. To verify that Pulumi was successfully installed, you can run the following command:

```
> pulumi version
```

This command will return the current version of the Pulumi CLI that is installed on your machine. However, if Pulumi does not exist on your machine because the installation wasn't successful, it will return an error message such as `'pulumi' is not recognized as an internal or external command, operable program or batch file`, or something similar. This indicates that either Pulumi was not installed correctly or it is not in your system's PATH. If you encounter this error, double-check the installation steps and ensure that the Pulumi binary is added to the PATH environment variable.

Installing Pulumi on macOS

To install Pulumi on macOS, you have multiple options depending on your preferred method: Homebrew, installation script, or manual installation. The following subsections contain step-by-step instructions for each approach.

Installing using Homebrew

Homebrew is a popular package manager for macOS that simplifies the installation of software by managing dependencies and versions. You can download it by running the installation command provided on the Homebrew website: `https://brew.sh`.

Once you have it installed, you can install Pulumi by running the following command:

```
$ brew install pulumi
```

This command will install the Pulumi CLI to the usual place (often, /usr/local/bin/pulumi) and add it to your path. To verify that Pulumi was successfully installed, you can run the following command:

```
$ pulumi version
```

This command will return the current version of the Pulumi CLI that is installed on your machine. However, if Pulumi does not exist on your machine because the installation wasn't successful, it will return an error message such as 'pulumi' is not recognized as an internal or external command, operable program or batch file, or something similar. This indicates that either Pulumi was not installed correctly or it is not in your system's PATH. If you encounter this error, double-check the installation steps and ensure that the Pulumi binary is added to the PATH environment variable.

Installing using the installation script

You can run this installation script in your terminal. Open a new window. In the window, run the following command to download and install Pulumi:

```
$ curl -fsSL https://get.pulumi.com | sh
```

If successful, this will install the Pulumi CLI to ~/.pulumi/bin and automatically add it to your system's PATH. If it cannot add Pulumi to your PATH automatically, you'll receive a prompt with instructions on how to add it manually. To verify that Pulumi was successfully installed, you can run the following command:

```
$ pulumi version
```

This command will return the current version of the Pulumi CLI that is installed on your machine. However, if Pulumi does not exist on your machine because the installation wasn't successful, it will return an error message such as 'pulumi' is not recognized as an internal or external command, operable program or batch file, or something similar. This indicates that either Pulumi was not installed correctly or it is not in your system's PATH. If you encounter this error, double-check the installation steps and ensure that the Pulumi binary is added to the PATH environment variable.

Installing manually

You can also manually install Pulumi by downloading the **binaries for macOS**. First, download the Pulumi binaries here: https://www.pulumi.com/docs/iac/download-install/versions.

After downloading the **tarball file**, extract its contents and move the binaries from the Pulumi directory to a folder that is already included in your system's $PATH. To verify that Pulumi was successfully installed, you can run the following command:

```
$ pulumi version
```

This command will return the current version of the Pulumi CLI that is installed on your machine. However, if Pulumi does not exist on your machine because the installation wasn't successful, it will return an error message such as 'pulumi' is not recognized as an internal or external command, operable program or batch file, or something similar. This indicates that either Pulumi was not installed correctly or it is not in your system's PATH. If you encounter this error, double-check the installation steps and ensure that the Pulumi binary is added to the PATH environment variable.

Installing Pulumi on Linux

To install Pulumi on Linux, you have two options depending on your preferred method: the installation script or manual installation. The following subsections contain step-by-step instructions for each approach.

Installing using the installation script

You can run this installation script in your Linux terminal. Run the following command in your terminal to download and install Pulumi:

```
$ curl -fsSL https://get.pulumi.com | sh
```

If successful, this will install the Pulumi CLI to ~/.pulumi/bin and automatically add it to your system's PATH. If it cannot add Pulumi to your PATH automatically, you'll receive a prompt with instructions on how to add it manually. You can verify the installation by running the following command:

```
$ pulumi version
```

This command will return the current version of the Pulumi CLI that is installed on your machine. However, if Pulumi does not exist on your machine because the installation wasn't successful, it will return an error message such as 'pulumi' is not recognized as an internal or external command, operable program or batch file, or something similar. This indicates that either Pulumi was not installed correctly or it is not in your system's PATH. If you encounter this error, double-check the installation steps and ensure that the Pulumi binary is added to the PATH environment variable.

Installing manually

You can also manually install Pulumi by downloading the binaries for Linux. First, download the Pulumi binaries here: `https://www.pulumi.com/docs/iac/download-install/versions`.

After downloading the tarball file, extract its contents and move the binaries from the Pulumi directory to a folder that is already included in your system's `$PATH`. To verify that Pulumi was successfully installed, you can run the following command:

```
$ pulumi version
```

This command will return the current version of the Pulumi CLI that is installed on your machine. However, if Pulumi does not exist on your machine because the installation wasn't successful, it will return an error message such as `'pulumi' is not recognized as an internal or external command, operable program or batch file`, or something similar. This indicates that either Pulumi was not installed correctly or it is not in your system's PATH. If you encounter this error, double-check the installation steps and ensure that the Pulumi binary is added to the PATH environment variable.

Installing dependencies

To follow along with the entire book, one important dependency you'll need to install is Node. js, as we'll be working with TypeScript for our Pulumi projects. Node.js provides the runtime environment needed to execute JavaScript and TypeScript code. Additionally, it comes with **npm** (short for **Node Package Manager**), which helps manage project dependencies and libraries.

To install Node.js, first visit the Node.js website at `https://nodejs.org` and download the latest stable version. For most users, the recommended version is the **long-term support** (**LTS**) version. Follow the installation prompts based on your operating system, whether you're using Windows, macOS, or Linux.

Once the installation is complete, open your terminal or Command Prompt to verify that Node.js and npm were installed correctly. You can do this by running node -v to check the Node.js version and npm -v to check the npm version. If both commands return version numbers, your installation was successful. With Node.js now installed, you are ready to work with TypeScript and Pulumi throughout the book.

Understanding resources and stacks

When working with cloud infrastructure, **resources** are the basic building blocks of your system. These resources represent services such as virtual machines, databases, networking components, and storage systems. Each of these elements is critical to making your applications run efficiently and at scale in the cloud. A **resource** in Pulumi represents a single cloud infrastructure component. For example, an Amazon EC2 instance, an Azure Blob Storage container, or a Google Cloud SQL instance can all be treated as resources in Pulumi.

Here's an example of a simple Pulumi TypeScript code to define an **Azure storage account** (a storage resource):

```
// Create an Azure resource group
const resourceGroup = new azure.resources.ResourceGroup("testgroup");

// Create an Azure storage account
const storage = new azure.storage.StorageAccount("teststorage", {
    resourceGroupName: resourceGroup.name,
    sku: {
        name: "Standard_LRS",
    },
    kind: "StorageV2",
});
```

In this example, we define a resource called `storage` using the `azure.storage.StorageAccount` class from Pulumi's **Azure Native** package. This code specifies that a storage account named `teststorage` will be created in Azure. When you run this Pulumi program, the resource is automatically provisioned in your Azure account.

Pulumi organizes resources into stacks. A **stack** in Pulumi represents an isolated instance of your cloud infrastructure, similar to how you might have separate environments for development, staging, and production. Each stack can have its own configuration settings, such as region, credentials, and environment variables. This enables you to deploy the same infrastructure code across different environments while keeping each environment isolated.

Let's say you have three environments: `dev`, `staging`, and `production`. You can create three separate stacks in Pulumi, each with its own set of configurations. These stacks might have the same resources but different sizes, configurations, or credentials. For example, your `production` environment might have more powerful resources than your `dev` environment.

♀ **Quick tip**: Enhance your coding experience with the **AI Code Explainer** and **Quick Copy** features. Open this book in the next-gen Packt Reader. Click the **Copy** button (1) to quickly copy code into your coding environment, or click the **Explain** button (2) to get the AI assistant to explain a block of code to you.

```
                                              Copy    Explain
function calculate(a, b) {                     1        2
   return {sum: a + b};
};
```

🔖 **The next-gen Packt Reader** is included for free with the purchase of this book. Scan the QR code OR visit packtpub.com/unlock, then use the search bar to find this book by name. Double-check the edition shown to make sure you get the right one.

Here's an example of how to create stacks using the Pulumi CLI:

```
pulumi stack init dev
pulumi stack init staging
pulumi stack init production
```

This command creates three separate stacks: dev, staging, and production. You can configure each stack individually. To set specific configurations for a stack, you can use the following CLI command:

```
pulumi config set azure:location westus --stack dev
pulumi config set azure:location eastus --stack production
```

In this example, we set the azure:location configuration to westus for the dev stack and eastus for the production stack. This flexibility allows you to target different Azure regions or services depending on the environment.

A stack can be deployed by running the `pulumi up` command, which provisions all the resources defined in your code for the selected stack, as in this example:

```
pulumi up --stack dev
```

This command applies the infrastructure changes to the dev stack. If you want to deploy your changes to the `production` environment, you simply switch to the `production` stack and run the command again:

```
pulumi up --stack production
```

Stack outputs can also be used to export useful information from a stack that might be needed by other services or applications. You can define stack outputs by exporting values in your Pulumi code:

```
export const storageAccountName = storageAccount.name;
export const blobContainerUrl = pulumi.
interpolate`https://${storageAccount.name}.blob.core.windows.
net/${container.name}`;
```

This `blobContainerUrl` value can then be used in other stacks or applications that need to access the **Azure Blob container**.

In large infrastructure setups, you might have several stacks working together, each responsible for a part of the system. For instance, you might have a *networking stack* that provisions the base network resources (such as virtual networks and subnets) and an *application stack* that deploys the application resources (such as web servers and databases). Pulumi allows you to reference outputs from one stack in another, making it easier to build complex, multi-stack setups.

Here's an example of referencing an output from another stack:

```
const infraStack = new pulumi.StackReference("org/project/stack");
const vnetId = infraStack.getOutput("vnetId");
const subnetId = infraStack.getOutput("subnetId");
```

The foundation of your Pulumi IaC journey is understanding stacks and knowing that they are the key to organizing, isolating, and managing environments. Stacks help you deploy consistent infrastructure across different stages of development while ensuring that your resources are provisioned in a repeatable, automated way. By mastering how stacks and resources work together, you gain full control over your cloud infrastructure, making it easier to scale, maintain, and evolve your systems over time.

Pulumi state and state management

One of the core concepts when working with IaC tools such as Pulumi is **state management**. Pulumi tracks the state of your cloud infrastructure, which is necessary to understand what resources exist, their current configuration, and how they relate to each other. This information is crucial when making updates or destroying resources, as it allows Pulumi to know exactly what needs to be created, modified, or deleted.

In Pulumi, **state** refers to a snapshot of the resources that have been deployed by Pulumi in a given stack. Pulumi keeps this state to ensure that it can compare the current live infrastructure with the desired infrastructure defined in your code. This state file is automatically updated whenever you make changes to your infrastructure by running commands such as pulumi up or pulumi destroy.

When you run pulumi up, Pulumi takes the infrastructure configuration you've defined in code (such as creating a virtual network or a storage account), compares it with the current state, and then performs the necessary actions (creates, updates, or deletes resources). This comparison ensures that only the differences between your desired state and actual infrastructure are applied, which prevents unnecessary changes and downtime.

Here's a simple example of what state looks like conceptually:

```
{
    "resources": [
        {
            "name": "myStorageAccount",
            "type": "azure:storage:Account",
            "id": "/subscriptions/.../mystorageaccount",
            "properties": {
                "resourceGroupName": "myResourceGroup",
                "location": "eastus"
            }
        },
        {
            "name": "myBlobContainer",
            "type": "azure:storage:BlobContainer",
            "id": "/subscriptions/.../mycontainer",
            "properties": {
```

```
                    "accountName": "myStorageAccount",
                    "publicAccess": "Blob"
            }
        }
    ]
}
```

This example state snippet shows that Pulumi is tracking two Azure resources: a storage account and a blob container. When you make changes to your code, Pulumi will look at this state to decide what needs to be updated.

Where is Pulumi state stored?

Pulumi state can be stored in several ways. By default, Pulumi stores the state in **Pulumi Cloud** (also called **Pulumi Service**), which is a managed backend for storing and managing your state files. However, you can also configure Pulumi to store the state in self-hosted options, such as an Amazon S3 bucket, Azure Blob Storage, or Google Cloud Storage.

Pulumi Cloud

Pulumi Cloud is the default option for storing your state. It's a fully managed service that securely stores your state files in the cloud. Here's how to use Pulumi Cloud:

- When you create a new Pulumi stack, the state is automatically saved in Pulumi Cloud. You don't need to configure anything special.

- To create a new stack using Pulumi Cloud, run the following:

```
pulumi stack init dev
```

This command will automatically set up your state in Pulumi Cloud, and you can view the stack's state by logging in to the Pulumi console at app.pulumi.com.

Self-hosted state backends

If you prefer not to use Pulumi Cloud, you can store your state in a self-hosted backend, such as Azure Blob Storage, Amazon S3, or Google Cloud Storage. This gives you more control over where your state files are stored, but it requires you to manage the storage and access policies yourself.

Let's take a closer look at configuring Pulumi to use Azure Blob Storage for state management:

1. First, create an Azure storage account and a blob container that will hold your state files. You can do that using the Azure portal or through your command line.

2. Once your storage account and blob container are created, you can configure Pulumi to store state there by setting the PULUMI_BACKEND_URL environment variable:

```
export PULUMI_BACKEND_URL=azblob://<container-path>?
storage_account=<account_name>
```

This tells Pulumi to use the specified Azure Blob Storage container and storage account to store its state files. Now, every time you run a command such as pulumi login, the context will be for the self-hosted backend, and if you run pulumi up, the state will be saved to the Azure Blob container instead of Pulumi Cloud.

You can also use Amazon S3 and Google Cloud Storage as your Pulumi backend. To use the Amazon S3 backend, pass s3://<bucket-name> as <backend-url>:

```
export PULUMI_BACKEND_URL=s3://<bucket-name>
```

To use the Google Cloud Storage backend pass gs://<bucket-path> as <backend-url>:

```
export PULUMI_BACKEND_URL=gs://<my-pulumi-state-bucket>
```

Using a self-hosted backend gives you full control over your state management and ensures that your state files are stored in an environment you manage.

Local state

Another option is to store the state file *locally* on your machine. This can be useful for testing or small projects where you don't need the full features of a remote backend. However, it's important to note that using local state comes with risks, such as losing state files if your local machine crashes or is wiped.

To configure Pulumi to use local state, set PULUMI_BACKEND_URL to a local file path:

```
export PULUMI_BACKEND_URL=file://~/.pulumi
```

This will save the state files locally on your machine in the ~/.pulumi directory. Be sure to secure and back up this directory if you choose to use local state, especially for anything beyond small or experimental projects.

Managing Pulumi state

To interact with your Pulumi state, you can use several commands provided by the Pulumi CLI:

- `pulumi stack export`: This command allows you to export the current state of your stack into a **JavaScript Object Notation (JSON)** file. This is useful if you want to manually inspect the state or back it up:

```
pulumi stack export --stack dev > dev-state.json
```

This will save the current state of the dev stack to a file called `dev-state.json`.

- `pulumi stack import`: If you have exported your state file and want to import it back into Pulumi, you can use the `import` command:

```
pulumi stack import --stack dev < dev-state.json
```

This will import the state from the `dev-state.json` file back into the dev stack.

- `pulumi stack rm`: If you no longer need a stack and want to remove its state file, you can delete the stack with this command:

```
pulumi stack rm dev
```

This removes the dev stack and its associated state file.

- `pulumi stack history`: Pulumi Cloud tracks the history of your stack's state. To view the history of a stack, you can use the `pulumi stack history` command:

```
pulumi stack history
```

- `pulumi state delete`: This command allows you to delete a resource from a stack's state without affecting the actual resource in the cloud. This is helpful if a resource was manually deleted outside of Pulumi, or if you want Pulumi to stop tracking a resource without deleting it. The following code snippet shows how to use it:

```
pulumi state delete "azure:storage/
account:Account::mystorageaccount"
```

In this example, the `mystorageaccount` resource is deleted from Pulumi's state file but not from the cloud. This means Pulumi will no longer manage or track this resource, and subsequent updates won't affect it. This command is useful when you have resources that you want to manage manually, or when a resource is no longer relevant to your stack but still exists in your cloud provider.

- `pulumi state move`: This command allows you to move resources from one stack to another. This can be helpful when you are splitting your infrastructure across multiple stacks or consolidating resources from multiple stacks into one. It ensures the resource is now associated with the correct stack without needing to be reprovisioned. The following code snippet shows how to use it:

```
pulumi state move --source dev --dest prod "azure:compute/virtualMac
hine:VirtualMachine::my-vm"
```

In this example, the virtual machine resource (`my-vm`) is moved from the dev stack to the prod stack. Pulumi will now manage this resource as part of the prod stack, and it will no longer be associated with the dev stack.

- `pulumi state rename`: This command allows you to rename a resource in the state file. This is particularly useful when you've refactored your code and renamed a resource in your program but need to align the existing state with the new name. The following code snippet shows how to use it:

```
pulumi state rename "azure:storage/
account:Account::mystorageaccount" "azure:storage/
account:Account::newstorageaccount"
```

In this example, `mystorageaccount` is renamed to `newstorageaccount` in Pulumi's state file. The resource itself is not modified, but Pulumi will now track it under the new name.

- `pulumi state unprotect`: This command removes the protection flag from a resource in your stack's state. In Pulumi, protected resources cannot be deleted unless their protection is explicitly removed. This command is useful when a resource was marked as protected to prevent accidental deletion, but you now want to allow it to be destroyed as part of a stack cleanup. The following code snippet shows how to use it:

```
pulumi state unprotect "azure:storage/
account:Account::mystorageaccount"
```

This command unprotects the specified Azure Storage Account resource (`mystorageaccount`), allowing it to be deleted in subsequent updates or during a stack teardown.

- `pulumi state upgrade`: This command migrates your stack's state to the latest supported version of the Pulumi backend. This is important when Pulumi introduces new features or changes to how state is handled, and you want to ensure your state is using the most up-to-date format.

  Upgrading your state can also help improve performance, ensure better compatibility with new resource providers, and take advantage of any state-related enhancements or bug fixes that have been introduced. It is a good practice to periodically upgrade your state, especially after upgrading the Pulumi CLI to a new major version.

  Before running this command, it's recommended to back up your current state to avoid any unforeseen issues. This is particularly important for production environments where stability is critical.

  The following code snippet shows how to use it:

  ```
  pulumi state upgrade
  ```

  Running this command will migrate your stack's state to the latest version, allowing you to fully benefit from the improvements and new capabilities provided by Pulumi.

The Pulumi programming model

The **Pulumi programming model** revolves around using standard programming constructs such as loops, conditionals, functions, and variables to define cloud infrastructure. The benefit of using familiar languages is that you can reuse libraries, apply business logic, and manage infrastructure in a more dynamic and flexible way.

At a high level, Pulumi works by taking the code you write, comparing it to the current state of your infrastructure, and then applying any necessary changes to reach the desired state. This is done through a series of steps:

1. **Write infrastructure code:** You define your cloud infrastructure using code in the programming language of your choice. For example, you might define virtual machines, storage accounts, databases, or networking resources.

2. **Pulumi CLI:** The Pulumi CLI is the command-line tool used to manage your Pulumi projects. When you run commands such as `pulumi up`, Pulumi takes your infrastructure code, converts it into API calls, and applies the changes to your cloud provider.

3. **State management**: Pulumi compares your code to the current state of your infrastructure, tracking what resources have been created, modified, or deleted. This is handled by Pulumi's state management system, which ensures that the infrastructure matches your code.

4. **Resource provisioning**: Pulumi sends the API requests to your cloud provider (e.g., Azure, AWS, or GCP) to provision, update, or destroy resources as needed. Pulumi takes care of managing dependencies between resources and ensures they are provisioned in the correct order.

The Pulumi programming model makes it easier to manage both your application code and your infrastructure code in one place, allowing developers to use the same tools and practices for both. This approach helps teams work more efficiently, as they can use familiar programming languages and apply the same methods they use for software development to managing cloud resources. It also makes it easier to automate infrastructure changes, integrate them into existing workflows, and ensure everything is consistent and well managed.

Pulumi CLI: key commands and operations

The Pulumi CLI is an essential tool when working with Pulumi. It provides the commands needed to *define*, *deploy*, and *manage* your infrastructure through code. Pulumi's CLI enables you to create, update, and destroy cloud resources, as well as manage the different stacks (environments) that you're working with.

In this section, we will explore the most important Pulumi CLI commands, how to use them, and what each one does. If you're working with Pulumi, becoming comfortable with the CLI is crucial, as it's where you'll spend most of your time deploying and managing your cloud infrastructure:

*   `pulumi new`: This command initializes a new Pulumi project. When you're starting a new infrastructure project, this is the first command you'll run. It sets up everything you need to begin writing code to manage your cloud resources. Here's how you can use it:

    ```
    pulumi new azure-typescript
    ```

This command creates a new Pulumi project that uses TypeScript and is set up for Azure using the `azure-typescript` template. Pulumi will prompt you for project details such as the project name and the cloud region. If you're not sure what project to use, you can run `pulumi new` and choose from the 220+ templates Pulumi has available.

```
nennenwodo@Nennes-MBP project % pulumi new
 Would you like to create a project from a template or using a Pulumi AI prompt? template
Please choose a template (227 total):
 [Use arrows to move, type to filter]
> aiven-go                       A minimal Aiven Go Pulumi program
  aiven-python                   A minimal Aiven Python Pulumi program
  aiven-typescript               A minimal Aiven TypeScript Pulumi program
  alicloud-csharp                A minimal AliCloud C# Pulumi program
  alicloud-fsharp                A minimal AliCloud F# Pulumi program
  alicloud-go                    A minimal AliCloud Go Pulumi program
  alicloud-javascript            A minimal AliCloud JavaScript Pulumi program
  alicloud-python                A minimal AliCloud Python Pulumi program
  alicloud-typescript            A minimal AliCloud TypeScript Pulumi program
  alicloud-visualbasic           A minimal AliCloud VB.NET Pulumi program
  alicloud-yaml                  A minimal AliCloud Pulumi YAML program
  auth0-csharp                   A minimal Auth0 C# Pulumi program
  auth0-go                       A minimal Auth0 Go Pulumi program
  auth0-javascript               A minimal Auth0 TypeScript Pulumi program
  auth0-python                   A minimal Auth0 Python Pulumi program
  auth0-typescript               A minimal Auth0 TypeScript Pulumi program
  auth0-yaml                     A minimal Auth0 Pulumi YAML program
  aws-csharp                     A minimal AWS C# Pulumi program
  aws-fsharp                     A minimal AWS F# Pulumi program
  aws-go                         A minimal AWS Go Pulumi program
  aws-java                       A minimal AWS Java Pulumi program
  aws-javascript                 A minimal AWS JavaScript Pulumi program
  aws-native-csharp              A minimal AWS C# Pulumi program
```

Figure 1.1: Pulumi templates

🔍 **Quick tip:** Need to see a high-resolution version of this image? Open this book in the next-gen Packt Reader or view it in the PDF/ePub copy.

📖 **The next-gen Packt Reader** is included for free with the purchase of this book. Scan the QR code OR go to packtpub.com/unlock, then use the search bar to find this book by name. Double-check the edition shown to make sure you get the right one.

- `pulumi up`: This command is one of the most important and frequently used commands in the Pulumi CLI. It deploys your cloud infrastructure based on the code you've written. When you run `pulumi up`, Pulumi compares your current state with the desired state defined in your code and then applies the necessary changes to match your infrastructure with your code. Pulumi will show a preview of the changes it will make, allowing you to confirm before actually applying them. After confirming, Pulumi will create, update, or delete resources as needed.

- `pulumi destroy`: If you want to tear down your infrastructure, the `pulumi destroy` command is used. This command deletes all the resources defined in your Pulumi project, returning your environment to its initial state. This command will show a preview of the resources that will be destroyed, and after confirmation, Pulumi will delete them.

- `pulumi stack`: This command is used to manage different stacks in Pulumi. In previous sections, you got exposed to some `pulumi stack` commands that you can use to manage your stack and state (e.g., `pulumi stack export`, `pulumi stack import`, `pulumi stack rm`, and `pulumi stack history`). Beyond those, there are some other commands.

For example, you can create a new stack using the following:

```
pulumi stack init dev
```

This command creates a new stack called dev. You can also list all available stacks with the following:

```
pulumi stack ls
```

To switch between stacks, use the following:

```
pulumi stack select dev
```

This command switches the current working stack to dev. After switching stacks, any changes you make will only apply to that stack.

- `pulumi config`: This command is used to *set*, *get*, and *manage* configuration values for your stacks. These configurations can include things such as cloud regions, resource names, or secrets such as API keys and passwords. We will cover more about configurations in the next section.

To set a configuration value, you can run the following:

```
pulumi config set azure:location eastus
```

This sets the azure:location configuration to eastus for the currently selected stack. If you're dealing with sensitive information such as passwords, you can store them securely using the --secret flag:

```
pulumi config set dbPassword mySecurePassword --secret
```

- pulumi preview: Before making changes to your cloud infrastructure, it's always a good idea to run a preview. The pulumi preview command shows what changes will be made without actually applying them. This is useful to verify what will happen before running pulumi up.

- pulumi refresh: This command is used to synchronize Pulumi's state with the real-world state of your cloud resources. This is helpful when changes have been made outside of Pulumi (for example, manually through a cloud provider's console), and you want Pulumi to reflect those changes in its state file.

- pulumi import: This command allows you to bring existing cloud resources under Pulumi management. For example, if you have already created a virtual machine in Azure manually, you can import it into Pulumi, so Pulumi starts managing it.

Here's how you can import a resource:

```
pulumi import azure:compute/virtualMachine:VirtualMachine my-vm /
subscriptions/xxxxx/resourceGroups/myResourceGroup/providers/Microsoft.
Compute/virtualMachines/my-vm
```

This command imports an existing Azure virtual machine into Pulumi so that you can manage it with your Pulumi program.

- pulumi state: This command allows you to interact directly with your Pulumi state. These commands were discussed in the previous section, and they are pulumi state delete, pulumi state move, pulumi state rename, pulumi state unprotect, and pulumi state upgrade.

- pulumi login and pulumi logout: To access Pulumi's managed backend (Pulumi Cloud) or to connect to your chosen backend storage (such as Azure Blob or S3), you need to log in. The pulumi login command is used for this purpose. To log in to Pulumi Cloud, run the following:

```
pulumi login
```

If you're using a self-hosted backend, you can specify it with a URL:

```
pulumi login azblob://my-state-container
```

This connects Pulumi to the backend where your state will be stored. If you want to disconnect from your backend, you can use the `pulumi logout` command. This is useful when you want to switch backends. To log out of Pulumi Cloud or your managed backend, run the following:

```
pulumi logout
```

- `pulumi cancel`: This command is used to cancel an ongoing update. If you realize mid-deployment that something has gone wrong or you want to stop the operation, you can cancel the update.
- `pulumi whoami`: If you're working with multiple Pulumi accounts or backends, you might want to check which account you're currently logged in to. The `pulumi whoami` command shows you the current logged-in user.
- `pulumi about`: This command provides information about your current Pulumi installation, including version details, backend configuration, and the language runtime being used.
- `pulumi version`: To check the version of the Pulumi CLI you're using, the `pulumi version` command is handy. Knowing the version helps in debugging and ensuring compatibility with your project's dependencies.
- `pulumi logs`: For debugging purposes, the `pulumi logs` command allows you to view logs from your Pulumi deployments. This is useful if you're trying to troubleshoot issues or see what happened during a failed deployment.
- `pulumi env`: The `pulumi env` command allows you to manage environments. An environment is a named collection of possibly secret, possibly dynamic data. There are some common subcommands: `pulumi env set`, `pulumi env get`, `pulumi env ls`, `pulumi env rm`, and more.

To set a value within an environment, you can use `pulumi env set` as illustrated here:

```
pulumi env set org/project/environment <name> <value>
```

To get a value within an environment, you can use `pulumi env get` as illustrated here:

```
pulumi env get org/project/environment[@version] <name>
```

To remove a value from an environment, you can use `pulumi env rm` as illustrated here:

```
pulumi env rm org/project/environment <name>
```

You can also list all the environments a logged-in user has access to. To do this, you can use the `pulumi env ls` command.

- `pulumi policy`: This command allows you to implement **policy-as-code** for your Pulumi projects. This feature enables you to define security and compliance policies that will be enforced when deploying infrastructure, ensuring that your infrastructure meets the required standards. Policies can help prevent misconfigurations, enforce best practices, or comply with security requirements.

Policies in Pulumi are written using familiar programming languages, and they can be applied to all of your stacks or just specific ones.

Some common subcommands are as follows:

- `pulumi policy new`: Creates a new policy pack
- `pulumi policy publish`: Publishes a policy pack for use in your organization
- `pulumi policy enable`: Enables a policy pack for a specific stack
- `pulumi policy disable`: Disables a policy pack for a stack
- `pulumi policy ls`: List all policy packs in your Pulumi organization

Chapter 14 will cover policy as code, and we will go over these in detail.

> What is a Pulumi organization?
>
> In Pulumi Cloud, a **Pulumi organization** is a way for teams to work together on cloud projects. It helps manage who can access different projects and control how resources are set up and maintained. With an organization, multiple people can collaborate on the same infrastructure, make sure everyone follows the same rules, and keep everything organized across different environments such as development or production. It's useful for teams or companies that need to manage cloud infrastructure together in a safe and structured way.

Input, output, and configuration

In Pulumi, **inputs**, **outputs**, and **configuration** are essential for managing cloud infrastructure. These concepts work together to allow for the dynamic handling of resources, their dependencies, and environment-specific values.

Inputs

Inputs in Pulumi represent values that are required to configure resources. These values can be *static* (e.g., hardcoded strings) or *dynamic*, such as the result of another resource's creation. Inputs allow Pulumi to manage dependencies between resources. When one resource depends on another (for example, a virtual machine depending on a network), Pulumi handles the ordering and passing of information between them.

Let's start with a simple example. Here, we create a storage account in Azure, passing the resource group name as an input:

```
// Create a resource group
const rgroup = new azure.resources.ResourceGroup("myResourceGroup");

// Create a storage account, referencing the resource group's name as an
// Input
const storageAccount = new azure.storage.
StorageAccount("mystorageaccount", {
    resourceGroupName: rgroup.name,   // This is pulumi.Input<string>
    sku: {
        name: "Standard_LRS",
    },
    kind: "StorageV2",
});
```

In this example, rgroup.name is an Input. Pulumi doesn't immediately know what the resource group's name will be because it's generated during the deployment process. However, Pulumi ensures that the name is properly passed to the storage account once the resource group is created.

Outputs

Outputs in Pulumi represent values that are produced after resources are created or updated. Outputs allow you to capture information about a resource (such as its name, ID, or IP address) and pass this information to other resources or systems. Outputs are important for connecting resources and exporting values from your Pulumi stack.

In this example, we'll modify the previous code to export the storage account name as an output:

```
// Create a resource group
const rgroup = new azure.resources.ResourceGroup("myResourceGroup");

// Create a storage account, referencing the resource group's name as an
// input
const storageAccount = new azure.storage.
StorageAccount("mystorageaccount", {
    resourceGroupName: rgroup.name,  // This is pulumi.Input<string>
    sku: {
        name: "Standard_LRS",
    },
    kind: "StorageV2",
});

// Export the storage account name as an output
export const storageAccountName = storageAccount.name;
```

Here, `storageAccount.name` is an `Output` that Pulumi resolves after the storage account is created. This value can be used in other parts of your program or exported as part of your stack's outputs.

Configuration in Pulumi

With configurations, you can manage environment-specific settings, such as cloud regions, API keys, or database URLs, without hardcoding these values in your code. Configuration values are set using the Pulumi CLI or stored in configuration files and are accessible within your Pulumi programs.

For example, you might want to set the region where resources are deployed:

```
pulumi config set azure:location eastus
```

In your Pulumi code, you can retrieve this configuration value:

```
import * as pulumi from "@pulumi/pulumi";

const config = new pulumi.Config();
const location = config.require("azure:location");

// Use the location as an input for a resource
```

```
const resourceGroup = new azure.resources.
ResourceGroup("myResourceGroup", {
    location: location,   // Input from configuration
});
```

Pulumi also allows you to store secrets securely in configuration, ensuring that sensitive data such as passwords or API keys is encrypted and not exposed in code or logs. For example, you can store a database password as a secret:

```
pulumi config set dbPassword mySecretPassword –secret
```

You can retrieve the secret in your code using `config.requireSecret()`:

```
const dbPassword = config.requireSecret("dbPassword");

// Use the secret as an input
const sqlServer = new azure.sql.Server("mySqlServer", {
    administratorLogin: "adminuser",
    administratorLoginPassword: dbPassword,   // Input using secret
});
```

This ensures that the secret is securely handled by Pulumi.

Summary

In this chapter, we covered essential concepts of IaC and the specific steps to get started with Pulumi. We learned how IaC solves issues such as configuration drift and manual errors by allowing infrastructure to be managed as code. The chapter outlined the installation process for Pulumi on different operating systems, followed by explanations of key topics such as resources, stacks, and state management. We also explored how Pulumi handles infrastructure changes by tracking the state and ensuring synchronization between code and the live environment. Important commands such as `pulumi up` and `pulumi stack` were discussed, helping you understand how to deploy, update, and destroy cloud resources, as well as manage multiple environments. This chapter provided a solid foundation to begin using Pulumi effectively in cloud projects.

In the next chapter, you will build your first Pulumi IaC project, and 'you'll be exposed to writing and organizing code, managing configurations, and handling common issues during deployment.

Questions

1. What is configuration drift, and how does IaC help prevent it?

2. How does IaC improve the reproducibility of infrastructure setups?

3. What are some of the main benefits of using code to manage cloud infrastructure instead of manual configuration?

4. How can you verify that Pulumi was installed correctly on your machine?

5. What is a resource in Pulumi, and how is it defined using code?

6. What is the purpose of stacks in Pulumi, and how do they relate to different environments?

7. How can you set specific configuration values for different stacks in Pulumi?

8. What does Pulumi use state files for, and why are they critical to the IaC process?

9. What are the default and alternative storage options for Pulumi state?

10. What does the `pulumi up` command do, and how does it manage infrastructure changes?

11. How can you preview changes before deploying them in Pulumi, and why is it important?

12. What command would you use to destroy all the resources in a Pulumi stack?

13. What are Inputs in Pulumi, and how are they used in defining cloud resources?

14. How do you set and retrieve configuration values in Pulumi for different environments?

15. What command is used to store sensitive information, such as database passwords, securely in Pulumi?

Further reading

To learn more about the basics of IaC using Pulumi, you can check out this blog post on the Pulumi website: `https://www.pulumi.com/what-is/what-is-infrastructure-as-code/`.

Unlock this book's exclusive benefits now

UNLOCK NOW

Scan this QR code or go to `packtpub.com/unlock`, then search for this book by name.

Note: Keep your purchase invoice ready before you start.

2

Creating Your First Pulumi IaC

Now that we've covered the fundamentals of **infrastructure as code (IaC)** and **Pulumi**, it's time to create your first IaC project using Pulumi. In this chapter, we'll walk you through building and deploying a simple cloud infrastructure project step by step. You'll start by *setting up a project*, *defining basic resources*, and *deploying* them using the **Pulumi CLI**. We'll explore the core concepts of writing and organizing your Pulumi code, managing configuration settings, and addressing common issues you might encounter during deployment.

By the end of this chapter, you'll have a functional Pulumi project and a solid grasp of the essential workflows involved in creating and managing cloud infrastructure. You'll also have learned valuable techniques for handling configurations, managing secrets securely, and implementing dynamic infrastructure that responds to changing conditions. This hands-on chapter will give you the foundational knowledge you need to tackle more complex IaC projects with confidence.

In this chapter, we're going to cover the following main topics:

- Kickstarting your first project
- Laying the foundation: Basic resource creation
- Secrets and configs: Managing sensitive data
- Smart infrastructure: Using conditional logic
- Scaling complexity: From simple to sophisticated

Technical requirements

If you would like to follow along with the examples in this chapter, you will require the following:

- The **Pulumi CLI** is required for executing commands. You can download it from here: `https://www.pulumi.com/docs/iac/download-install/`.

- Pulumi supports multiple programming languages, but for this chapter, we'll be using **JavaScript/TypeScript**, which requires **Node.js**. You can download and install it from the Node.js official site here: `https://nodejs.org/`.

- Since we'll be deploying resources to **Microsoft Azure**, you'll need an Azure account. You can sign up for a free account or use your existing Azure subscription. For more details, visit `https://azure.microsoft.com/en-us/free/`.

- The **Azure CLI** is required to interact with Azure resources from your local machine. You can install the Azure CLI by following the instructions here: `https://docs.microsoft.com/en-us/cli/azure/install-azure-cli`.

Kickstarting your first project

Now that you're ready to begin, let's kickstart your very first Pulumi project! In this section, we'll guide you through creating a new Pulumi project, understanding its structure, and setting up a basic infrastructure definition using TypeScript. Don't worry if this seems overwhelming—by the end of this section, you'll have a working project and a clear understanding of the essential pieces involved. To follow along with this chapter, you should log in to your Azure account by typing the following command in your terminal:

```
$ az login
```

This command will open a browser window where you can sign in with your Azure credentials. Once signed in, you're ready to use Pulumi with Azure.

Now that your environment is set up, it's time to create your first Pulumi project. Pulumi projects are the foundation of your IaC work, and they help organize your code and configuration.

To create a new project, open your terminal and navigate to the directory where you want your project to live. Then, run the following command to create a new project:

```
$ pulumi new azure-typescript
```

Pulumi will guide you through a series of prompts to configure your project:

- **Project name**: This will be the name of your Pulumi project
- **Project description**: You can give a short description of the project
- **Stack name**: Stacks are different environments for your infrastructure (e.g., dev, prod)
- **Azure location**: Choose the Azure region where you want to deploy resources (e.g., WestEurope, EastUS)

Once these prompts are completed, Pulumi will generate a new project folder with some starter files, and you'll be able to take a look at the basic structure of your new Pulumi project. You should see a few key files in your project folder:

- Pulumi.yaml: This file contains the project configuration, including the project name and description.
- Pulumi.<stack-name>.yaml: This file stores stack-specific configuration, such as environment variables and settings.
- index.ts: This is the main file where you'll write your infrastructure code. By default, Pulumi has already placed some starter code here.

Here's what your project might look like:

```
my-first-pulumi-project/
|
|— Pulumi.dev.yaml    # Configuration for the "dev" stack
|— Pulumi.yaml        # Project configuration
|— index.ts           # Main infrastructure code file
|— node_modules/      # Installed dependencies
|— package.json       # Project dependencies
|__ tsconfig.json      # TypeScript configuration
```

As we can tell from the folder structure, this is a Pulumi TypeScript project, and we need to install dependencies using npm. To install them, run the following command inside your project folder:

```
$ npm install
```

This will download and install all the necessary packages defined in your package.json file. Once that's done, you're ready to start defining infrastructure.

Each file plays an important role, but the most critical file for now is index.ts, where we'll define the cloud resources.

Laying the foundation: Basic resource creation

Now that the project setup is complete, you can open your index.ts (the entry point) file and start writing infrastructure declarations. This is where you'll define the cloud resources that Pulumi will create for you. For TypeScript projects like this one, the index.ts file is the main file where all your infrastructure code goes. However, if you're using other supported languages, such as Python, Go, or C#, the entry point will be different (__main__.py for **Python**, main.go for **Go**, etc.). For this chapter, we're sticking with TypeScript.

A common resource in cloud projects is a storage account. Let's add a simple **Azure storage account** to our project. In your index.ts file, start by adding the following code:

```
import * as pulumi from "@pulumi/pulumi";
import * as azure from "@pulumi/azure-native";

// Create an Azure Resource Group
const resourceGroup = new azure.resources.
ResourceGroup("myResourceGroup", {
    location: "WestEurope",
});

// Create an Azure Storage Account
const storageAccount = new azure.storage.
StorageAccount("mystorageaccount", {
    resourceGroupName: resourceGroup.name,
    location: resourceGroup.location,
    sku: {
        name: "Standard_LRS",
    },
    kind: "StorageV2",
});
```

This code does a couple of things:

- We define an Azure resource group called myResourceGroup in the WestEurope region
- We create a storage account named myStorageAccount inside that resource group
- The Standard_LRS SKU specifies that we want a locally redundant storage account, and StorageV2 is the account type

Once you've added the code, you can preview the changes before deployment. This is a good habit because it helps you understand what Pulumi is about to create. You can run the preview using the following command:

```
$ pulumi preview
```

Pulumi will show you a preview of the changes—specifically, that it will create a new resource group and a storage account. When you run the preview, your terminal should look like the following screenshot:

```
nennenwodo@Nennes-MBP chapter2 % pulumi preview
Previewing update (dev)

View in Browser (Ctrl+O): https://app.pulumi.com/adorahack/chapter2/dev/previews/18
98c-87739d76211c

     Type                                      Name              Plan
 +   pulumi:pulumi:Stack                       chapter2-dev      create
 +     ├─ azure-native:resources:ResourceGroup  myResourceGroup   create
 +     └─ azure-native:storage:StorageAccount   myStorageAccount  create

Resources:
    + 3 to create
```

Figure 2.1: Pulumi preview

> **Note**
>
> To successfully run pulumi preview, you may need to run pulumi login and az login first. This is to authenticate you to the Pulumi CLI as well as the Azure CLI (or the CLI for any other cloud you are using).

If everything looks good, go ahead and deploy the resources by running the following command:

```
$ pulumi up
```

Pulumi will now create these resources in Azure. Once the deployment is complete, you should see your storage account and resource group in the Azure portal.

Next, let's expand our infrastructure by adding an Azure **Virtual Network** (**VNet**). VNets allow your resources to communicate with each other securely.

Add the following code to your `index.ts` file, just below the storage account:

```
const vnet = new azure.network.VirtualNetwork("myVnet", {
    resourceGroupName: resourceGroup.name,
    location: resourceGroup.location,
    addressSpace: {
        addressPrefixes: ["10.0.0.0/16"],
    },
});
```

This creates a VNet named myVnet in the same resource group and region as your other resources. The `addressSpace` specifies the IP range for the network; in this case, we're using a range of `10.0.0.0/16`.

Now that we have a VNet, let's add a subnet. A subnet is a range of IP addresses within a VNet, and it allows you to segment your network for better management:

```
const subnet = new azure.network.Subnet("exampleSubnet", {
        resourceGroupName: resourceGroup.name,
        virtualNetworkName: vnet.name,
        addressPrefix: "10.0.1.0/24"
});
```

As usual, preview your changes before deploying:

```
$ pulumi preview
```

If everything looks good, deploy the resources:

```
$ pulumi up
```

Once the deployment is complete, you'll have a VNet with a subnet. You can view these in the Azure portal under the resource group you created.

Let's take a moment to talk about how resources are configured in Pulumi. Every resource you create has a set of properties that define its behavior. These properties are typically organized into blocks such as `resourceGroupName`, which specifies the Azure resource group where the resource will be created; `location`, which indicates the geographical region for the resource; and `sku`, which defines the pricing tier or performance level. You've already seen this with the storage account and VNet, but it applies to every resource you create.

For example, if you wanted to create a more complex **virtual machine** (**VM**), you would provide detailed configurations for things such as size, storage, and networking. Pulumi's declarative approach makes it easy to define these configurations in code.

Secrets and configs: Managing sensitive data

Now that you've deployed your first infrastructure using Pulumi, it's time to talk about dynamic infrastructure and sensitive data. In real-world projects, you'll often work with secrets such as **API keys, database passwords,** and other **sensitive information**. Storing these values in plain text can pose serious security risks. Luckily, Pulumi offers a way to manage sensitive data securely using its built-in secrets management system.

In this section, we'll explore how to manage secrets and configurations in Pulumi, ensuring that your infrastructure remains secure.

Configurations in Pulumi allow you to customize the behavior of your infrastructure by setting parameters such as **environment names, resource sizes,** and **credentials**. These settings are stored in your Pulumi stack and can be accessed programmatically within your code.

To set configurations, Pulumi provides a `pulumi config` command, which we'll explore shortly. The configuration values can be either plain text (such as region names) or encrypted secrets (such as passwords).

Pulumi treats sensitive data differently from regular configuration values. By marking a value as a **secret**, Pulumi ensures that it's encrypted and stored securely in your Pulumi state file. This means that even if someone accesses your state file, they won't be able to see the actual value of the secret.

Let's go through how to use both configurations and secrets in your Pulumi project.

To start working with configurations, you'll use the `pulumi config` command. For example, if you want to set the location of your Azure resources as a configurable value, you can do so by running the following:

```
$ pulumi config set azure:location WestEurope
```

This stores the WestEurope location in your configuration file, which you can reference in your code. In your `index.ts` file, modify the code to use this configuration:

```
const config = new pulumi.Config();
const location = config.require("azure:location");
const rg = new azure.resources.ResourceGroup("testrg", {
    location: location,
});
```

Here, `config.require()` retrieves the value you stored using the `pulumi config set` command.

Now, let's look at how to securely manage sensitive data such as passwords. Suppose you need to store a database password. You can mark it as a secret by using the `pulumi config set` command with the `--secret` flag:

```
$ pulumi config set dbPassword --secret mySecretPassword
```

This ensures that `mySecretPassword` is encrypted and stored securely in your Pulumi configuration. You can now retrieve this secret in your code using the `requireSecret()` method:

```
const dbPassword = config.requireSecret("dbPassword");
// Export the secret as output (this will remain encrypted in outputs)
export const password = dbPassword;
```

Even though the password is retrieved and used in your infrastructure code, it remains encrypted when stored in the Pulumi state file and in the output logs.

Secrets can be applied to various aspects of your infrastructure. For instance, if you're setting up an **Azure SQL database** and need to provide a password for the admin user, you can use the secret you stored:

```
const sqlServer = new azure.sql.Server("mySqlServer", {
    resourceGroupName: resourceGroup.name,
    location: resourceGroup.location,
    administratorLogin: "adminUser",
    administratorLoginPassword: dbPassword, // Use the secret password
                                            // here
});
```

By using `dbPassword` as the admin password, Pulumi ensures that it's not exposed in plain text, even in the deployment logs.

One of Pulumi's great features is how it handles sensitive data in the state file. When you store a secret using `pulumi config set --secret`, Pulumi encrypts that value. If you look at your stack configuration file (e.g., `Pulumi.dev.yaml`), you'll see something like this:

```
config:
  myproject:dbPassword:
    secure: v1:k0x$s97... # Encrypted secret value
```

The *secure key* indicates that the value is encrypted, making it unreadable without the proper decryption keys. Pulumi handles this encryption behind the scenes, ensuring your secrets stay safe.

As you can see, the Pulumi configuration files, such as `Pulumi.dev.yaml`, often contain references to sensitive data. Although these values are encrypted, it's still good practice to keep configuration files out of source control. You can add them to your `.gitignore` file to prevent accidental exposure:

```
# Ignore Pulumi stack configs
Pulumi.*.yaml
```

This helps ensure that your secrets don't accidentally end up in a public repository.

Dynamic infrastructure with configs

When provisioning cloud infrastructure, *flexibility* is essential. You don't want to hardcode values such as resource sizes, regions, or environment-specific details in your code. Pulumi's configuration system allows you to create dynamic infrastructure by making these values configurable, meaning they can be easily adjusted without changing your core infrastructure code. This flexibility allows you to reuse the same *code base* across different environments (e.g., development, testing, and production) while making specific adjustments, such as selecting the appropriate region or VM size, based on the needs of each environment.

Let's look at an example where we use Pulumi configurations to dynamically adjust the size of a VM, which is a virtualized instance that runs an operating system and applications, based on the environment. Instead of hardcoding the VM size in your `index.ts` file, you can use a configuration value that can be changed depending on the stack or environment to which you are deploying. To do this, start by setting a configuration value for the VM size using the Pulumi CLI:

```
pulumi config set vmSize Standard_B2s
```

This command stores `Standard_B2s` as the size for the VM in the Pulumi configuration for the current stack. You can use different sizes for different stacks (e.g., smaller sizes for dev and larger ones for prod).

Once you've set the configuration, you can use it in your TypeScript code to define the VM size. In `index.ts`, you can retrieve the configuration value and apply it to your infrastructure:

```
const config = new pulumi.Config();
const vmSize = config.
require("vmSize");  // Require ensures the value is mandatory

// Create a Virtual Machine using the dynamic VM size
```

```
const virtualMachine = new azure.compute.VirtualMachine("myVM", {
    resourceGroupName: resourceGroup.name,
    location: resourceGroup.location,
    vmSize: vmSize, // Use the config value for VM size
    // more code here ...
});
```

In this example, we have the following:

- vmSize is pulled from the Pulumi configuration
- We use the value to dynamically determine the size of the VM

This approach allows you to create flexible infrastructure code that can be adapted to different environments by simply changing the configuration value without modifying the underlying code. You can set different configuration values for different environments (stacks). For instance, you might want to use a smaller VM in your development environment and a larger one in production. To achieve this, you can set the vmSize configuration for each stack.

For the development environment, set a smaller VM size:

```
pulumi stack select dev
pulumi config set vmSize Standard_B1s
```

For the production environment, set a larger VM size:

```
pulumi stack select prod
pulumi config set vmSize Standard_D2s_v3
```

Now, depending on which stack you deploy (dev or prod), Pulumi will use the appropriate configuration for the VM size. This makes it easy to adjust your infrastructure across different environments without touching the code.

Using dynamic configurations like this has some key benefits:

- **Reusability:** You can reuse the same infrastructure code across multiple environments with different configurations
- **Flexibility**: Configuration changes are quick and don't require changes to the infrastructure code itself, making deployments more flexible
- **Environment-specific behavior**: Configurations allow for environment-specific settings (e.g., using different resource sizes for dev and prod environments), improving cost-efficiency and performance optimization

This dynamic approach is a best practice in IaC, as it ensures you adhere to the **don't repeat yourself (DRY)** principle and that infrastructure changes are simple and manageable.

Accessing configuration values

In previous sections, we've seen how configuration values can be accessed using the Config class. However, there are two primary methods for retrieving these values: require() and get(). Let's explore the differences and see how you can use them effectively.

Using require() for mandatory values

The require() method is used when a configuration value is *essential* for your infrastructure and should always be provided. If the configuration value is not set, Pulumi will throw an error, ensuring that you don't accidentally deploy incomplete or incorrect infrastructure.

Here's an example where we use require() to retrieve a mandatory configuration value for the Azure region:

```
const config = new pulumi.Config();
const region = config.require("azure:location");   // Fails if
                                                    // 'azure:location' is
                                                    // not set


// Create an Azure Resource Group using the region from config
const resourceGroup = new azure.resources.
ResourceGroup("myResourceGroup", {
    location: region,
});
```

In this code, config.require("azure:location") retrieves the region value that you set using pulumi config set azure:location WestEurope. If the configuration value is missing, Pulumi will stop the deployment and raise an error, prompting you to provide the necessary configuration.Using get() for optional values.

The get() method is used for optional configuration values. If the value is not set, Pulumi returns undefined, allowing you to provide default values or handle the absence of the configuration gracefully.

Here's an example where get() is used to retrieve an optional setting for enabling diagnostics in a VM:

```
const config = new pulumi.Config();
const enableDiagnostics = config.
get("enableDiagnostics") === "true";  // Optional config

// Create a Virtual Machine with optional diagnostics
const virtualMachine = new azure.compute.VirtualMachine("myVM", {
    resourceGroupName: resourceGroup.name,
    location: resourceGroup.location,
    vmSize: "Standard_B2s",
    diagnosticsProfile: enableDiagnostics ? {
        bootDiagnostics: {
            enabled: true,
        },
    } : undefined,   // If diagnostics are not enabled, no diagnostics
                     // profile is provided
});
```

In this case, config.get("enableDiagnostics") returns the value of the enableDiagnostics configuration if it exists. If the value is not set, it returns undefined, and we provide a default behavior (no diagnostics). This allows you to create infrastructure that adapts based on whether certain optional configurations are provided.

Combining require() and get()

In many cases, you might need to combine both require() and get() in your infrastructure code. For example, you might have a mandatory setting such as a resource region but an optional setting such as resource tags:

```
const config = new pulumi.Config();
const region = config.require("azure:location"); // Required
const tags = config.get("resourceTags");  // Optional
  const resourceGroup = new azure.resources.
ResourceGroup("myResourceGroup", {
    location: region,
    tags: tags ? JSON.parse(tags) : undefined,   // If tags are provided,
                                                 //  use them
});
```

In this example, `config.require("azure:location")` ensures that the region is always specified, while `config.get("resourceTags")` allows you to optionally provide tags. This combination helps balance flexibility with ensuring that essential settings are provided.

Next, let's look at how you can provide default values for optional configurations to ensure that your infrastructure behaves predictably even when certain settings are not explicitly set.

Providing default values

Sometimes, when a configuration value is not set, you may want to provide a *default value*. This can be useful when a configuration is optional, but you still want the infrastructure to behave in a certain way if the value isn't provided.

You can provide default values by using JavaScript's || (OR) operator, like so:

```
const config = new pulumi.Config();
const vmSize = config.get("vmSize") || "Standard_B1s";  // Default to
                                                        // 'Standard_B1s'
const virtualMachine = new azure.compute.VirtualMachine("myVM", {
    resourceGroupName: resourceGroup.name,
    location: resourceGroup.location,
    vmSize: vmSize,
});
```

In this case, if the `vmSize` config is not set, the VM will use the default size of `Standard_B1s`. This provides flexibility while ensuring your infrastructure still works if certain configurations are missing.

Retrieving secret configurations

When working with sensitive data, such as passwords or API keys, Pulumi allows you to retrieve secrets securely using `requireSecret()` or `getSecret()`. These methods work similarly to `require()` and `get()`, but they handle sensitive data securely by marking them as secrets.

For example, you might need to retrieve a secret database password:

```
const config = new pulumi.Config();
const dbPassword = config.requireSecret("dbPassword"); // Retrieves secret
const sqlServer = new azure.sql.Server("mySqlServer", {
    resourceGroupName: resourceGroup.name,
    location: resourceGroup.location,
    administratorLogin: "adminUser",
```

```
            administratorLoginPassword: dbPassword,   // Securely use the secret
                                                      // password
    });
```

In this example, `requireSecret("dbPassword")` ensures that the database password is treated as a secret, meaning it will be encrypted and handled securely throughout the deployment process.

Now that we understand how to handle sensitive data securely, let's explore how to make our infrastructure smarter by using conditional logic to adapt to different environments or requirements.

Smart infrastructure: Using conditional logic

When building cloud infrastructure, you often need to make decisions based on certain conditions, such as whether you're deploying to a production or development environment, or whether certain resources should exist based on configuration. Pulumi gives you the flexibility to create smart infrastructure by using conditional logic and loops directly within your code. This allows you to build infrastructure that adapts to different environments or requirements.

In this section, we'll explore how to implement conditional logic and loops in Pulumi using TypeScript, making your infrastructure more dynamic and responsive.

In many cloud environments, you may need to make decisions based on the current configuration or environment. Take the following examples:

- You might only want to create certain resources in a production environment
- You could conditionally enable or disable features, such as logging or diagnostics
- You may need to loop over a list of items, such as creating multiple VMs or storage accounts

Here, you'd be able to use familiar programming constructs (such as `if` statements and loops) to make these decisions dynamically as you define your infrastructure.

Conditional logic

Let's start with an example of **conditional logic**. Suppose you want to create an **Azure storage account** only if you're deploying to a production environment. First, you can set a configuration value to indicate the environment type:

```
pulumi config set env prod
```

Now, in your `index.ts` file, you can use this configuration to conditionally create the storage account:

```
const config = new pulumi.Config();
const environment = config.require("env");
if (environment === "prod") {
    const storageAccount = new azure.storage.
StorageAccount("prodstorageaccount", {
        resourceGroupName: resourceGroup.name,
        location: resourceGroup.location,
        sku: {
            name: "Standard_LRS",
        },
        kind: "StorageV2",
    });
}
```

In this example, the storage account will only be created if the env configuration is set to prod. If you're working in a different environment (e.g., dev or test), the storage account won't be created.

Using loops

If you need to create several VMs or storage accounts based on a list of names, you can use a loop to define these resources in one go. Let's create multiple storage accounts based on a list of environment names:

```
const environments = ["dev", "test", "prod"];
environments.forEach(env => {
    const storageAccount = new azure.storage.StorageAccount(`${env}
StorageAccount`, {
        resourceGroupName: resourceGroup.name,
        location: resourceGroup.location,
        sku: {
            name: "Standard_LRS",
        },
        kind: "StorageV2",
    });
});
```

In this example, we have the following:

- A loop iterates over a list of environments (dev, test, and prod)
- For each environment, a new storage account is created with a name that includes the environment name

This pattern is useful when you need to create multiple similar resources without duplicating code.

Scaling complexity: From simple to sophisticated

Now that you've mastered the basics of building infrastructure with Pulumi, it's time to scale up and handle more complex scenarios. As your project grows, you'll likely move from simple setups to more sophisticated architectures. In this section, we'll explore how to manage larger infrastructure projects by organizing resources into multi-tier architectures.

A common architectural pattern in cloud infrastructure is the **multi-tier architecture**, where different parts of your application are separated into layers. For example, a web application might have the following:

- A **frontend tier** for serving web content
- A **backend tier** for processing data and handling logic
- A **database tier** for storing information

In Pulumi, you can define each of these tiers as separate resources, creating a well-organized structure for your infrastructure.

Let's start by creating a simple web server for the frontend tier. You can use an Azure app service to host your frontend:

```
const appServicePlan = new azure.web.AppServicePlan("appServicePlan", {
    resourceGroupName: resourceGroup.name,
    location: resourceGroup.location,
    sku: {
        name: "B1",
        tier: "Basic",
    },
});

const webApp = new azure.web.WebApp("frontendApp", {
    resourceGroupName: resourceGroup.name,
    location: resourceGroup.location,
```

```
        serverFarmId: appServicePlan.id,
        siteConfig: {
            alwaysOn: true,
        },
    });
```

Here, you've created a basic Azure App Service plan and a web app that will serve as the frontend of your multi-tier architecture.

Next, let's add a backend API tier. You can use an **Azure Functions app** to handle the backend logic:

```
const storageAccount = new azure.storage.
StorageAccount("backendStorage", {
    resourceGroupName: resourceGroup.name,
    location: resourceGroup.location,
    sku: {
        name: "Standard_LRS",
    },
    kind: "StorageV2",
});

const functionApp = new azure.web.WebApp("backendFunctionApp", {
    resourceGroupName: resourceGroup.name,
    location: resourceGroup.location,
    serverFarmId: appServicePlan.id,
    siteConfig: {
        appSettings: [
            {
                name: "AzureWebJobsStorage",
                value: "STORAGE_ACCOUNT_CONNECTION_STRING",
            },
            {
                name: "FUNCTIONS_EXTENSION_VERSION",
                value: "~3",
            },
            {
                name: "WEBSITE_RUN_FROM_PACKAGE",
                value: "1",
            },
```

```
        ],
        alwaysOn: true,
    },
});
```

The backend is connected to an Azure storage account, which serves as a storage layer for the function app. This separation allows your application logic to be handled in the backend, independent of the frontend.

For the database tier, you can add an Azure SQL database to store data for the application:

```
const sqlServer = new azure.sql.Server("sqlServer", {
    resourceGroupName: resourceGroup.name,
    location: resourceGroup.location,
    administratorLogin: "adminUser",
    administratorLoginPassword: "Admin123!",
});

const sqlDatabase = new azure.sql.Database("appDatabase", {
    resourceGroupName: resourceGroup.name,
    serverName: sqlServer.name
});
```

With this, you've added a relational database to your architecture. The frontend and backend tiers can now interact with this database to store and retrieve data. As your infrastructure becomes more complex, it's a good idea to organize your code into modules. Modules allow you to break up your infrastructure into logical components, making the project easier to manage.

For example, you could separate your project into different files for each tier:

- frontend.ts for the web app
- backend.ts for the function app
- database.ts for the SQL database

Here's how you could import and use these modules in your index.ts file:

```
import { createFrontend } from "./frontend";
import { createBackend } from "./backend";
import { createDatabase } from "./database";
const frontendApp = createFrontend(resourceGroup);
const backendApp = createBackend(resourceGroup);
const database = createDatabase(resourceGroup);
```

This approach keeps your code clean and maintainable, especially as your infrastructure grows.

Summary

In this chapter, we covered the essential steps to create your first IaC project using Pulumi. You learned how to set up a basic project, define and deploy resources to Microsoft Azure, and configure your Pulumi project with dependencies.

We demonstrated creating fundamental resources such as Azure resource groups and storage accounts using TypeScript, previewing and deploying the changes. We also explained how to securely manage sensitive data, such as passwords, using Pulumi's secrets management system.

Additionally, we explored making infrastructure flexible through configuration, accessing both mandatory and optional values, and providing defaults. We introduced smart infrastructure techniques using conditional logic and loops, enabling you to adapt your code to different environments. Finally, we discussed scaling infrastructure complexity by organizing code for larger, multi-tier setups.

In the next chapter, you will learn how to use Pulumi to deploy and manage infrastructure on Amazon Web Services.

Questions

1. What are the key files in a Pulumi TypeScript project, and what is the role of each file?
2. How does Pulumi manage multiple environments using stacks, and how do you switch between them?
3. What is the purpose of the `pulumi preview` command, and why is it important to run it before `pulumi up`?
4. How does Pulumi handle sensitive data, and how would you securely store a database password using Pulumi?
5. What is the difference between using `require()` and `get()` when accessing configuration values in Pulumi? In what scenarios would you use each?
6. Explain how you would dynamically change the size of a VM using Pulumi's configuration system.
7. Describe how you can conditionally create resources based on the environment (e.g., only create certain resources in production). Provide a code example.

Unlock this book's exclusive benefits now

Scan this QR code or go to packtpub.com/unlock, then search for this book by name.

Note: Keep your purchase invoice ready before you start.

Part 2

Deploying Infrastructure Across Major Cloud Providers

The second part of the book focuses on using Pulumi to deploy infrastructure across the four most widely used cloud platforms. It moves from foundational concepts into practical, provider-specific implementations, demonstrating how to apply Pulumi's capabilities in real environments.

You will start with AWS, learning how to provision and configure core services such as compute, storage, and networking. From there, you will work with Azure to deploy resources that take advantage of its integrated ecosystem and enterprise features. The journey continues with Google Cloud, where you will build and manage infrastructure using Pulumi's Google Cloud provider.

Finally, you will explore Kubernetes deployments with Pulumi, creating and managing clusters and resources with the same programming language driven approach used for cloud services.

By the end of this part, you will be confident in using Pulumi to deliver infrastructure on any of these major platforms, applying consistent practices while adapting to each provider's unique capabilities.

This part of the book includes the following chapters:

- *Chapter 3, Deploying with Pulumi on AWS*
- *Chapter 4, Deploying with Pulumi on Azure*
- *Chapter 5, Deploying with Pulumi on Google Cloud*
- *Chapter 6, Deploying with Pulumi on Kubernetes*

3

Deploying with Pulumi on AWS

The introductions are out of the way, and it's now time to use Pulumi to deploy infrastructure across the major cloud providers. **AWS** is one of the most widely used cloud platforms in the world, offering a broad range of services and resources that can be deployed and managed with Pulumi. In this chapter, you will learn how to set up your AWS environment, configure Pulumi to work with AWS, and deploy a variety of AWS resources in a *secure, scalable*, and *efficient* manner.

We'll start by configuring your **AWS credentials** and setting up your Pulumi environment to ensure secure and seamless interaction with **AWS services**. From there, we'll move on to deploying core AWS resources, such as **EC2 instances**, **S3 buckets**, and **IAM roles**, guiding you through hands-on examples to help you master these essentials.

Once you're comfortable with the basics, we'll explore how to define and deploy custom AWS resources tailored to your specific needs. These reusable components will allow you to streamline your Pulumi projects and maximize efficiency.

Finally, we'll dive into automation and continuous integration, demonstrating how to integrate Pulumi with **CI/CD pipelines** to automate AWS deployments, handle updates, and ensure smooth rollbacks when necessary.

By the end of this chapter, you'll have the knowledge and confidence to deploy and manage AWS infrastructure using Pulumi, leveraging automation to ensure your infrastructure is scalable, reliable, and easy to maintain.

In this chapter, we're going to cover the following main topics:

- Setting up your AWS environment
- Creating and managing core AWS resources
- Creating custom AWS resources
- Automation and continuous integration

Technical requirements

If you would like to follow along with the examples in this chapter, you will require the following:

- The Pulumi CLI is required for executing commands. You can download it here: `https://www.pulumi.com/docs/iac/download-install/`.
- Pulumi supports multiple programming languages, but for this chapter, we'll be using JavaScript/TypeScript, which requires Node.js. You can download and install it from the Node.js official site here: `https://nodejs.org/`.
- Since we'll be deploying resources to AWS, you'll need an AWS account. You can sign up for a free account or use your existing AWS account. For more details, visit `https://aws.amazon.com/`.
- The AWS CLI is required to interact with AWS resources from your local machine. You can install the AWS CLI by following the instructions here: `https://aws.amazon.com/cli/`.
- The final section of this chapter is about automation and continuous integration, so you'll need a **GitHub account** so that you can create a GitHub Actions workflow. You can create an account here: `https://github.com/`.

Setting up your AWS environment

Before you can deploy any infrastructure with Pulumi on AWS, you need to configure your AWS environment and set up Pulumi to interact with AWS services securely. In this section, we'll walk through the steps to configure AWS credentials, set up your Pulumi environment, and ensure everything is ready for deployment.

The first step is to install the **AWS Command Line Interface (CLI)**. This tool allows you to interact with AWS directly from your terminal and is essential for configuring your environment. To install the AWS CLI, run the following command based on your operating system.

For macOS or Linux, use the following:

```
curl "https://awscli.amazonaws.com/AWSCLIV2.pkg" -o "AWSCLIV2.pkg"
sudo installer -pkg AWSCLIV2.pkg -target /
```

If you don't want to run the preceding command, or if you're on a Windows machine, download and run the installer from the official AWS CLI installation page: https://docs.aws.amazon.com/cli/latest/userguide/getting-started-install.html

Once the AWS CLI is installed, the next step is to configure your AWS credentials. These credentials are required for Pulumi to interact with AWS securely. In your terminal, run the following:

```
aws configure sso
```

This command will prompt you for the following information:

- **AWS Access Key ID**: You can create or retrieve this from the **AWS Management Console** under **IAM (Identity and Access Management)**.
- **AWS Secret Access Key**: This is the secret key associated with your access key ID.
- **Default region name**: Choose the region where you want to deploy resources, such as us-west-2 or eu-central-1.
- **Default output format**: You can set this to json, text, or table. For most cases, json is recommended.

After entering this information, your AWS credentials will be saved locally and used by both the AWS CLI and Pulumi.

You should already have the Pulumi CLI installed, and once you have the AWS CLI as well, you will be able to set up your first Pulumi project for AWS. Navigate to the directory where you want to store your project, and run the following command to create a new project:

```
pulumi new aws-typescript
```

This command will prompt you for several details:

- **Project name**: Choose a name for your Pulumi project
- **Project description**: Optionally, you can add a brief description of your project
- **Stack name**: You can choose dev, prod, or another environment name for this stack
- **AWS region**: Enter the AWS region where your resources will be deployed, such as us-west-2

Once completed, Pulumi will generate a project folder with several files, including `Pulumi.yaml` and `index.ts`, where you will define your infrastructure.

In Pulumi, the AWS provider is what connects your Pulumi code to AWS. By default, Pulumi uses the AWS credentials and region configured through the AWS CLI. If you need to customize the AWS provider, you can do so in your Pulumi code.

Here's an example of how to explicitly configure the AWS provider in your `index.ts` file:

```typescript
import * as aws from "@pulumi/aws";

// Set up the AWS provider with a specific region
const provider = new aws.Provider("aws", {
    region: "us-west-2",
});
```

This example configures the AWS provider to deploy resources to the `us-west-2` region. You can adjust the region or other provider settings as needed.

Before deploying any resources, it's important to verify that your AWS credentials and Pulumi environment are properly configured. You can do this by running the following command:

```
pulumi config
```

This will display the current configuration for your Pulumi stack, including the AWS region. If everything is correctly configured, you're ready to start deploying resources. The following screenshot shows what a config may look like.

```
nennenwodo@Nennes-MBP chapter3 % pulumi config
KEY              VALUE
aws:region       us-east-1
pulumi:tags      {"pulumi:template":"aws-typescript"}
```

Figure 3.1: Pulumi config output

Creating and managing core AWS resources

Now that you've set up your AWS environment with Pulumi, it's time to start creating and managing core **AWS resources**. In this section, we'll walk through deploying essential AWS resources such as **S3 buckets**, **EC2 instances**, **IAM roles**, and **VPCs**. These resources form the backbone of most AWS deployments, and you'll get hands-on experience defining and managing them using Pulumi and TypeScript.

Creating an S3 bucket

Let's start with one of the most common AWS resources—an S3 bucket. S3 is AWS's *object storage service*, used for storing data such as files, backups, and media. In your Pulumi index.ts file, add the following code to create a basic S3 bucket:

```
import * as aws from "@pulumi/aws";

// Create an S3 bucket
const bucket = new aws.s3.Bucket("testBucket", {
    bucket: "test-pulumi-bucket",
    acl: "private",  // Set access control to private
});

// Export the bucket name
export const bucketName = bucket.id;
```

This code creates a new S3 bucket with private access, meaning only authorized users can access it. Make sure you replace testBucket here with your own unique storage bucket name to avoid conflicts. To deploy this resource, run the following:

```
pulumi preview
pulumi up
```

This will create the S3 bucket in AWS, and the bucket name will be exported as an output (see *Figure 3.2*).

```
nennenwodo@Nennes-MBP chapter3 % pulumi up
Updating (dev)

View in Browser (Ctrl+O): https://app.pulumi.com/adorahack/chapter3/de

     Type                        Name              Status
     pulumi:pulumi:Stack         chapter3-dev
 +   └─ aws:s3:Bucket            testAdorasBucket  created (2s)

Outputs:
   + bucketName: "testadorsas-pulumi-bucket"

Resources:
     + 1 created
     1 unchanged

Duration: 10s
```

Figure 3.2: pulumi up output

To further control access to the S3 bucket, you can attach *policies* that define who can access the bucket and what actions they can perform. Here's how to add a bucket policy that allows public read access to objects in the bucket:

```
// Block public access configuration
const blockPublicAccess = new aws.
s3.BucketPublicAccessBlock("blockPublicAccess", {
    bucket: bucket.bucket,
    blockPublicAcls: false,
    ignorePublicAcls: false,
    blockPublicPolicy: false,
    restrictPublicBuckets: false,
});

// Define the bucket policy
const bucketPolicy = new aws.s3.BucketPolicy("bucketPolicy", {
    bucket: bucket.bucket, // Referencing the bucket created above
    policy: bucket.bucket.apply(bucketName => JSON.stringify({
        Version: "2012-10-17",
        Statement: [{
            Effect: "Allow",
```

```
            Principal: "*",
            Action: [
                "s3:GetObject"
            ],
            Resource: [
                `arn:aws:s3:::${bucketName}/*`
            ]
        }]
    }))
}, { dependsOn: blockPublicAccess });
```

This policy allows anyone to read objects in the bucket, which is useful for hosting static websites. You can modify the policy as needed to restrict or expand access.

Creating an EC2 instance

Next, let's create an EC2 instance, which is a *virtual server* that allows you to run applications in the cloud. First, you'll need to define a security group that controls inbound and outbound traffic to the instance. Add this code to your index.ts file:

```
const securityGroup = new aws.ec2.SecurityGroup("webSecurityGroup", {
    description: "Allow HTTP traffic",
    ingress: [{
        protocol: "tcp",
        fromPort: 80,
        toPort: 80,
        cidrBlocks: ["0.0.0.0/0"], // Allow traffic from anywhere
    }],
    egress: [{
        protocol: "-1",
        fromPort: 0,
        toPort: 0,
        cidrBlocks: ["0.0.0.0/0"], // Allow all outbound traffic
    }],
});
```

Now, define the EC2 instance itself:

```
// Get the most recent Amazon Linux 2 AMI ID
const ami = aws.ec2.getAmi({
    filters: [
        { name: "name", values: ["amzn2-ami-hvm-*-x86_64-gp2"] },
    ],
    owners: ["amazon"],
    mostRecent: true,
}).then(ami => ami.id);


const ec2Instance = new aws.ec2.Instance("myInstance", {
    instanceType: "t2.micro",
    ami: ami,
    vpcSecurityGroupIds: [securityGroup.id],
    tags: {
        Name: "PulumiEC2Instance",
    },
});
```

To deploy the EC2 instance and security group, run the following:

```
pulumi preview
pulumi up
```

Once the deployment is complete, the public IP of the instance will be displayed, allowing you to SSH into the server or access it via a web browser if you've installed a web server.

Working with IAM roles

Identity and Access Management (IAM) roles in AWS allow you to *manage permissions* for AWS services. For example, you may need to create an IAM role that allows an EC2 instance to access S3 buckets. Here's how to define an IAM role and attach a policy to allow S3 access:

```
const role = new aws.iam.Role("ec2S3AccessRole", {
    assumeRolePolicy: JSON.stringify({
        Version: "2012-10-17",
        Statement: [{
            Action: "sts:AssumeRole",
            Effect: "Allow",
            Principal: {
```

```
                Service: "ec2.amazonaws.com",
            },
        }],
    }),
});

const policy = new aws.iam.RolePolicy("ec2S3AccessPolicy", {
    role: role.id,
    policy: JSON.stringify({
        Version: "2012-10-17",
        Statement: [{
            Action: ["s3:ListBucket", "s3:GetObject"],
            Effect: "Allow",
            Resource: "*"
        }],
    }),
});
```

There are so many AWS resources that you can create and manage with Pulumi, and although we cannot cover everything in this book, the goal is to get you thinking about how you can use Pulumi to simplify and automate your cloud infrastructure deployments. The hands-on examples in this section are just the beginning. With Pulumi, you can leverage a wide range of AWS services and integrate them seamlessly into your projects, whether it's for storage, compute, networking, databases, or security. To see more resources and explore all the possibilities, check out the Pulumi AWS documentation:

`https://www.pulumi.com/registry/packages/aws/api-docs`.

Creating custom AWS resources

In this section, we'll explore how to define and deploy custom AWS resources that can be reused across Pulumi projects. Creating **custom resources** allows you to package common infrastructure patterns into modular, reusable components. This approach not only makes your code easier to maintain but also helps ensure consistency and scalability across multiple deployments.

We'll introduce how to build these custom resources using Pulumi's ComponentResource and explore why creating modular, reusable infrastructure can be a game-changer in managing complex cloud environments.

Why create custom resources?

As your infrastructure grows, you'll often find yourself repeatedly creating the same AWS resources, such as S3 buckets, EC2 instances, or VPCs. While defining these resources manually works in small projects, it quickly becomes inefficient and error-prone in larger setups. This is where custom resources come in.

Custom resources allow you to encapsulate the logic for creating cloud resources into reusable modules. Instead of duplicating code for every project, you can create a custom resource that wraps the complexity and offers a clean, simplified interface for deploying infrastructure. By using custom resources, you do the following:

- **Increase consistency**: Ensure that resources follow best practices (e.g., security settings, encryption, naming conventions) across all projects.

- **Improve reusability**: Build once, use everywhere. Custom resources let you reuse the same infrastructure logic across different teams or environments.

- **Simplify maintenance**: If you need to update infrastructure (e.g., a security policy change), you can update the custom resource once and apply it across all projects that use it.

For example, if you're frequently deploying S3 buckets with versioning and encryption enabled, you can wrap this logic into a custom resource and use it across all your projects without having to rewrite the same configuration.

Custom resources with Pulumi's ComponentResource

Pulumi's ComponentResource is a powerful feature that allows you to define custom resources as reusable components. It helps you *group together multiple AWS resources*, such as an S3 bucket and its associated policies, and treat them as a single logical unit.

Using ComponentResource allows you to create more complex infrastructure setups that are still easy to manage and deploy. While ComponentResource is a key part of creating reusable modules, it's not the only tool for doing so—it just helps organize the resources effectively.

Let's walk through a simple example of creating a custom S3 bucket resource. In this example, we'll create an S3 bucket with versioning and encryption enabled. We'll then package this logic into a custom resource that can be reused in different Pulumi projects.

First, create a new file called customS3Bucket.ts:

```typescript
import * as pulumi from "@pulumi/pulumi";
import * as aws from "@pulumi/aws";

export interface CustomS3BucketArgs {
    bucketName: string;
}

export class CustomS3Bucket extends pulumi.ComponentResource {
    public readonly bucket: aws.s3.Bucket;

    constructor(name: string, args: CustomS3BucketArgs, opts?:
    pulumi.ResourceOptions) {
        super("custom:resource:CustomS3Bucket", name, {}, opts);

        // Create the S3 bucket with versioning and encryption
        this.bucket = new aws.s3.Bucket(name, {
            bucket: args.bucketName,
            versioning: {
                enabled: true,
            },
            serverSideEncryptionConfiguration: {
                rule: {
                    applyServerSideEncryptionByDefault: {
                        sseAlgorithm: "AES256",
                    },
                },
            },
        });

        // Register outputs for the bucket name
        this.registerOutputs({
            bucketName: this.bucket.bucket,
        });
    }
}
```

Here's what's happening in this code:

- CustomS3BucketArgs: This *interface* defines the inputs for the custom resource, such as the S3 bucket name.

- CustomS3Bucket: This *class* extends ComponentResource, allowing us to group related resources together. We use this class to create an S3 bucket with versioning and encryption enabled.

- registerOutputs(): This *function* registers any outputs (such as the bucket name), which can be accessed by other parts of your infrastructure.

Once you've created your custom resource, you can use it in any Pulumi project. Here's how to instantiate the custom S3 bucket in index.ts:

```
import { CustomS3Bucket } from "./customS3Bucket";

// Create a custom S3 bucket
const myCustomBucket = new CustomS3Bucket("myCustomBucket", {
    bucketName: "my-custom-pulumi-bucket",
});

// Export the bucket name
export const bucketName = myCustomBucket.bucket.bucket;
```

By using this custom S3 bucket, you ensure that every bucket you create follows the same standards (versioning, encryption) without having to repeat the same code.

One of the benefits of creating custom resources is the ability to extend them easily. Let's enhance the custom S3 bucket by adding an event notification that triggers a **Lambda function** when an object is uploaded.

- In customS3Bucket.ts, update the code as follows:

```
export class CustomS3BucketWithNotifications extends
pulumi.ComponentResource {
    public readonly bucket: aws.s3.Bucket;

    constructor(name: string, args: CustomS3BucketArgs, opts?:
    pulumi.ResourceOptions) {
        super(
            "custom:resource:CustomS3BucketWithNotifications",
            name,
```

```
        {},
        Opts
    );

    // Create the S3 bucket
    this.bucket = new aws.s3.Bucket(name, {
        bucket: args.bucketName,
        versioning: {
            enabled: true,
        },
        serverSideEncryptionConfiguration: {
            rule: {
                applyServerSideEncryptionByDefault: {
                    sseAlgorithm: "AES256",
                },
            },
        },
    });

    // Add an event notification to trigger a Lambda function
    const notification = new aws.s3.BucketNotification(
        `${name}-notification`,
        {
            bucket: this.bucket.id,
            lambdaFunctions: [{
                lambdaFunctionArn: lambdaFunction.arn,
                events: ["s3:ObjectCreated:*"],
            }],
        });

    this.registerOutputs({
        bucketName: this.bucket.bucket,
    });
    }
}
```

- Now, this custom resource not only creates an S3 bucket but also triggers a Lambda function when objects are created in the bucket.

Organizing and sharing custom resources

Once you've created several custom resources, you'll want to organize them in a way that makes it easy to share and reuse them across projects. A good practice is to package your custom resources into *modules* and *libraries*, which you can then publish to **npm** or a private repository.

For example, you might structure your project like this:

```
my-custom-aws-resources/
|
|— customS3Bucket.ts
|— customVpc.ts
|— customEc2.ts
```

By organizing custom resources into a directory structure like this, you can easily import and use them in any Pulumi project.

Versioning custom resources

As your infrastructure evolves, you'll likely need to update your custom resources. When making changes, it's important to version your custom modules. **Versioning** ensures that different projects can continue using older versions of the resource without breaking, while newer projects can take advantage of updates.

For example, if you enhance CustomS3Bucket with additional functionality (such as lifecycle policies), you can release a new version of the module. Projects that rely on the older version can continue working as expected.

Automation and continuous integration

Automation in AWS deployments helps reduce manual errors, as CI/CD pipelines ensure that every infrastructure change is applied consistently. This *consistency* also speeds up deployments, allowing infrastructure updates to be deployed faster with less manual intervention. Additionally, automation enables *rollbacks*; if something goes wrong during a deployment, a well-configured pipeline allows you to quickly revert to a previous stable version. By ensuring consistency across environments, automation makes it easy to replicate infrastructure changes in different environments such as development, staging, and production, helping maintain reliability across the board.

To get started, you'll need to create a **GitHub Actions workflow** that runs Pulumi commands to manage your AWS infrastructure. First, ensure your Pulumi project is already set up in your repository.

Next, create a new file called `.github/workflows/pulumi.yml` to define the GitHub Actions workflow.

Here's a basic example of a GitHub Actions workflow that deploys AWS infrastructure using Pulumi:

```yaml
name: Pulumi AWS Deploy
on:
  push:
    branches:
      - main
jobs:
  deploy:
    runs-on: ubuntu-latest
    steps:
      - name: Checkout repository
        uses: actions/checkout@v2
      - name: Set up Node.js
        uses: actions/setup-node@v2
        with:
          node-version: '14'
      - name: Install Pulumi
        run: |
          curl -fsSL https://get.pulumi.com | sh
          export PATH=$PATH:$HOME/.pulumi/bin
      - name: Install dependencies
        run: npm install
      - name: AWS Configure
        uses: aws-actions/configure-aws-credentials@v1
        with:
          aws-access-key-id: ${{ secrets.AWS_ACCESS_KEY_ID }}
          aws-secret-access-key: ${{ secrets.AWS_SECRET_ACCESS_KEY }}
          aws-region: us-west-2
      - name: Pulumi Preview
        run: pulumi preview
      - name: Pulumi Deploy
        run: pulumi up --yes
```

Here's a breakdown of the key parts of the GitHub Actions workflow:

- **on: push**: This tells GitHub Actions to trigger the workflow whenever changes are pushed to the main branch.
- **jobs**: The deploy job runs on the ubuntu-latest environment, meaning the workflow will be executed in a Linux virtual machine.
- **Set up Node.js and Pulumi**: The workflow installs Node.js (required for TypeScript Pulumi projects) and Pulumi.
- **AWS Configure**: This step configures the AWS credentials using the secrets stored in your GitHub repository (AWS_ACCESS_KEY_ID and AWS_SECRET_ACCESS_KEY). Make sure you add these credentials as secrets in your GitHub repo settings.
- **Pulumi Preview and Deploy**: Finally, the workflow runs pulumi preview to show the planned changes and pulumi up --yes to apply the changes and deploy your AWS resources.

The workflow example provided here is just the beginning—there are many ways to customize and extend these workflows to fit your needs. We'll dive deeper into CI/CD best practices and other automation techniques using other CI/CD tools later in the book. For now, you're equipped to start automating your AWS deployments with Pulumi and GitHub Actions.

Summary

This chapter covered how to deploy infrastructure on AWS using Pulumi. We started by setting up the AWS environment and configuring Pulumi to interact securely with AWS services. You learned how to create core AWS resources such as S3 buckets, EC2 instances, and IAM roles, and how to automate the process using continuous integration with GitHub Actions. The chapter also explored creating custom AWS resources that can be reused across projects, making your infrastructure deployments more modular and scalable.

In the next chapter, you will learn how to use Pulumi to deploy and manage infrastructure on Microsoft Azure.

Questions

1. How do you initialize a new Pulumi project for AWS using TypeScript?

2. What is the purpose of the AWS provider in Pulumi, and how is it configured?

3. Describe how to create an S3 bucket using Pulumi in TypeScript.

4. How do you create an EC2 instance in Pulumi?

5. What is the significance of IAM roles in AWS, and how are they created with Pulumi?

6. What are the key benefits of creating custom AWS resources using Pulumi's `ComponentResource`?

7. Explain the structure of a GitHub Actions workflow for deploying AWS infrastructure using Pulumi.

8. How do you configure AWS region settings explicitly in Pulumi?

9. What role does automation play in Pulumi deployments, and how can it be integrated with CI/CD?

4

Deploying with Pulumi on Azure

Azure is one of the most widely used cloud platforms in the world, offering a broad range of services and resources that can be deployed and managed with Pulumi. In this chapter, you will learn how to set up your Azure environment, configure Pulumi to work with Azure, and deploy a variety of Azure resources in a secure, scalable, and efficient manner.

We'll start by configuring your Azure credentials and setting up your Pulumi environment to ensure secure and seamless interaction with Azure services. From there, we'll move on to deploying core Azure resources.

Once you're comfortable with the basics, we'll explore how to define and deploy custom Azure resources tailored to your specific needs. These reusable components will allow you to streamline your Pulumi projects and maximize efficiency.

Finally, we'll dive into automation and continuous integration, demonstrating how to integrate Pulumi with CI/CD pipelines to automate Azure deployments, handle updates, and ensure smooth rollbacks when necessary.

By the end of this chapter, you'll have the knowledge and confidence to deploy and manage Azure infrastructure using Pulumi, leveraging automation to ensure that your infrastructure is scalable, reliable, and easy to maintain.

In this chapter, we're going to cover the following main topics:

- Setting up your Azure environment
- Creating and managing core Azure resources
- Creating custom Azure resources
- Automation and continuous integration

Technical requirements

If you would like to follow along with the examples in this chapter, you will require the following:

- The Pulumi CLI is required for executing commands. You can download it from `https://www.pulumi.com/docs/iac/download-install/`.
- Pulumi supports multiple programming languages, but for this chapter, we'll be using JavaScript/TypeScript, which requires Node.js. You can download and install it from the Node.js official site here: `https://nodejs.org/`.
- Since we'll be deploying resources to Azure, you'll need an Azure account. You can sign up for a free account or use your existing Azure account. For more details, visit the Azure website here:
- `https://azure.microsoft.com/en-us/pricing/purchase-options/azure-account`.
- The Azure CLI is required to interact with Azure resources from your local machine. You can install the Azure CLI by following the instructions here: `https://learn.microsoft.com/en-us/cli/azure/install-azure-cli`.
- The final section of this chapter is about automation and continuous integration, so you'll need a GitHub account so that you can create a GitHub Actions workflow. You can create an account here: `https://github.com/`.

Setting up your Azure environment

Before you can start deploying infrastructure to Azure with Pulumi, you need to configure your Azure environment and ensure that Pulumi can interact securely with Azure services. In this section, we'll guide you through setting up Azure credentials, configuring the Pulumi environment, and preparing everything for deployment.

The first step is to install the Azure **Command-Line Interface** (**CLI**), which is essential for managing your Azure account and configuring authentication for Pulumi.

For Linux, use the following command to install the Azure CLI:

```
curl -sL https://aka.ms/InstallAzureCLIDeb | sudo bash
```

For macOS, it's recommended to install the Azure CLI using Homebrew. Run the following command:

```
brew update && brew install azure-cli
```

For Windows, you can download the installer from the Azure CLI installation page: `https://learn.microsoft.com/en-us/cli/azure/install-azure-cli-windows`.

Once installed, verify the Azure CLI is working by running the following:

```
az --version
```

Once you've verified that the Azure CLI has been installed, you need to log in to your Azure account. Run the following command to initiate the login process:

```
az login
```

This will open a web browser where you can enter your Azure credentials. After successfully logging in, the Azure CLI will display the details of your account and subscriptions. Depending on your version of the Azure CLI, it will prompt you to choose a subscription, as displayed in *Figure 4.1*.

```
nennenwodo@Nennes-MBP chapter4 % az login
A web browser has been opened at https://login.microsoftonline.com/organizations/oauth2/v2.0/authoriz
e. Please continue the login in the web browser. If no web browser is available or if the web browser
 fails to open, use device code flow with `az login --use-device-code`.

Retrieving tenants and subscriptions for the selection...

[Tenant and subscription selection]

No    Subscription name          Subscription ID                               Tenant
----  -------------------------  --------------------------------------------  -----------------
[1] *                                                                          Default Directory

The default is marked with an *; the default tenant is 'Default Directory' and subscription is

Select a subscription and tenant (Type a number or Enter for no changes): 1

Tenant: Default Directory
Subscription:
```

Figure 4.1: Azure CLI subscription selection

However, if that doesn't happen, you can set a default subscription using the following command:

```
az account set --subscription "YOUR_SUBSCRIPTION_ID"
```

You should already have the Pulumi CLI installed, and once you have the Azure CLI as well, you will be able to set up your first Pulumi project for Azure. Navigate to the directory where you want to store your project, and run the following command to create a new project:

```
pulumi new azure-typescript
```

This command will prompt you to provide the following:

- **Project name**: Choose a name for your Pulumi project
- **Project description**: Optionally, add a description of your project
- **Stack name**: Select an environment for the stack, such as dev or prod
- **Azure location**: Choose a region for your resources, such as **WestEurope** or **EastUS**

Once complete, Pulumi will generate a basic project with several files, including `Pulumi.yaml` (project settings) and `index.ts` (your main infrastructure code file).

Pulumi uses the Azure credentials configured through the Azure CLI to authenticate with Azure services. By default, Pulumi will automatically pick up your Azure credentials from the CLI, but if you need to specify additional options (such as different *tenants* or *subscriptions*), you can configure this directly in your Pulumi code.

Here's an example of how you can configure the Azure provider within your Pulumi project:

```
const provider = new azure.Provider("azure", {
    subscriptionId: process.env.AZURE_SUBSCRIPTION_ID,
    tenantId: process.env.AZURE_TENANT_ID,
});
```

In this example, environment variables such as `AZURE_SUBSCRIPTION_ID` and `AZURE_TENANT_ID` can be used to specify credentials explicitly, which is especially useful in automation environments such as CI/CD.

Let's verify that everything is working by creating a simple Azure resource. Resource groups are used to group related resources together in Azure. In your `index.ts` file, add the following code to create an Azure resource group:

```
const resourceGroup = new azure.resources.
ResourceGroup("myResourceGroup", {
    location: "WestEurope",
});
```

♀ **Quick tip**: Enhance your coding experience with the **AI Code Explainer** and **Quick Copy** features. Open this book in the next-gen Packt Reader. Click the **Copy** button (1) to quickly copy code into your coding environment, or click the **Explain** button (2) to get the AI assistant to explain a block of code to you.

```
                                                    Copy      Explain
function calculate(a, b) {                           1          2
    return {sum: a + b};
};
```

📱 **The next-gen Packt Reader** is included for free with the purchase of this book. Scan the QR code OR visit packtpub.com/unlock, then use the search bar to find this book by name. Double-check the edition shown to make sure you get the right one.

To deploy this resource, run the following commands in your terminal:

```
pulumi preview
pulumi up
```

Pulumi will show you the planned changes and then deploy the resource group to Azure.

Creating and managing core Azure resources

In this section, we'll explore how to deploy and manage essential Azure resources using Pulumi. While you may be familiar with resources such as storage accounts and virtual networks, we'll focus on more advanced Azure services that are crucial for building robust cloud infrastructure. Through hands-on examples, you'll learn how to define and manage resources such as **Azure Kubernetes Service (AKS)**, **Azure Key Vault**, and **Azure Load Balancer**.

Creating an AKS cluster

AKS is a managed Kubernetes service that simplifies deploying, managing, and scaling containerized applications. Let's create an AKS cluster using TypeScript.

In your index.ts file, add the following code:

```
const aksCluster = new azure.containerservice.
ManagedCluster("myAKSCluster", {
    resourceGroupName: resourceGroup.name,
    location: resourceGroup.location,
    agentPoolProfiles: [{
        count: 2,
        vmSize: "Standard_DS2_v2",
        mode: "System",
        name: "agentpool",
    }],
    dnsPrefix: "myakscluster",
    identity: {
        type: "SystemAssigned",
    },
    kubernetesVersion: "<latest-version>",
    enableRBAC: true,
});
```

This code sets up an AKS cluster with two nodes using the Standard_DS2_v2 VM size. You can
adjust the *cluster size*, *Kubernetes version*, and other parameters depending on your requirements.
You can deploy the cluster by running pulumi up.

Creating an Azure key vault

Azure Key Vault is a secure storage service for secrets, keys, and certificates. You can use Key Vault
to store sensitive information such as *API keys*, *passwords*, and *certificates* securely. Here's how to
create an Azure key vault in your Pulumi project:

```
const keyVault = new azure.keyvault.Vault("myKeyVault", {
    resourceGroupName: resourceGroup.name,
    location: resourceGroup.location,
    properties: {
        sku: {
```

```
                 family: "A",
                 name: "standard",
           },
           tenantId: azure.authorization.getClientConfig().then(config =>
           config.tenantId),
           accessPolicies: [],
       },
   });
```

Once deployed, you can add secrets, certificates, and keys to the key vault for secure management.

Creating an Azure web app (Azure App Service)

Azure App Service is a fully managed platform for building, deploying, and scaling web applications. You can deploy a web app with Pulumi by creating an **App Service plan** and then deploying the app itself. Here's how to set up Azure App Service:

```
const appServicePlan = new azure.web.AppServicePlan("myAppServicePlan", {
    resourceGroupName: resourceGroup.name,
    location: resourceGroup.location,
    sku: {
        name: "B1",
        tier: "Basic",
    },
});
 const webApp = new azure.web.WebApp(" mytestweb-app", {
    name: "mytestweb-app",
    resourceGroupName: resourceGroup.name,
    location: resourceGroup.location,
    serverFarmId: appServicePlan.id,
    kind: "app"
});
```

The preceding code creates a basic web application hosted on an App Service plan. You can adjust the SKU to scale up or down based on your needs. You can also add app settings and other configurations you might need.

Configuring an Azure Load Balancer

Azure Load Balancer distributes incoming traffic across multiple servers, helping you build high-availability systems. Here's how to create an Azure load balancer using Pulumi:

```
const publicIP = new azure.network.PublicIPAddress("myPublicIP", {
    resourceGroupName: resourceGroup.name,
    location: resourceGroup.location,
    sku: {
        name: "Basic",
    }
});
const loadBalancer = new azure.network.LoadBalancer("myLoadBalancer", {
    resourceGroupName: resourceGroup.name,
    location: resourceGroup.location,
    sku: {
        name: "Basic",
    },
    frontendIPConfigurations: [{
        name: "myFrontendIP",
        publicIPAddress: { id: publicIP.id }
    }],
});
```

This creates a public-facing load balancer that can be used to distribute traffic across multiple backend resources. To deploy it, you can run the `pulumi up` command.

There are so many Azure resources that you can create and manage with Pulumi, and although we cannot cover everything in this book, the goal is to get you thinking about how you can use Pulumi to simplify and automate your cloud infrastructure deployments. The hands-on examples in this section are just the beginning. With Pulumi, you can leverage a wide range of Azure services and integrate them seamlessly into your projects, whether it's for storage, compute, networking, databases, or security. To see more resources and explore all the possibilities, check out the Pulumi Azure documentation: `https://www.pulumi.com/registry/packages/azure-native/api-docs/`.

Creating custom Azure resources

In this section, we will explore how to define and deploy custom Azure resources that can be re-used across different Pulumi projects. Custom resources allow you to encapsulate infrastructure configurations into reusable components, simplifying your setup and ensuring consistency across your deployments. While we previously introduced ComponentResource in *Chapter 3*, we'll apply similar concepts here but focus on creating and customizing Azure resources.

Creating custom Azure resources is useful for managing infrastructure at scale. If you find your-self repeatedly deploying the same types of resources (such as storage accounts, app services, or databases), you can encapsulate the logic for these resources into reusable components. This not only saves time but also ensures that all your deployments follow best practices and are consistent across multiple environments, such as development, staging, and production.

Let's begin with something small: a custom Azure storage account. We'll create a storage account with custom settings such as replication, access tier, and encryption. The goal is to define these settings once and reuse them across different projects.

Here's how you can define a custom Azure storage account in a custom file you create. You can call it customStorageAccount.ts:

```typescript
// import needed libraries
export class CustomStorageAccount {
    public readonly storageAccount: azure.storage.StorageAccount;

    constructor(name: string, resourceGroupName: pulumi.
Input<string>, location: pulumi.Input<string>) {
        this.storageAccount = new azure.storage.StorageAccount(name, {
            resourceGroupName: resourceGroupName,
            location: location,
            sku: {
                name: "Standard_LRS"
            },
            kind: "StorageV2",
            accessTier: "Hot",
            enableHttpsTrafficOnly: true,
            allowBlobPublicAccess: false,
            encryption: {
                services: {
```

```
                    blob: {
                        enabled: true,
                    },
                },
                keySource: "Microsoft.Storage",
            },
        });
    }
}
```

In this code, we define a `CustomStorageAccount` class that encapsulates the logic for creating a storage account with custom settings such as **locally redundant storage (LRS)**, a Hot access tier, and HTTPS-only access. You can reuse this class across your projects by passing different resource group names and locations.

To use this custom storage account in your Pulumi project, instantiate the class and pass in the required arguments, such as the resource group name and location. Here's how to use it in your `index.ts` file:

```
import { CustomStorageAccount } from "./customStorageAccount";
const storageAccount = new CustomStorageAccount("customstore",
resourceGroup.name, resourceGroup.location);
```

This setup creates a storage account with predefined settings, ensuring that you don't need to rewrite the same code every time you need a storage account in a different project. To deploy this, run `pulumi up`.

Now, let's extend this concept. Suppose you want to deploy a web app to an Azure **App Service Environment (ASE)** with custom configurations. ASE provides an isolated and highly scalable environment for running your web applications.

We can create a custom web app that is deployed into an ASE with specific settings, such as scaling configurations and custom domains.

Here's how to define a custom web app class that deploys to an ASE:

```
export class CustomWebApp {
    public readonly webApp: azure.web.WebApp;
    constructor(name: string, resourceGroupName: pulumi.
Input<string>, location: pulumi.Input<string>, aseId: pulumi.
Input<string>) {
```

```
        const appServicePlan = new azure.web.AppServicePlan(`${name}-
plan`, {
            resourceGroupName: resourceGroupName,
            location: location,
            sku: {
                name: "I1",  // Isolated SKU for ASE
                tier: "Isolated",
            },
            hostingEnvironmentProfile: {
                id: aseId,
            },
        });
        this.webApp = new azure.web.WebApp(name, {
            resourceGroupName: resourceGroupName,
            location: location,
            serverFarmId: appServicePlan.id,
            httpsOnly: true,
            siteConfig: {
                alwaysOn: true,
                minTlsVersion: "1.2",
            },
        });
    }
}
```

In this code, we define a CustomWebApp class that encapsulates the logic for creating a web app in an ASE. The web app has custom settings such as HTTPS-only access, TLS 1.2 enforcement, and an isolated SKU for better scalability. Once you have successfully created your custom web app, you can also use it in index.ts.

Automation and continuous integration

Automating Azure deployments ensures that updates are applied consistently across different environments such as development, staging, and production. This means you don't need to manually apply every change, which helps avoid mistakes. **Automation** also makes deployments faster and smoother, allowing updates to happen as soon as the code is changed. If something goes wrong, CI/CD pipelines make it easy to roll back to a previous working version, ensuring minimal downtime.

We can create a *GitHub Actions workflow* that runs Pulumi commands automatically when you push code to your repository's main branch. Let's create a simple GitHub Actions workflow to automate the deployment process.

First, create a file called `.github/workflows/pulumi.yml` in your GitHub repository and add the following content:

```yaml
name: Pulumi Azure Deploy
on:
  push:
    branches:
      - main
jobs:
  deploy:
    runs-on: ubuntu-latest
    steps:
      - name: Checkout repository
        uses: actions/checkout@v2
      - name: Set up Node.js
        uses: actions/setup-node@v2
        with:
          node-version: '14'
      - name: Install Pulumi
        run: |
          curl -fsSL https://get.pulumi.com | sh
          export PATH=$PATH:$HOME/.pulumi/bin
      - name: Azure CLI Login
        uses: azure/login@v1
        with:
          creds: ${{ secrets.AZURE_CREDENTIALS }}
      - name: Install dependencies
        run: npm install
      - name: Pulumi Preview
        run: pulumi preview
      - name: Pulumi Deploy
        run: pulumi up --yes
```

Let's break down the key parts of the GitHub Actions workflow:

- **on: push**: This tells GitHub Actions to trigger the workflow whenever changes are pushed to the `main` branch.
- **jobs**: The `deploy` job runs the actual steps needed to deploy your Azure infrastructure using Pulumi.
- **Set up Node.js and Install Pulumi**: Since Pulumi uses Node.js for TypeScript projects, the workflow installs Node.js and the Pulumi CLI.
- **Azure CLI Login**: This step logs in to Azure using a service principal. Make sure to add your Azure credentials as secrets in the GitHub repository.
- **Pulumi Preview** and **Pulumi Deploy**: The workflow first runs `pulumi preview` to show planned changes, then runs `pulumi up` to deploy those changes automatically.

The workflow example provided here is just the beginning. There are many ways to customize and extend these workflows to fit your needs. We'll dive deeper into CI/CD best practices and other automation techniques using other CI/CD tools in the *Chapter 7*. For now, you're equipped to start automating your Azure deployments with Pulumi and GitHub Actions.

Summary

In this chapter, we covered how to set up Pulumi for deploying and managing resources on Azure. We started by configuring the Azure environment, setting up the Azure CLI, and ensuring that Pulumi could securely connect to Azure services. After that, we explored how to create and manage core Azure resources, such as Kubernetes clusters, key vaults, and web apps. The chapter also explained how to define custom Azure resources for reuse across projects, helping streamline deployments. Finally, we discussed integrating Pulumi with automation tools such as GitHub Actions to automate deployments through CI/CD pipelines, making infrastructure management more efficient and scalable.

In the next chapter, we will cover using Pulumi to deploy resources to Google Cloud.

Questions

1. What command is used to create a new Pulumi project for Azure, and what key details are required during project initialization?
2. How does Pulumi automatically pick up Azure credentials from the CLI, and how can you manually configure Azure credentials in a Pulumi project?

3. How can you define an AKS cluster in Pulumi using TypeScript, and what are some of the key parameters for configuring the cluster?

4. How does the reuse of custom resources improve consistency and follow best practices across multiple Pulumi projects?

5. What are the benefits of automating Azure deployments using CI/CD pipelines?

5

Deploying with Pulumi on Google Cloud

Google Cloud is one of the most widely used cloud platforms in the world, offering a broad range of services and resources that can be deployed and managed with Pulumi. In this chapter, you will learn how to set up your Google Cloud environment, configure Pulumi to work with Google Cloud, and deploy a variety of Google Cloud resources in a secure, scalable, and efficient manner, similar to previous chapters with AWS and Microsoft Azure.

We'll start by configuring your Google Cloud credentials and setting up your Pulumi environment to ensure secure and seamless interaction with Google Cloud services. From there, we'll move on to deploying core Google Cloud resources.

Once you're comfortable with the basics, we'll explore how to define and deploy custom Google Cloud resources tailored to your specific needs. These reusable components will allow you to streamline your Pulumi projects and maximize efficiency.

Finally, we'll dive into automation and continuous integration, demonstrating how to integrate Pulumi with CI/CD pipelines to automate Google Cloud deployments, handle updates, and ensure smooth rollbacks when necessary.

By the end of this chapter, you'll have the knowledge and confidence to deploy and manage Google Cloud infrastructure using Pulumi, leveraging automation to ensure your infrastructure is scalable, reliable, and easy to maintain.

In this chapter, we're going to cover the following main topics:

- Setting up your Google Cloud environment
- Creating and managing core Google Cloud resources
- Creating custom Google Cloud resources
- Automation and continuous integration

Technical requirements

If you would like to follow along with the examples in this chapter, you will require the following:

- The Pulumi CLI is required for executing commands. You can download it here: `https://www.pulumi.com/docs/iac/download-install/`.

- Pulumi supports multiple programming languages, but for this chapter, we'll be using JavaScript/TypeScript, which requires Node.js. You can download and install it from the Node.js official site here: `https://nodejs.org/`.

- Since we'll be deploying resources to Google Cloud, you'll need a **Google Cloud** account. You can sign up for a free account or use your existing Google Cloud account. For more details, visit the Google Cloud website here: `https://cloud.google.com/gcp`.

- The Google Cloud CLI is required to interact with Google Cloud resources from your local machine. You can install the Google Cloud CLI by following the instructions here: `https://cloud.google.com/sdk/docs/install`.

- The final section of this chapter is about automation and continuous integration, so you'll need a GitHub account so that you can create a GitHub Actions workflow. You can create an account here: `https://github.com/`.

Setting up your Google Cloud environment

Before you can start deploying infrastructure to Google Cloud with Pulumi, you need to configure your Google Cloud environment and ensure that Pulumi can interact securely with Google Cloud services. In this section, we'll guide you through setting up Google Cloud credentials, configuring the Pulumi environment, and preparing everything for deployment.

The first step is to install the Google Cloud CLI/SDK. This tool allows you to interact with Google Cloud directly from your terminal and is essential for configuring your environment.

To install the CLI, run the following command based on your operating system:

```
curl -O https://dl.google.com/dl/cloudsdk/channels/rapid/downloads/google-
cloud-cli-<VERSION>-<OS>.tar.gz
tar -xf google-cloud-cli-<VERSION>-<OS>.tar.gz
./google-cloud-sdk/install.sh
```

If you don't want to run the preceding command, or if you're on a Windows machine, you can either try other options or download and run the installer from the official Google Cloud CLI installation page: `https://cloud.google.com/sdk/docs/install`.

Once the Google Cloud CLI is installed, the next step is to authenticate with Google Cloud so that you are able to use Pulumi with Google Cloud. The following command shows how to authenticate with Google Cloud:

```
gcloud auth login
```

Once you've successfully authenticated, you can configure gcloud to interact with your Google Cloud project. To do so, use the following commands:

```
gcloud config set project <PROJECT_ID>
pulumi config set gcp:project <PROJECT_ID>
```

Replace `<PROJECT_ID>` with the ID of the project you want to use. This ensures that all subsequent operations target this project. Next, enable **application default credentials (ADC)**, which allows Pulumi to authenticate and interact with your Google Cloud resources. Use this command:

```
gcloud auth application-default login
```

Once authenticated, you need to ensure that the required Google Cloud APIs are enabled for your project. Pulumi uses these APIs to provision and manage resources. For example, to enable **Compute Engine and Cloud Storage APIs**, run the following commands:

```
gcloud services enable compute.googleapis.com
gcloud services enable storage.googleapis.com
```

If you plan to use other Google Cloud services, enable their respective APIs in the same manner.

You should already have the Pulumi CLI installed, and once you have the gcloud CLI as well, you will be able to set up your first Pulumi project for Google Cloud. Navigate to the directory where you want to store your project, and run the following command to create a new project:

```
pulumi new gcp-typescript
```

This command initializes a new Pulumi project using the Google Cloud TypeScript template. You'll be prompted to provide a project name, stack name, and some optional configuration values. Follow the prompts to complete the setup. Pulumi will create a set of starter files, including a `Pulumi.yaml` configuration file, a `Pulumi.<stack-name>.yaml` file for storing stack-specific configuration, and a program file (`index.ts`) where you will define your infrastructure.

Open the `index.ts` file and define the infrastructure you want to deploy. For example, to create a Google Cloud Storage bucket, you can edit the file to include the following:

```typescript
import * as pulumi from "@pulumi/pulumi";
import * as gcp from "@pulumi/gcp";

// Create a Google Cloud Storage Bucket
const bucket = new gcp.storage.Bucket("my-bucket", {
    location: "US",
    forceDestroy: true, // Deletes the bucket and contents when destroyed
});

// Export the bucket name
export const bucketName = bucket.name;
```

This code snippet creates a new storage bucket in the US region and ensures that the bucket and its contents are deleted when the stack is destroyed.

After defining your infrastructure, you can preview and deploy the resources. First, preview the changes by running this:

```
pulumi preview
```

This will show you what resources Pulumi will create, update, or delete. When you are satisfied with the preview, deploy the stack by running this:

```
pulumi up
```

Pulumi will prompt you to confirm the deployment. Once you confirm it, the resources will be provisioned in your Google Cloud project. After the deployment, Pulumi will display the outputs, including the bucket name, which you can verify in the Google Cloud console.

Creating and managing core Google Cloud resources

Now that you've set up your Google Cloud environment with Pulumi, it's time to start creating and managing core Google Cloud resources. In this section, we'll walk through deploying essential **Google Cloud resources** such as **Compute Engine instances**, **Cloud SQL databases**, **Cloud functions**, and **Cloud Pub/Sub topics**. These resources form the backbone of most Google Cloud deployments, and you'll get hands-on experience defining and managing them using Pulumi and TypeScript.

Creating a Compute Engine instance

Let's start with creating a **Compute Engine instance**. Compute Engine instances are virtual machines that provide the flexibility to run workloads of all types. You can run web applications, data processing pipelines, and more.

For example, you might use a Compute Engine instance to host a small web server, act as a backend for your mobile app, or serve as a node in a larger distributed system. It has options ranging from lightweight machine types optimized for cost to high-performance instances with GPUs for machine learning.

To create a Compute Engine instance in your Pulumi project, open the `index.ts` file and add the following code:

```
import * as pulumi from "@pulumi/pulumi";
import * as gcp from "@pulumi/gcp";
const instance = new gcp.compute.Instance("my-instance", {
    machineType: "e2-micro",
    zone: "us-central1-a",
    bootDisk: {
        initializeParams: {
            image: "debian-cloud/debian-11",
        },
    },
    networkInterfaces: [{
        network: "default",
        accessConfigs: [{}],
    }],
});
```

```
export const instanceName = instance.name;
export const instanceIP = instance.networkInterfaces.apply(interfaces
=> interfaces[0].accessConfigs![0].natIp);
```

This code sets up a virtual machine with the *e2-micro machine type*, which is a good choice for lightweight workloads such as testing, development, or running a small server. It's configured with a Debian 11 boot disk and is connected to the default network. The external IP address allows you to access the instance over the internet.

Once you've added this code, deploy the instance using Pulumi. First, preview the changes to see what will be created:

```
pulumi preview
```

When everything looks good, deploy the infrastructure:

```
pulumi up
```

Pulumi will ask for confirmation before proceeding. Once you confirm, the instance will be created in your Google Cloud project. Pulumi will also output the instance's name and public IP address, which you can use to SSH into the instance or deploy applications.

Creating a Cloud SQL database

Next, let's create a **Cloud SQL database instance**, which is a fully managed relational database service on Google Cloud. Cloud SQL makes it easy to set up and manage databases such as MySQL, PostgreSQL, and SQL Server without worrying about the underlying infrastructure. It handles things such as backups, scaling, and updates automatically, so you can focus on building your application instead of managing databases.

For example, you can use Cloud SQL to host the database for a web application, manage e-commerce data, or store analytics results. It's also great for migrating existing databases to the cloud because it takes care of a lot of the heavy lifting, such as security patches and scaling, for you.

Here's how you can create a Cloud SQL database instance in Pulumi. Open your index.ts file and add the following code:

```
import * as pulumi from "@pulumi/pulumi";
import * as gcp from "@pulumi/gcp";

const sqlInstance = new gcp.sql.DatabaseInstance("my-sql-instance", {
    databaseVersion: "MYSQL_8_0",
```

```
        region: "us-central1",
        settings: {
            tier: "db-f1-micro",
            backupConfiguration: {
                enabled: true,
            },
        },
    });

    // Export the connection name so it can be used by applications
    export const sqlInstanceConnectionName = sqlInstance.connectionName;
```

This code creates a MySQL database instance in the us-central1 region. The key parameter here is databaseVersion. Its value is set to MYSQL_8_0, meaning that the instance will use MySQL version 8.0 as its database engine. You can adjust this parameter to specify a different database engine if MySQL isn't the right fit for your application.

For example, if you want to create a **PostgreSQL database**, you can set databaseVersion to POSTGRES_14 to use PostgreSQL version 14. Here's how the code would look:

```
    const sqlInstance = new gcp.sql.DatabaseInstance("my-postgres-instance", {
        databaseVersion: "POSTGRES_14",
        region: "us-central1",
        settings: {
            tier: "db-f1-micro",
            backupConfiguration: {
                enabled: true,
            },
        // other properties...
        },
    });

    export const sqlInstanceConnectionName = sqlInstance.connectionName;
```

If your application requires SQL Server, you can configure the database for Microsoft's relational database engine. For instance, setting databaseVersion to SQLSERVER_2019_STANDARD will create an SQL Server 2019 Standard Edition instance.

Here's an example:

```
const sqlInstance = new gcp.sql.DatabaseInstance("my-sqlserver-
instance", {
    databaseVersion: "SQLSERVER_2019_STANDARD",
    region: "us-central1",
    settings: {
        tier: "db-custom-2-3840",
        backupConfiguration: {
            enabled: true,
        },
    },
});

export const sqlInstanceConnectionName = sqlInstance.connectionName;
```

Each engine—MySQL, PostgreSQL, and SQL Server—has its own use cases and strengths. MySQL is widely supported and efficient for many general-purpose applications. PostgreSQL offers advanced features such as JSON support, making it great for complex or modern workloads. SQL Server is ideal for enterprise applications, especially those deeply integrated with the Microsoft ecosystem.

The process of deploying these database instances remains the same. Update `databaseVersion` to match the engine you need, run `pulumi up`, and the appropriate database instance will be provisioned in your Google Cloud project.

Beyond creating the database, let's imagine that your team comes with an extra requirement to ensure the database is backed up daily at a specific time. Instead of navigating the Cloud console and manually enabling this, you can define the backup schedule directly in your infrastructure code. Here's how you can incorporate this into the `gcp.sql.DatabaseInstance` definition:

```
const sqlInstance = new gcp.sql.DatabaseInstance("my-sql-instance", {
    databaseVersion: "MYSQL_8_0",
    region: "us-central1",
    settings: {
        tier: "db-f1-micro",
        backupConfiguration: {
            enabled: true,
            startTime: "03:00", // Schedule backups at 3AM
```

```
        },
        // More code here
    },
});
```

Now, suppose there's another requirement to secure the database by keeping it isolated within a private network, preventing it from being accessed publicly. You can handle this by adding a private network configuration to the same instance:

```
const sqlInstance = new gcp.sql.DatabaseInstance("my-sql-instance", {
    databaseVersion: "MYSQL_8_0",
    region: "us-central1",
    settings: {
        tier: "db-f1-micro",
        ipConfiguration: {
            privateNetwork: "projects/{project}/global/networks/{network}",
        },
        // More code here
    },
});
```

With these configurations added, you've integrated automated backups and secure networking into your database setup.

In the next section, you will see how to create infrastructure for Cloud functions.

Creating your Cloud functions infrastructure

Like other serverless functions from different cloud providers, Google Cloud functions let you run small, event-driven bits of code without worrying about managing servers. They're great for things such as processing files, handling HTTP requests, or responding to events from Google Cloud services such as Pub/Sub or Cloud Storage.

To deploy a Cloud function, the first thing you'll need is a place to store the function's source code. For Google Cloud functions, the source code can be in a Cloud Storage bucket, so we'll create one.

```
const bucket = new gcp.storage.Bucket("my-storage-bucket");
```

Next, upload the zipped source code for the function to the bucket. This makes the code accessible for deployment.

```
const archive = new gcp.storage.BucketObject("source-archive", {
    bucket: bucket.name,
    source: new pulumi.asset.FileAsset("./function-source.zip"), // Path
to the zip file
});
```

Here, archive represents the uploaded file. FileAsset points to the local path of your zipped function code, which Pulumi packages and uploads to the bucket. This saves you from manually uploading the file through the console or CLI, keeping the entire process defined in your project.

Now that the source code is stored in the bucket, you can define the Cloud function itself.

```
const cloudFunction = new gcp.cloudfunctions.Function("my-function", {
    runtime: "nodejs<XX>",
    entryPoint: "handler",
    sourceArchiveBucket: bucket.name,
    sourceArchiveObject: archive.name,
    triggerHttp: true,
    availableMemoryMb: 128,
    // other properties ...
});
```

This defines a Cloud function called my-function. Let's break this down:

- runtime: "nodejs<XX>" specifies the environment the function runs in. You should set it to the environment and version you want to use (e.g., Node.js version 22).
- entryPoint: "handler" tells Google Cloud the name of the function to execute. This should match the exported function name in your source code.
- sourceArchiveBucket and sourceArchiveObject link the function to the storage bucket and the uploaded code.
- triggerHttp: true sets up an HTTP trigger, making the function accessible via a URL.
- availableMemoryMb: 128 allocates 128 MB of memory for the function, which can be adjusted based on your requirements.

Finally, export the function's URL so you can use it in your application or testing.

```
export const functionUrl = cloudFunction.httpsTriggerUrl;
```

This outputs the URL for accessing the function, making it immediately available after deployment without needing to locate it in the cloud console.

In the next section, you will see how to create a cloud pub/sub topic.

Creating a Cloud Pub/Sub topic

This is another commonly used infrastructure component in cloud-native applications. A **Cloud Pub/Sub topic** is essentially a messaging system that allows one service to send messages to other services in a decoupled way. It's used to build scalable, event-driven architectures where one part of your application can publish events, and other parts can subscribe to them. For example, you might have a service publishing user activity events, while another service processes those events asynchronously, ensuring the two services don't need to interact directly.

To create a Cloud Pub/Sub topic with Pulumi, start by defining it in your code. Here's how you can add a Pub/Sub topic to your infrastructure:

```
const topic = new gcp.pubsub.Topic("my-topic");
```

Let's imagine that the topic gets events from a backend service whenever a new user signs up. The backend would publish a message to the topic with details about the new user. Now, we want to trigger an existing Cloud function whenever such a message is published to the topic. To do this, we'll set up a subscription that connects the topic to the Cloud function.

```
const subscription = new gcp.pubsub.Subscription("my-subscription", {
    topic: topic.name,
    pushConfig: {
        pushEndpoint: cloudFunction.httpsTriggerUrl,
    },
});
```

In this code, pushEndpoint is set to the Cloud function's URL, so any message published to the topic is pushed directly to the function. The subscription acts as the bridge between the topic and the function, ensuring that messages are delivered reliably.

With this setup, the backend publishes a message when a user signs up, the topic receives the event, and the subscription pushes it to the Cloud function. The function can then process the message to send a welcome email, log the event, or perform any other required action.

In the next section, you will learn how to create custom Google Cloud resources.

Creating custom Google Cloud resources

As we've said in previous chapters, custom resources allow you to encapsulate infrastructure logic into reusable modules. This simplifies deployments, ensures consistency, and makes your code more maintainable. Here, we'll define a concept we're calling an **Archive Function App**. This custom resource bundles everything a serverless function needs—such as a storage bucket for its source code, the function definition, and its trigger configuration—into one reusable component.

The idea is to streamline the process of deploying serverless applications. Instead of defining a Cloud function, creating a storage bucket, and uploading the source code as separate steps, an Archive Function App wraps these into a *single resource*. This abstraction not only saves time but also ensures that the function is always deployed with the correct dependencies and configurations.

Let's define the Archive Function App using Pulumi's `ComponentResource`. The following code creates a reusable resource that includes a Cloud function, its source code bucket, and support for both HTTP and Pub/Sub triggers. For the first step, you can create the arguments that the custom resource will need:

```
export interface ArchiveFunctionArgs {
    name: string;
    runtime: string;
    entryPoint: string;
    sourcePath: string;
    region: string;
    memory?: number;
    triggerType: "http" | "pubsub";
    topicName?: string;
}
```

The `ArchiveFunctionArgs` interface defines the arguments that can be passed to this custom resource. It includes options for the function's runtime, entry point, deployment region, source code path, memory allocation, and trigger type (either HTTP or Pub/Sub). If the trigger is Pub/Sub, you can optionally specify a topic name.

Now, let's define the `ArchiveFunctionApp` class:

```
export class ArchiveFunctionApp extends pulumi.ComponentResource {
    public readonly functionUrl?: pulumi.Output<string>;
    constructor(name: string, args: ArchiveFunctionArgs, opts?:
    pulumi.ResourceOptions) {
```

```
            super("custom:resource:ArchiveFunctionApp", name, {}, opts);
            const bucket = new gcp.storage.Bucket(
            `${name}-source-bucket`, {}, { parent: this }
            );
            const sourceArchive = new gcp.storage.BucketObject(
            `${name}-source-archive`, {
                ... }, { parent: this });
    const funcArgs: gcp.cloudfunctions.FunctionArgs = { ... };
    if (args.triggerType === "http") {
            funcArgs.triggerHttp = true;
        } else if (args.triggerType === "pubsub" && args.topicName) {
            const topic = new gcp.pubsub.Topic(args.topicName, {},
            { parent: this });
            funcArgs.eventTrigger = {
                eventType: "google.pubsub.topic.publish",
                resource: topic.name,
            };
        }

        const cloudFunction = new gcp.cloudfunctions.Function(name,
        funcArgs, { parent: this });

    }

}
```

This custom resource encapsulates the following:

- A Cloud Storage bucket for the function's source code
- The Cloud function definition, including runtime, entry point, and memory allocation
- Configurable triggers, supporting both HTTP and Pub/Sub

To use the Archive Function App, you can instantiate it like this:

```
import { ArchiveFunctionApp } from "./archiveFunctionApp";

// HTTP-triggered function
const httpFunction = new ArchiveFunctionApp("my-http-function", {
    name: "my-http-function",
    runtime: "nodejs16",
    entryPoint: "handler",
```

```
        sourcePath: "./function-source.zip",
        region: "us-central1",
        triggerType: "http",
});

// Pub/Sub-triggered function
const pubsubFunction = new ArchiveFunctionApp("my-pubsub-function", {
        name: "my-pubsub-function",
        runtime: "nodejs16",
        entryPoint: "handler",
        sourcePath: "./function-source.zip",
        region: "us-central1",
        triggerType: "pubsub",
        topicName: "my-topic",
});
```

In this example, we deploy two functions: one triggered by HTTP and the other by Pub/Sub. Both functions include everything they need—source code, storage bucket, and trigger configuration—all managed in a single component. This abstraction keeps your infrastructure code clean, reduces repetition, and simplifies updates across projects.

Automation and continuous integration

Let's also look at a basic way to automate your Google Cloud and Pulumi infrastructure deployments using GitHub Actions. **Automation** ensures that deployments are consistent and reliable while also integrating seamlessly with your development workflow. In this example, we'll set up a GitHub Actions workflow to authenticate with Google Cloud, configure Pulumi, and deploy infrastructure whenever changes are pushed to the repository.

Here's the full workflow file for .github/workflows/deploy.yml:

```
name: Deploy Infrastructure
on:
  push:
    branches:
      - main
jobs:
  deploy:
    runs-on: ubuntu-latest
```

```
    steps:
      - name: Checkout repository
        uses: actions/checkout@v3


      - name: Authenticate with Google Cloud
        uses: google-github-actions/auth@v1
        with:
          credentials_json: ${{ secrets.GCP_CREDENTIALS }}


      - name: Set up gcloud CLI
        uses: google-github-actions/setup-gcloud@v1
        with:
          project_id: ${{ secrets.GCP_PROJECT_ID }}
          service_account_key: ${{ secrets.GCP_CREDENTIALS }}
          export_default_credentials: true


      - name: Install Pulumi
        run: |
          curl -fsSL https://get.pulumi.com | sh
          export PATH=$PATH:$HOME/.pulumi/bin


      - name: Install project dependencies
        run: npm install


      - name: Deploy with Pulumi
        run: pulumi up --yes
        env:
          PULUMI_ACCESS_TOKEN: ${{ secrets.PULUMI_ACCESS_TOKEN }}
```

This workflow begins by defining when it should be triggered. In this case, it looks out for pushes to the main branch. This ensures that infrastructure deployments are tied directly to changes merged into the primary branch, aligning with best practices for managing production infrastructure. The on: push block specifies this trigger condition.

The first step in the workflow uses the actions/checkout action to pull the latest version of your code repository into the runner. This ensures that the deployment is based on the most recent changes.

The next step authenticates with Google Cloud using the `google-github-actions/auth` action. This action leverages a service account key stored in the GitHub secret `GCP_CREDENTIALS`. By securely accessing this key, the workflow gains the permissions needed to deploy resources to Google Cloud.

Once authentication is complete, the `google-github-actions/setup-gcloud` action is used to install and configure the `gcloud` CLI. This sets up the project ID and service account credentials, allowing the runner to interact with Google Cloud APIs. The configuration also exports default credentials, enabling other tools, such as Pulumi, to use them seamlessly during the deployment process.

Pulumi is then installed in the workflow environment using its official installation script. This ensures the Pulumi CLI is available for subsequent steps. The workflow also updates the system `PATH` to include the Pulumi installation directory. With Pulumi installed, the workflow runs `npm install` to install any project-specific dependencies, such as Pulumi packages or other required modules, ensuring the project is ready for deployment.

The deployment itself happens in the final step, where the `pulumi up` command is executed. This applies the infrastructure changes defined in your project. The command uses the `PULUMI_ACCESS_TOKEN` secret to authenticate with Pulumi's backend for state management, ensuring a smooth deployment process. The `--yes` flag is used to bypass interactive prompts, making the workflow fully automated.

To make this setup work, you need to configure three GitHub secrets in your repository: `GCP_CREDENTIALS` (a JSON key for a Google Cloud service account), `GCP_PROJECT_ID` (your Google Cloud project ID), and `PULUMI_ACCESS_TOKEN` (a token for Pulumi's backend). These secrets securely store sensitive information and make it accessible only to the workflow. Adding these secrets can be done via the repository: **Settings > Secrets and variables > Actions page**.

By integrating Pulumi and Google Cloud with GitHub Actions, this workflow ensures that your infrastructure is deployed automatically and consistently. Whenever changes are pushed to the repository, the pipeline handles authentication, configuration, and deployment, freeing you from manual intervention while maintaining reliability.

Summary

This chapter covered how to deploy infrastructure on Google Cloud using Pulumi. We started by setting up the Google Cloud environment and configuring Pulumi to interact securely with Google Cloud services.

You learned how to create core Google Cloud resources such as Google Cloud Storage buckets, Compute Engine instances, Cloud SQL databases, Cloud functions, and Cloud Pub/Sub topics, and how to automate the process using continuous integration with GitHub Actions. The chapter also explored creating custom Google Cloud resources that can be reused across projects, making your infrastructure deployments more modular and scalable.

In the next chapter, you will learn how to use Pulumi to deploy and manage infrastructure on Kubernetes.

Questions

1. How do you initialize a new Pulumi project for Google Cloud using TypeScript?

2. Describe how to create a Cloud Storage bucket using Pulumi in TypeScript.

3. How do you create a Compute Engine instance in Pulumi?

4. How do you create a Cloud SQL database in Pulumi?

5. How do you create an instance of the Google Cloud functions infrastructure in Pulumi?

6. How do you create a Google Cloud Pub/Sub topic in Pulumi?

7. What are the key benefits of creating custom Google Cloud resources using Pulumi's ComponentResource?

8. Explain the structure of a GitHub Actions workflow for deploying Google Cloud infrastructure using Pulumi.

9. What role does automation play in Pulumi deployments, and how can it be integrated with CI/CD for Google Cloud?

6

Deploying with Pulumi on Kubernetes

Kubernetes is a powerful tool that helps developers and DevOps teams manage containerized applications. It allows you to automate the deployment, scaling, and management of applications across different environments. However, working with Kubernetes can get complicated, especially when you have to deal with multiple cloud providers. This is where Pulumi makes a big difference. Pulumi lets you define your Kubernetes infrastructure using familiar programming languages, such as *TypeScript*, *Python*, *Go*, or *C#*. Instead of writing long YAML files, you can use real code to create and manage your Kubernetes clusters and workloads in a more organized and efficient way.

In this chapter, you'll learn how to set up a Kubernetes environment and connect it to Pulumi. You'll be guided through creating a cluster and configuring it so that it's ready for use. You'll also see how to define and deploy important Kubernetes resources such as **Pods**, **Services**, and **ingress controllers**. These are key parts of running containerized applications, and you'll get hands-on experience in managing them with Pulumi.

Later in the chapter, you'll cover how to handle Kubernetes clusters across different cloud providers such as **Amazon Web Services (AWS)**, Azure, and Google Cloud. You'll learn how to manage clusters on multiple clouds using a single approach. This is important for companies that use more than one cloud platform or want to avoid being locked into one provider. By the end, you'll be able to create, manage, and deploy Kubernetes clusters no matter where they're running.

By the time you finish this chapter, you'll know how to set up Kubernetes clusters, deploy applications on them, and manage them on multiple clouds.

In this chapter, we're going to cover the following main topics:

- Setting up your Kubernetes environment
- Defining and deploying Kubernetes resources
- Multi-cloud Kubernetes management

Technical requirements

If you would like to follow along with the examples in this chapter, you will require the following:

- The Pulumi CLI is required for executing commands. You can download it from here: `https://www.pulumi.com/docs/iac/download-install/`.

- Pulumi supports multiple programming languages, but for this chapter, we'll be using JavaScript/TypeScript, which requires Node.js. You can download and install it from the Node.js official site here: `https://nodejs.org/`.

- You'll need access to a Kubernetes cluster to deploy resources. Here, you have multiple options. This can be a local Kubernetes cluster, such as **minikube** (`https://minikube.sigs.k8s.io/docs/start`) or **kind** (`https://kind.sigs.k8s.io/`), or a cloud-hosted Kubernetes cluster such as **AWS Elastic Kubernetes Service (EKS)**, **Azure Kubernetes Service (AKS)**, or **Google Kubernetes Engine (GKE)**. You can choose the option that best fits your environment.

- If you are running Kubernetes locally, you also need to have a **Docker container** or a **virtual machine (VM)** environment set up. To install Docker, you can follow the instructions here: `https://docs.docker.com/engine/install/`.

- The **kubectl** command-line tool is required to interact with your Kubernetes cluster. It allows you to view cluster details, debug workloads, and verify that your deployments are working as expected. You can install `kubectl` by following the instructions here: `https://kubernetes.io/docs/tasks/tools/`.

- A **kubeconfig** file is needed to authenticate with and access your Kubernetes cluster. This file contains the credentials and configuration details required to connect to your cluster. You can set up kubeconfig by following these instructions: `https://kubernetes.io/docs/concepts/configuration/organize-cluster-access-kubeconfig/`.

Setting up your Kubernetes environment

Before you can start deploying infrastructure to Kubernetes with Pulumi, you need to configure your environment and ensure that Pulumi can interact securely with Kubernetes. This section will guide you through everything required to get your environment ready for Kubernetes deployments.

To start, you'll need a working Kubernetes cluster. If you don't have access to a managed Kubernetes service such as Amazon EKS, AKS, or GKE, you can create a local Kubernetes cluster using tools such as Minikube or `kind`. These tools allow you to run Kubernetes locally on your machine. To create a cluster with Minikube, run the following command:

```
minikube start
```

This command starts a local Kubernetes cluster, which can be used for development and testing purposes. If you're working with a cloud-hosted Kubernetes cluster, the process is different. For example, with AWS, you can create an EKS cluster using the AWS CLI or the AWS Management Console. Once your cluster is up, you'll need access to it via `kubeconfig`, which contains the credentials and endpoint details for connecting to the cluster.

> NOTE
>
> To interact with your Kubernetes cluster, you'll need `kubectl`, the command-line tool for Kubernetes. If you don't already have it installed, follow the instructions in the official Kubernetes installation guide: `https://kubernetes.io/docs/tasks/tools/`.

Once installed, verify that it's working by running the following:

```
kubectl version --client
```

This will display the version of the `kubectl` client installed on your machine. If you see an error, make sure it's correctly installed and included in your system's `PATH` environment variable.

If you're using a local Kubernetes cluster with Minikube, you can configure `kubectl` to use the Minikube context. Run the following command:

```
kubectl config use-context minikube
```

This sets the active `kubeconfig` context to Minikube, and this means that all `kubectl` commands will target your local Kubernetes cluster. If you're working with a cloud-hosted cluster, such as Amazon EKS, AKS, or GKE, you'll need to download and configure the `kubeconfig` file for your cluster.

For Amazon EKS, you can run the following command to configure your kubeconfig file:

```
aws eks update-kubeconfig
--region <region>
--name <cluster>
```

Replace `<region>` and `<cluster>` with the appropriate AWS region and cluster name. This command updates the `kubeconfig` file with the connection details for your EKS cluster.

For AKS, you can configure your kubeconfig file using the Azure CLI. Run the following command to download the `kubeconfig` file for your AKS cluster:

```
az aks get-credentials
--resource-group <resource-group-name>
--name <aks-cluster-name>
```

Replace `<resource-group-name>` with the name of the resource group where your AKS cluster is located and `<aks-cluster-name>` with the name of your AKS cluster. This command merges the AKS cluster configuration with your existing `kubeconfig` file.

For GKE, you can configure your kubeconfig file using the Google Cloud CLI. Run the following command to get the credentials for your GKE cluster:

```
gcloud container clusters get-credentials <cluster-name>
--region <region-name>
--project <project-id>
```

Replace `<cluster-name>`, `<region-name>`, and `<project-id>` with your cluster name, the region where the cluster is running, and your Google Cloud project ID. This command retrieves the credentials and updates the `kubeconfig` file, allowing `kubectl` to connect to your GKE cluster.

After running the respective commands for your cloud provider, you can verify access to your cluster by running the following:

```
kubectl get nodes
```

If everything is set up correctly, you'll see a list of nodes in your cluster. This confirms that kubectl is successfully connected to your Kubernetes cluster.

At this point, you're ready to connect Pulumi to Kubernetes. Pulumi automatically uses the kubeconfig file that kubectl relies on, so no additional configuration is required. To verify that Pulumi can connect to Kubernetes, you'll create a new Pulumi project. First, create a directory for your project and initialize it with Pulumi:

```
mkdir pulumi-k8s && cd pulumi-k8s
pulumi new kubernetes-typescript
```

The pulumi new kubernetes-typescript command creates a new Pulumi project set up to work with Kubernetes using TypeScript. As you run this command, Pulumi will ask you to log in (if you haven't already) and enter a name for your project stack.

To check that Pulumi is connected to your Kubernetes cluster, you can list all the pods in your cluster. This requires using Pulumi's query functionality, which is designed specifically for reading existing Kubernetes resources. First, install the required package:

```
npm install @pulumi/query-kubernetes
```

Then, open the index.ts file in a text editor and replace its contents with the following code:

```
import * as pulumi from "@pulumi/pulumi";
import * as kq from "@pulumi/query-kubernetes";

// List all existing pods in the cluster
const pods = kq.list("v1", "Pod");
export const allPods = pods;
```

To run the script, use the following command:

```
pulumi up
```

This command will connect to your Kubernetes cluster using your current kubeconfig context and display all pods running in the default namespace. If the connection is successful, you'll see a list of pod objects, confirming that Pulumi can communicate with your cluster. If there are no pods in the default namespace, the command will return an empty list, which still indicates a successful connection.

Defining and deploying Kubernetes resources

In this section, you'll learn how to define and deploy Kubernetes resources using Pulumi. Instead of working with YAML files, you'll use TypeScript to write resource definitions in a more familiar and flexible way. This approach makes it easier to organize your configurations and reuse parts of your code where needed.

You'll start by understanding key Kubernetes resources such as Pods, Services, Deployments, and ingress controllers. Each of these resources plays a role in how applications are run, scaled, and accessed within a Kubernetes cluster. Once you know their purpose, you'll see how to define them using Pulumi.

After defining the resources, you'll learn how to deploy them to a Kubernetes cluster. You'll see how to use Pulumi commands to preview, apply, and verify changes in your cluster. This process ensures that you know what's changing before any updates are made.

Introduction to Kubernetes resources

When building and running an application on Kubernetes, there are some important resources you need to understand. Each of these resources plays a specific role in making sure your application is always running, can be accessed by users, and is easy to update. When you understand these resources, you'll be able to manage your application more effectively.

Let's say you're building a website where people can ask and answer questions—similar to an online forum or Q&A platform. The first key resource you'll need is a **pod**. A pod is the smallest part of a Kubernetes application and runs the container that holds your application code. For example, if you have a service that handles user interactions such as posting questions, submitting answers, and voting, Kubernetes will run it inside a pod. Sometimes, you may want more than one container in a pod. For instance, you might have the main Q&A service and a logging tool running together inside the same pod so that they can share storage and network access. If a pod stops working (maybe the server it's on crashes), Kubernetes will automatically create a new pod to keep the application running. This way, users can always post questions and submit answers without interruptions.

Next, you'll want a **deployment**. While pods handle running containers, a deployment makes sure you have the right number of pods running at all times. For your Q&A website, you might want at least three pods running for the user interaction service so that if one pod goes down, your app stays available. The deployment will automatically replace any pods that fail and keep the total number of pods at three. Deployments also make it easy to update your app.

For example, if you release a new version of your user interaction service, the deployment will slowly update each pod, one at a time, instead of shutting everything down all at once. This process, called a *rolling update*, makes sure users don't see any downtime while the update happens. Without deployments, you would have to manage each pod manually, which would be time-consuming and error-prone.

While a deployment works great for stateless services (services that don't have a data store), such as the user interaction service, it's not enough when you have services that need to store data, such as a database. Here, you'd need a **StatefulSet**. A StatefulSet is similar to a deployment, but it's designed to handle stateful applications such as databases. For a Q&A website, you'll probably need a database to store user profiles, questions, answers, and votes. Unlike regular pods that can be created and destroyed without issue, database pods must maintain their data and identity. For example, if a database pod crashes and a new one is created, it must keep the same data and hostname as before. StatefulSets ensure that each pod has a unique, stable identifier (such as db-0, db-1, db-2), and they attach persistent storage to each pod. This means if db-0 crashes, Kubernetes will replace it but attach it to the same storage volume, so no data is lost. Without StatefulSets, your database pods would lose their data every time they restart, which would be a disaster for a site where user questions and answers must be saved permanently.

Once your pods are running, you'll need a way for users to access them. You can use a **service** for this. A service acts like a bridge between the pods and the outside world. For your Q&A website, you want users to access the user interaction service no matter which pod is handling it. Pods can move between nodes or restart, but the service provides a single, stable entry point for the user. If you've ever typed a website URL such as www.thisismywebsite.com, you've used something like a service. The service makes sure that users are always connected to the right pod, even if that pod changes. There are different types of services. If you only want your app to be accessible inside the cluster (such as internal APIs), you would use a **ClusterIP** service. If you want users outside the cluster (such as your website visitors) to access your app, you'd use a **LoadBalancer** service, which makes your app available on the internet.

Now, if you want users to access specific pages in your Q&A site, such as /questions to browse questions or /profile to view user profiles, you'll need an **ingress**. An ingress works like a *traffic controller* for web traffic. Instead of exposing every part of your app separately, the ingress allows you to route all traffic through a single entry point. For example, users could visit myquestionswebsite.com/questions to see a list of questions or myquestionswebsite.com/profile to access their user profile. Without ingress, you'd need to create multiple services, which would be more complex to manage.

You'll also need **ConfigMaps** and **Secrets**. These two resources help you store settings and sensitive information separately from your application code. For example, if your user interaction service connects to an external API to analyze trending questions, you don't want to hardcode the API URL, username, or password directly in your app. Instead, you can store this information in a ConfigMap (for general configuration) or a Secret (for sensitive data such a passwords). When the pods start, they can load this information automatically. This makes it easier to manage different environments, such as development, staging, and production, where the API URL or credentials might change.

These Kubernetes resources work together to run, update, and protect your application. Now that you know about them in theory, let's see how to define them using Pulumi.

Defining Kubernetes resources with Pulumi

Now that you understand the Kubernetes resources needed for your Q&A website, it's time to define them using Pulumi.

To start, let's define a pod. In Pulumi, you define a pod using `k8s.core.v1.Pod`. The `metadata` section allows you to specify a name and labels for the pod, which are useful for identifying it in the cluster. The `spec` section defines the containers that the pod will run. Here's an example of a pod definition with two containers:

```
import * as k8s from "@pulumi/kubernetes";

const qaPod = new k8s.core.v1.Pod("qa-pod", {
    metadata: {
        name: "qa-service-pod",
        labels: { app: "qa-service" },
    },
    spec: {
        containers: [
            {
                name: "qa-container",
                image: "myrepo/qa-service:latest",
                ports: [{ containerPort: 80 }]
            },
            {
                name: "logging-container",
                image: "myrepo/logging-agent:latest",
                ports: [{ containerPort: 8080 }]
```

```
            }
        ]
    }
});
```

Here, the `containers` array defines two containers inside the pod. Each container specifies an image to use and a port that it listens on: the main container that runs the Q&A service and a logging container that tracks user activity. Each container has its own port configuration. The labels in the `metadata` section allow other Kubernetes resources, such as services, to connect to this pod.

Next, let's look at a deployment. A deployment is defined using `k8s.apps.v1.Deployment`. The `spec` section includes the number of replicas and the container template that defines what each pod will look like. Here's how you create a deployment that ensures three replicas of the Q&A service are always running:

```
const qaDeployment = new k8s.apps.v1.Deployment("qa-deployment", {
    metadata: {
        name: "qa-service-deployment",
    },
    spec: {
        replicas: 3,
        selector: {
            matchLabels: { app: "qa-service" }
        },
        template: {
            metadata: {
                labels: { app: "qa-service" }
            },
            spec: {
                containers: [
                    {
                        name: "qa-container",
                        image: "myrepo/qa-service:latest",
                        ports: [{ containerPort: 80 }]
                    }
                ]
            }
        }
    }
});
```

In this deployment, the `replicas` field specifies that three pods should always be running. The `selector` field ensures that only pods with the app: `qa-service` label are controlled by this deployment. The container template is similar to the pod definition, but since this is a deployment, Kubernetes automatically creates and manages multiple pods.

For managing persistent data, you'll need a StatefulSet. A StatefulSet uses `k8s.apps.v1.StatefulSet` and requires volume configuration to persist data across pod restarts. Here's an example for defining a PostgreSQL database:

```
const qaDatabase = new k8s.apps.v1.StatefulSet("qa-db", {
  metadata: { name: "qa-db" },
  spec: {
    serviceName: "qa-db-service",
    replicas: 1,
    selector: {
        matchLabels: { app: "qa-db" }
    },
    template: {
        metadata: {
            labels: { app: "qa-db" }
        },
        spec: {
          containers: [{
                name: "postgres",
                image: "postgres:14",
                ports: [{ containerPort: 5432 }],
                env: [
                  {
                    name: "POSTGRES_DB",
                    value: "qadb"
                  },
                  {
                    name: "POSTGRES_USER",
                    value: "qauser"
                  },
                  {
                    name: "POSTGRES_PASSWORD",
                    value: "qapassword"
```

```
                          },
                          {
                             name: "PGDATA",
                             value: "/var/lib/postgresql/data/pgdata"
                          }],
                          volumeMounts: [{
                             name: "db-storage",
                             mountPath: "/var/lib/postgresql/data"
                          }]
                       }
                    ]
                 }
              },
              volumeClaimTemplates: [{
                    metadata: {
                       name: "db-storage"
                    },
                    spec: {
                       accessModes: ["ReadWriteOnce"],
                       resources: {
                          requests: {
                             storage: "10Gi"
                          }
                       }
                    }
              }]
           }
        });
```

The key part of this StatefulSet is the volumeClaimTemplates part, which requests 10 Gi of storage for each pod. The volumeMounts part attaches the volume to the container at /var/lib/postgresql/data. This ensures that the database data is retained even if the pod restarts.

Once your services are running, you'll need a service to expose them. A service is defined using k8s.core.v1.Service, and it allows you to route traffic to your pods.

Here's how you can define a LoadBalancer service that exposes the Q&A service to the internet:

```
const qaService = new k8s.core.v1.Service("qa-service", {
    metadata: {
        name: "qa-service"
    },
    spec: {
        type: " ClusterIP",
        ports: [{ port: 80, targetPort: 80 }],
        selector: { app: "qa-service" }
    }
});
```

In this service definition, type: ClusterIP creates an internal service that's only accessible within the cluster. The selector field tells the service to route traffic to pods labeled app: qa-service. This type of service is ideal when you're using an ingress controller to manage external access, as the ingress will handle routing internet traffic to your ClusterIP services internally.

If you want to route users to specific pages, you'll need an **ingress** resource. Before creating an ingress, you must first install an ingress controller, such as ingress-nginx or Traefik, in your cluster, as most Kubernetes clusters don't include one by default. The ingress controller handles the actual traffic routing based on your Ingress rules.

An ingress is defined using k8s.networking.v1.Ingress and allows you to define URL paths that route traffic to specific services. Here's how to define an ingress for paths such as /questions and /profile:

```
const qaIngress = new k8s.networking.v1.Ingress("qa-ingress", {
    metadata: {
        name: "qa-ingress",
        annotations: { "nginx.ingress.kubernetes.io/rewrite-target": "/" }
    },
    spec: {
        rules: [
            {
                host: "myquestionswebsite.com",
                http: {
                    paths: [
                        {
```

```
                            path: "/questions",
                            pathType: "Prefix",
                            backend: {
                                service: {
                                    name: "qa-service",
                                    port: { number: 80 }
                                }
                            }
                        },
                        {
                            path: "/profile",
                            pathType: "Prefix",
                            backend: {
                                service: {
                                    name: "qa-service",
                                    port: { number: 80 }
                                }
                            }
                        }
                    ]
                }
            }
        ]
    }
});
```

This ingress specifies rules to route traffic to /questions and /profile, sending it to qa-service. Each path uses pathType: Prefix, which matches requests that start with the given path.

To manage application configuration and sensitive data, you'll need ConfigMaps and Secrets. ConfigMaps store general settings, while Secrets store encrypted sensitive data such as passwords. Here's how you define them:

```
const qaConfigMap = new k8s.core.v1.ConfigMap("qa-config", {
    metadata: {
        name: "qa-config"
    },
    data: {
        "app.environment": "production",
```

```
                "api.baseUrl": "https://api. myquestionswebsite.com"
    }
});


const qaSecret = new k8s.core.v1.Secret("qa-secret", {
    metadata: {
        name: "qa-secret"
    },
    stringData: {
        "dbUser": "admin",
        "dbPassword": "hello123"
    }
});
```

The qaConfigMap field defines two configuration keys that are loaded into the app, while the qaSecret field stores the database username and password securely. The stringData field is used to provide the Secret values in plain text. Kubernetes encrypts this data before storing it. Although this example writes this information in plain text just for illustration, you shouldn't do this in a real environment. Instead, you should use a more secure approach for handling sensitive data. A more secure approach would be to use Pulumi's built-in secrets management functionality to encrypt sensitive values automatically or integrate Kubernetes with a cloud-native secrets store such as Azure Key Vault, AWS Secrets Manager, or Google Secret Manager. These tools allow for encryption at rest, access policies, and automatic rotation of secrets.

Pulumi has **Environment, Secrets, and Configuration (ESC)**, a concept we will discuss in more detail in *Chapter 11*, which can help you manage configuration values and secrets securely across multiple environments such as development, staging, and production. ESC allows you to encrypt secrets directly in Pulumi's configuration files and manage them centrally. You can use ESC or store the secret in the configuration as a secret using the regular Pulumi CLI (we covered this in *Chapter 2*).

To securely manage sensitive information such as database credentials using Pulumi ESC, you can follow these steps:

1. **Set up Pulumi ESC:** Begin by setting up Pulumi ESC in your project. This involves creating an environment that will hold your configuration and secrets. You can do this using the Pulumi ESC CLI:

    ```
    esc env init myproject/dev
    ```

This command initializes a new environment named dev within the myproject project.

2. **Define secrets in the environment**: Next, add your sensitive data, such as database credentials, to the environment. Pulumi ESC allows you to define secrets that are encrypted and securely stored. You can set a secret using the following command:

```
esc env set myproject/dev dbPassword hello123 --secret
```

The --secret flag ensures that the value is treated as a secret and encrypted accordingly.

3. **Access secrets in your Pulumi program**: Now that you have the secret saved in your environment, you can access it in your Pulumi program by referencing the environment in your stack configuration and then accessing the secret, like this:

```
import * as pulumi from "@pulumi/pulumi";

const config = new pulumi.Config();
const dbPassword = config.requireSecret("dbPassword");
```

The requireSecret function retrieves the secret value securely, and this ensures that it is not exposed in logs or outputs.

4. **Use secrets in resource definitions**: When defining resources that require a secret, such as a Kubernetes Secret, you can pass the retrieved secret value directly. Here's an example:

```
const qaSecret = new k8s.core.v1.Secret("qa-secret", {
    metadata: {
        name: "qa-secret"
    },
    stringData: {
        "dbPassword": dbPassword
    }
});
```

In this example, dbPassword is securely injected into the Kubernetes secret without exposing its plain-text value.

With these definitions and your secure secret referenced properly, you now have all the key Kubernetes resources required for your Q&A website. Now that you have the resources defined, it's time to deploy them to your Kubernetes cluster.

Deploying Kubernetes resources with Pulumi

Once you've defined all the Kubernetes resources for your Q&A website, the next step is to deploy them to a Kubernetes cluster. You can do this by running the following command:

```
pulumi up
```

When you run `pulumi up`, Pulumi will analyze the changes required to achieve the desired state and present a preview of the resources it will create, update, or delete. Here's an example of what you might see when you run `pulumi up` for the first time:

```
Previewing update (dev):
    Type                          Name              Plan
 +  pulumi:pulumi:Stack           qa-platform-dev   create
 +  kubernetes:core/v1:Pod               qa-pod     create
 +  kubernetes:apps/v1:Deployment qa-deployment     create
 +  kubernetes:apps/v1:StatefulSet  qa-database     create
 +  kubernetes:core/v1:Service       qa-service     create
 +  kubernetes:networking/v1:Ingress qa-ingress     create
 +  kubernetes:core/v1:Secret        qa-secret      create

Resources:
    + 7 to create
```

The + symbol indicates that these resources will be created. Pulumi shows you what will happen before making any changes. This gives you an opportunity to review and confirm the update. If everything looks correct, proceed with the deployment. Pulumi will then create the resources in your Kubernetes cluster.

Once the deployment is complete, Pulumi provides a summary of the changes it made. The output might look like this:

```
Updating (dev):
Type                             Name              Status
 +  pulumi:pulumi:Stack          qa-platform-dev   created
 +  kubernetes:core/v1:Pod              qa-pod     created
 +  kubernetes:apps/v1:Deployment  qa-deployment   created
 +  kubernetes:apps/v1:StatefulSet  qa-database    created
 +  kubernetes:core/v1:Service       qa-service    created
 +  kubernetes:networking/v1:Ingress qa-ingress    created
```

```
+ kubernetes:core/v1:Secret       qa-secret        created

Outputs:

Resources:
    + 7 created

Duration: 45s
```

This output confirms that Pulumi successfully created seven resources. After running `pulumi up`, you can verify the state of the resources directly in Kubernetes using `kubectl`. Pulumi tracks the desired state, but Kubernetes itself maintains the running state of the resources. To check if your pods are running, use the following command:

```
kubectl get pods
```

This command returns a list of pods that are currently running in your Kubernetes cluster. The output might look like this:

```
NAME                          READY   STATUS    RESTARTS   AGE
qa-pod                        1/1     Running   0          2m
qa-service-deployment-7xx     1/1     Running   0          2m
qa-service-deployment-748     1/1     Running   0          2m
qa-service-deployment-7c7     1/1     Running   0          2m
qa-database-0                 1/1     Running   0          2m
```

This output shows that several pods are running. The READY column tells you how many containers in each pod are running. For example, 1/1 means one container is running, and the pod is fully operational. The `qa-service-deployment` pod has multiple pods running since it's a deployment with three replicas. The `qa-database-0` pod is part of a StatefulSet, and its name reflects its index (starting from 0) to maintain order.

To verify the status of services, you can run the following command:

```
kubectl get services
```

The output might look like this:

```
NAME        TYPE          CLUSTER IP    EXTERNAL-IP    PORT(S)    AGE
kubernetes  ClusterIP     10.96.0.1     <none>         443/TCP    2d
qa-service  LoadBalancer  10.0.170.75   34.75.210.58   80:31/TCP  2m
```

This output shows the `qa-service` service, which is exposed as a `LoadBalancer` service. The `EXTERNAL-IP` value is the public IP address you can use to access the service. If you navigate to `http://34.75.210.58` (or what your `EXTERNAL-IP` value is when you do your own deployment), you should be able to access the Q&A website. Note that it may take a few minutes for the external IP to become available as the cloud provider sets up the `LoadBalancer` service.

If you want to see the current state of deployments, you can run the following command:

```
kubectl get deployments
```

The output will look like this:

```
NAME                    READY     UP-TO-DATE     AVAILABLE     AGE
qa-service-deployment   3/3       3              3             2m
```

This output shows that `qa-service-deployment` has three pods running. The `UP-TO-DATE` column confirms that all three replicas are running the latest version of the image. The `AVAILABLE` column confirms that all three pods are available and ready to serve traffic.

To check the status of the StatefulSet, you can run the following:

```
kubectl get statefulsets
```

The output will look like this:

```
NAME          READY     AGE
qa-database   1/1       2m
```

This output shows that the `qa-database` StatefulSet has one pod running, and it is ready. If the database pod is deleted for any reason, Kubernetes will automatically re-create it, ensuring that it stays available.

If you want to see the ingress routing rules, you can run the following:

```
kubectl get ingress
```

The output will look like this:

```
NAME         CLASS    HOSTS                       ADDRESS       PORTS   AGE
qa-ingress   <none>   myquestionswebsite.com      34.75.210.58  80      2m
```

This output shows the ingress resource for your Q&A website. The HOSTS column indicates that traffic to myquestionswebsite.com will be routed according to the rules defined in the ingress. The ADDRESS value is the IP address of the LoadBalancer service used to expose the ingress. If you've configured DNS to point myquestionswebsite.com to this IP, users will be able to access the site at https:// myquestionswebsite.com.

Pulumi maintains the state of all these resources. If you make changes to your Pulumi definitions (such as updating the container image for the Q&A service), Pulumi will automatically detect the changes when you run pulumi up. It will only modify the parts of the infrastructure that need updating.

Once you are done trying out different things with your Pulumi x Kubernetes configuration and you want to delete all the resources, you can use the following command:

```
pulumi destroy
```

Pulumi will show you a preview of all the resources that will be deleted and ask for confirmation. After you confirm, all the resources will be deleted from your Kubernetes cluster, and Pulumi will update its state file to reflect that the resources no longer exist.

Updating and managing existing resources

Once your Q&A website is deployed, you'll likely need to make updates to your Kubernetes resources. This could be as simple as adding a new configuration or updating an existing one. To illustrate this, let's work with a ConfigMap. Suppose you originally created a ConfigMap with the following Pulumi code:

```
const qaConfigMap = new k8s.core.v1.ConfigMap("qa-config", {
  metadata: {
      name: "qa-config"
  },
  data: {
      "app.environment": "production",
      "api.baseUrl": "https://api.myquestionswebsite.com"
  }
});
```

This ConfigMap defines two configuration keys: `app.environment` and `api.baseUrl`. Let's say you want to add a new configuration key called `featureFlags.enableVoting`, which will be used to enable or disable a voting feature on your Q&A site. To make this change, you update the data section of the ConfigMap to include the new key, like this:

```
const qaConfigMap = new k8s.core.v1.ConfigMap("qa-config", {
    metadata: {
        name: "qa-config"
    },
    data: {
        "app.environment": "production",
        "api.baseUrl": "https://api.myquestionswebsite.com",
        "featureFlags.enableVoting": "true"
    }
});
```

Notice that only one line was added: `"featureFlags.enableVoting": "true"`. This change updates the ConfigMap to include a new feature flag, which can be used to control the behavior of your Q&A application.

To apply this update, you run the following:

```
pulumi up
```

Pulumi will detect that the `qa-config` resource has changed. Instead of deleting and recreating the ConfigMap, Pulumi will issue an update to modify only the data section. The preview output might look like this:

```
Previewing update (dev):
    Type                            Name       Plan
~   kubernetes:core/v1:ConfigMap   qa-config  update


Resources:
    ~ 1 to update
```

The ~ symbol indicates that the resource will be updated. Unlike destructive changes (which require deletion and recreation), this change only modifies the data field of the ConfigMap. This approach ensures no downtime and avoids unnecessary re-creation of resources.

If everything looks correct, apply the changes. Pulumi will display a log of the update process, which might look like this:

```
Updating (dev):
    Type                            Name        Status
~   kubernetes:core/v1:ConfigMap   qa-config   updated


Resources:
    ~ 1 updated
```

The log confirms that Pulumi successfully updated the ConfigMap. No other Kubernetes resources were affected, and the update was applied efficiently.

To verify the changes in Kubernetes, you can use kubectl to view the contents of the ConfigMap. Run the following command:

```
kubectl get configmap qa-config -o yaml
```

The output will look like this:

```
apiVersion: v1
data:
  app.environment: production
  api.baseUrl: https://api.myquestionswebsite.com
  featureFlags.enableVoting: "true"
kind: ConfigMap
metadata:
  name: qa-config
  namespace: default
```

You can see that the new key, featureFlags.enableVoting, has been added to the data section of the ConfigMap. This confirms that the update was applied successfully.

Beyond ConfigMaps, you can manage and update the declarations of your Kubernetes resources using Pulumi. Whether you're updating container images, scaling deployments, or modifying StatefulSets, Pulumi tracks only the changes you make and updates them efficiently. Now that you've seen how to use Pulumi to create and manage your Kubernetes resources, let's go over best practices for managing Kubernetes in a multi-cloud setting.

Multi-cloud Kubernetes management

Managing Kubernetes across multiple cloud providers can be challenging, but it also provides significant benefits, such as increased redundancy and the ability to avoid vendor lock-in. With a multi-cloud approach, you can run your Kubernetes workloads on different cloud providers such as AWS, Azure, and Google Cloud, ensuring that your application remains highly available, even if one cloud provider experiences an outage. However, managing Kubernetes clusters across multiple providers requires consistent configurations, secure secrets management, and a way to orchestrate changes across all environments.

Pulumi simplifies multi-cloud Kubernetes management by allowing you to define, deploy, and update Kubernetes resources on multiple clouds from a single program. Instead of managing separate configurations for each provider, you can use Pulumi to write a unified, reusable script that works across AWS, Azure, and Google Cloud. This eliminates the complexity of using different cloud-native tools.

To manage Kubernetes across multiple cloud providers, the first step is to define multiple Kubernetes providers in Pulumi. Each provider is linked to a specific Kubernetes cluster. For example, you might have an **Amazon EKS cluster**, an **AKS cluster**, and a **GKE cluster**. Here's how you can configure providers for each of these clouds:

```
import * as pulumi from "@pulumi/pulumi";
import * as k8s from "@pulumi/kubernetes";

// AWS Kubernetes Provider (EKS)
const awsProvider = new k8s.Provider("aws-k8s", {
    kubeconfig: "eks-kubeconfig-contents"
});

// Azure Kubernetes Provider (AKS)
const azureProvider = new k8s.Provider("azure-k8s", {
    kubeconfig: " aks-kubeconfig-contents"
});

// Google Cloud Kubernetes Provider (GKE)
const gcpProvider = new k8s.Provider("gcp-k8s", {
    kubeconfig: " gke-kubeconfig-contents "
});
```

Once you have multiple providers set up, you can define shared resources across multiple clusters. For example, suppose you want to deploy a simple Kubernetes service on all three clouds. Instead of writing the service three times, you can define it once and use it across all the providers. Here's how to do it:

```
function createService(name: string, provider: k8s.Provider) {
    return new k8s.core.v1.Service(name, {
        metadata: {
            name: name
        },
        spec: {
            type: "LoadBalancer",
            ports: [{ port: 80, targetPort: 80 }],
            selector: { app: name }
        }
    }, { provider });
}


// Create the same service on AWS, Azure, and GCP
const awsService = createService("qa-service-aws", awsProvider);
const azureService = createService("qa-service-azure", azureProvider);
const gcpService = createService("qa-service-gcp", gcpProvider);
```

In this code, the createService function defines a Kubernetes service. The function is called three times, each time using a different provider. This creates identical LoadBalancer services on AWS, Azure, and Google Cloud. Each cloud provider will allocate a public IP address for the service, giving you three independent endpoints for your Q&A website.

Synchronizing configurations across clouds is one of the most difficult parts of multi-cloud management. You want to ensure that your Kubernetes resources remain consistent across all clouds. One approach to this is to use Pulumi's environment configuration. With Pulumi, you can store configurations for each cloud provider in the Pulumi.<stack>.yaml file. For example, you might define different configurations for development, staging, and production environments.

Here's an example of what a configuration file might look like:

```
# Pulumi.dev.yaml
config:
  aws:region: "us-east-1"
  azure:region: "eastus"
  gcp:region: "us-central1"
  replicas: 2
```

This configuration defines the region for each cloud provider and the number of replicas you want for each cluster. You can access these configuration values in your Pulumi program like this:

```
import * as pulumi from "@pulumi/pulumi";

const config = new pulumi.Config();
const replicas = config.requireNumber("replicas");

const deployment = new k8s.apps.v1.Deployment("qa-deployment", {
    metadata: { name: "qa-service-deployment" },
    spec: {
        replicas: replicas,
        selector: { matchLabels: { app: "qa-service" } },
        template: {
            metadata: { labels: { app: "qa-service" } },
            spec: {
                containers: [
                    {
                        name: "qa-container",
                        image: "myrepo/qa-service:latest",
                        ports: [{ containerPort: 80 }]
                    }
                ]
            }
        }
    }
});
```

When you run pulumi up, the number of replicas will be set based on the environment configuration. For development, you might have two replicas, but in production, you could have five replicas.

With these, you can more efficiently manage Kubernetes clusters across multiple clouds.

Summary

In this chapter, we covered how to define, deploy, and manage Kubernetes resources using Pulumi. You learned how to set up a Kubernetes environment, define essential resources such as Pods, Deployments, StatefulSets, Services, ConfigMaps, and Secrets, and deploy them using `pulumi up`. We also explored how to manage updates efficiently without re-creating resources and how to verify deployments using `kubectl`. Finally, we discussed multi-cloud Kubernetes management, where you learned how to manage clusters on AWS, Azure, and Google Cloud from a single Pulumi program. These skills will equip you to build, update, and maintain Kubernetes infrastructure with consistency and control.

In the next chapter, we will cover integrating Pulumi with **continuous integration/continuous deployment (CI/CD)** pipelines.

Questions

1. Explain the process of connecting Pulumi to a cloud-hosted Kubernetes cluster and how `kubeconfig` is used in this process.

2. How does Pulumi's approach to defining Kubernetes resources differ from using YAML manifests, and what are the key benefits of this approach?

3. How would you handle environment-specific configuration for a Kubernetes Deployment across development, staging, and production environments using Pulumi?

4. In multi-cloud Kubernetes management, how would you ensure that Kubernetes resources remain consistent across AWS, Azure, and GCP? Describe your strategy for handling configuration differences.

5. When creating a Kubernetes Service in Pulumi, explain how to expose it to the internet using a `LoadBalancer` service. What configurations are required in the Service definition?

Part 3

Integration and Cross-Provider Capabilities

The third part of the book focuses on taking Pulumi beyond single-provider deployments and integrating it into broader workflows. It shows how to combine automation, governance, and cross platform flexibility to manage complex infrastructure at scale.

You will begin by integrating Pulumi into CI/CD pipelines, enabling automated delivery of infrastructure changes alongside application code. From there, you will explore Pulumi's provider ecosystem, extending your automation to services beyond the major cloud platforms, including SaaS tools and on-premises systems.

Next, you will learn strategies for managing infrastructure across multiple regions and environments, ensuring consistency, reliability, and repeatability. This leads to multi cloud and hybrid scenarios, where Pulumi's flexibility allows you to orchestrate resources across different providers and environments from a single codebase.

By the end of this part, you will be able to design and implement infrastructure that spans providers, regions, and environments while maintaining control, security, and operational efficiency.

This part of the book includes the following chapters:

- *Chapter 7, Integrating Pulumi with CI/CD Pipelines*
- *Chapter 8, Exploring Pulumi's Provider Ecosystem*
- *Chapter 9, Managing your IaC in Multiple Regions and Environments*
- *Chapter 10, Managing Multi-Cloud and Hybrid Scenarios*

7

Integrating Pulumi with CI/CD Pipelines

Up until this point, all the Pulumi CLI commands have been executed directly from your local terminal. While this is a great way to learn and experiment, it is not a viable approach for production environments. This is because production-grade infrastructure demands consistency, repeatability, and the ability to scale changes across multiple environments without manual intervention. Relying on local execution can introduce human error, delay deployments, and make it difficult to track changes or maintain auditability. To address these challenges, modern development teams rely on **continuous integration/continuous deployment (CI/CD)** pipelines to automate the process of building, testing, and deploying **infrastructure as code (IaC)**. These pipelines ensure that infrastructure updates are consistent, traceable, and can be rolled back in the event of a failure.

In this chapter, we will explore how to integrate Pulumi into CI/CD environments to enable seamless, automated workflows for infrastructure management. You will learn how to configure CI/CD pipelines to build, test, and deploy Pulumi projects, ensuring that infrastructure changes are applied consistently across development, staging, and production environments. We will walk through the process of setting up secure access to sensitive information such as API keys and credentials, which are essential for pipeline execution. Additionally, we'll cover how to handle deployment errors and rollbacks, a crucial aspect of ensuring high availability and stability in production environments. Security is a key focus throughout this chapter, as we'll highlight best practices to prevent unauthorized access and maintain a secure CI/CD process for your Pulumi projects.

By the end of this chapter, you will be equipped to integrate Pulumi with popular CI/CD tools, enabling fully automated infrastructure deployments. You will know how to securely manage secrets, handle rollbacks, and establish a secure, efficient CI/CD process that can be applied across multiple environments. With this knowledge, you'll be able to increase the reliability and speed of your infrastructure delivery workflows, ultimately enhancing the overall efficiency of your development lifecycle.

In this chapter, we're going to cover the following main topics:

- Setting up Pulumi in CI/CD environments
- Automating build, test, and deployment processes
- Managing secrets and secure access
- Handling rollbacks and error management
- Best practices for pipeline security and efficiency

Technical requirements

If you would like to follow along with the examples in this chapter, you will require the following:

- The Pulumi CLI is required for executing commands. You can download it from here: `https://www.pulumi.com/docs/iac/download-install/`.
- Pulumi supports multiple programming languages, but for this chapter, we'll be using JavaScript/TypeScript, which requires Node.js. You can download and install it from the Node.js official site here: `https://nodejs.org/`.
- Access to a GitHub account (for using GitHub Actions) is required. You can create your GitHub account here: `https://github.com`.
- Access to a CircleCI account is required. You can create your CircleCI account here: `https://circleci.com/`.
- Access to an Azure DevOps account is required. You can create one here: `https://azure.microsoft.com/en-gb/products/devops`.
- We'll be deploying resources to Azure for this chapter, so you'll need an Azure account. You can sign up for a free account or use your existing Azure account. For more details, visit the Azure website here: `https://azure.microsoft.com/en-us/pricing/purchase-options/azure-account`.

- You will need a text editor or **integrated development environment** (IDE) such as Visual Studio Code, which provides syntax highlighting and other development aids for Pulumi configuration files.

- Familiarity with Git, YAML files, and simple scripting concepts is needed to understand CI/CD pipeline definitions and automation scripts.

Setting up Pulumi in CI/CD environments

You must create processes for automated, reliable, and traceable infrastructure deployments as you integrate Pulumi into your CI/CD setup. These processes guarantee that modifications are repeatable and error-free while enabling smooth infrastructure updates across development, staging, and production environments.

Here's how to set up Pulumi with GitHub Actions, CircleCI, and Azure DevOps:

1. To use GitHub Actions, start by creating a `.github/workflows` directory at the root of your repository.

2. Inside this directory, create a file called `pulumi.yml`. This file defines the CI/CD steps for GitHub to follow when a change is made to the repository's `main` branch. The pipeline runs automatically as long as the file is in the `.github/workflows` directory and contains a valid on trigger, which tells GitHub Actions when to execute the workflow. Here is an example configuration:

```yaml
name: Pulumi CI/CD
on:
  push:
    branches:
      - main
jobs:
  build:
    runs-on: ubuntu-latest
    steps:
      - uses: actions/checkout@v3
      - name: Set up Pulumi CLI
        uses: pulumi/actions@v3
        with:
          command: preview
      - name: Run Pulumi Preview
        run: pulumi preview
```

♀ **Quick tip**: Enhance your coding experience with the **AI Code Explainer** and **Quick Copy** features. Open this book in the next-gen Packt Reader. Click the **Copy** button

(1) to quickly copy code into your coding environment, or click the **Explain** button

(2) to get the AI assistant to explain a block of code to you.

```
function calculate(a, b) {
  return {sum: a + b};
};
```

Copy   Explain
 ①   ②

🔖 **The next-gen Packt Reader** is included for free with the purchase of this book. Scan the QR code OR visit packtpub.com/unlock, then use the search bar to find this book by name. Double-check the edition shown to make sure you get the right one.

3. To store sensitive information such as PULUMI_ACCESS_TOKEN, navigate to **Settings | Secrets and Variables** in the GitHub repository and add the necessary secrets.

4. If you're using CircleCI, you'll need to create a .circleci/config.yml file in the root of your project. This file defines how CircleCI will run your jobs and workflows. Unlike GitHub Actions, CircleCI requires that you activate the project in CircleCI's dashboard.

5. After logging in to CircleCI, you'll select your project, enable CircleCI for that repository, and then CircleCI will begin monitoring changes. Once a `.circleci/config.yml` file is present in the repository and the project is activated in CircleCI, pipelines will automatically run when a commit is pushed to the configured branches. A sample CircleCI configuration for running `pulumi preview` will look like the following code snippet:

```
version: 2.1
jobs:
  build:
    docker:
      - image: circleci/node:latest
    steps:
      - checkout
      - run: npm install -g pulumi
      - run: pulumi login --local
      - run: pulumi preview
workflows:
  version: 2
  build-and-preview:
    jobs:
      - build
```

6. To run this, you may also need environment variables such as `PULUMI_ACCESS_TOKEN` and the credentials for the cloud provider you are trying to log in to. To secure these environment variables, go to CircleCI, open **Project Settings**, and add the values under **Environment Variables**.

7. For Azure DevOps, you'll create a pipeline using an `azure-pipelines.yml` file at the root of your repository. This file specifies how to run the pipeline. To make the pipeline run, you'll need to create a pipeline in the Azure DevOps UI. Navigate to **Pipelines | New Pipeline**, select your repository, and link it to the `azure-pipelines.yml` file. Once the pipeline is created, Azure DevOps will detect and run it automatically on every commit to the configured branch.

8. Here's an example configuration:

```
trigger:
  branches:
    include:
      - main
pool:
  vmImage: 'ubuntu-latest'
steps:
  - task: UseNode@1
    inputs:
      version: '14.x'
  - script: npm install -g pulumi
    displayName: 'Install Pulumi CLI'
  - script: pulumi login --local
    displayName: 'Login to Pulumi'
  - script: pulumi preview
    displayName: 'Pulumi Preview'
```

9. To store pipeline variables and secrets in Azure DevOps, navigate to **Pipelines | Library** to create variable groups. Add environment variables such as PULUMI_ACCESS_TOKEN and any cloud provider credentials required for deployments. These values are referenced securely in the pipeline.

This section showed you how to set up Pulumi in CI/CD environments such as GitHub Actions, CircleCI, and Azure DevOps. Now, let's see how to automate testing, builds, and deployment processes.

Automating build, test, and deployment processes

To effectively automate the process of building, testing, and deploying infrastructure using Pulumi, you need a CI/CD pipeline that ensures code quality, reliable infrastructure changes, and smooth deployments. In this section, we'll explore how to set up a complete CI/CD pipeline to automate the process from start to finish. The pipeline will handle everything from building a backend application, running unit and integration tests, provisioning cloud infrastructure, and finally, deploying the app to a live environment using a blue-green deployment strategy. This strategy is important for minimizing downtime and allowing for seamless rollbacks if issues arise after deployment. This strategy allows traffic to be shifted to a new, fully tested environment only when everything works as expected.

Follow these steps:

1. The process begins with building the hypothetical backend application, which, in this case, is written in TypeScript. The first step is to ensure that the application is compiled and packaged correctly. The following code snippet shows how to install dependencies and build the application:

    ```
    # GitHub Actions
    - name: Install dependencies
      run: npm install
    - name: Build the application
      run: npm run build


    # Azure DevOps
    - task: Npm@1
      inputs:
        command: 'install'
    - script: npm run build
      displayName: 'Build the application'


    # Circle CI
    - run: npm install
    - run: npm run build
    ```

2. Once the application is built, the next stage is running unit tests. Unit tests are essential for validating the logic of individual components in the application. This ensures that the app's core functions work as intended before proceeding. If any of these tests fail, the pipeline stops immediately, preventing broken code from being deployed. The process is similar across all platforms, using npm test to execute the tests. The following code snippet shows you how this is done across the three pipelines:

    ```
    # GitHub Actions
    - name: Run unit tests
      run: npm test


    # Azure DevOps
    - script: npm test
    ```

```
        displayName: 'Run unit tests'

    # Circle CI
    - run: npm test
```

3. Once the unit tests pass, the process shifts to logging in to Azure before proceeding with infrastructure changes. Azure login is a critical step that must happen before Pulumi can access and preview or apply changes to Azure resources. This step provides the authentication required for Pulumi to access and manipulate the cloud infrastructure. The following code snippet shows you how this is done across the three pipelines:

```
# GitHub Actions
- name: Login to Azure
  uses: azure/login@v1
  with:
    creds: ${{ secrets.AZURE_CREDENTIALS }}

# Azure DevOps
- task: AzureCLI@2
  inputs:
    azureSubscription: 'My Azure Subscription'
    scriptType: 'bash'
    scriptLocation: 'inlineScript'
    inlineScript: |
      az login --service-principal
-u $(AZURE_CLIENT_ID)
-p $(AZURE_CLIENT_SECRET)
--tenant $(AZURE_TENANT_ID)

# CircleCI
- run: |
    az login --service-principal
-u $AZURE_CLIENT_ID
-p $AZURE_CLIENT_SECRET
--tenant $AZURE_TENANT_ID
```

4. After logging in to Azure, it's time to preview the infrastructure changes using `Pulumi Preview`. This step shows what resources will be created, updated, or deleted, giving developers a chance to review and approve changes. The pipeline stops if there are any misconfigurations or if unexpected changes are detected. `Pulumi Preview` provides visibility into what will change in the infrastructure, and each platform implements this step using the respective CI/CD commands. The following code snippet shows you how this is done across the three pipelines:

```
# GitHub Actions
- name: Run Pulumi Preview
  env:
    PULUMI_ACCESS_TOKEN: ${{ secrets.PULUMI_ACCESS_TOKEN }}
  run: |
    pulumi login
    pulumi preview

# Azure DevOps
- script: |
    pulumi login
    pulumi preview
  displayName: 'Run Pulumi Preview'
  env:
    PULUMI_ACCESS_TOKEN: $(PULUMI_ACCESS_TOKEN)

# CircleCI
- run: |
    pulumi login
    pulumi preview
  environment:
    PULUMI_ACCESS_TOKEN: $PULUMI_ACCESS_TOKEN
```

5. If the preview is successful, the next stage is to apply the infrastructure changes using `Pulumi Up`. This command creates or updates resources such as virtual machines, databases, and storage. Using the `--yes` flag ensures that the pipeline doesn't require manual confirmation. This process is essential for provisioning all the cloud resources required for the application. This step is similar for GitHub Actions, Azure DevOps, and CircleCI.

The following code snippet shows how it's done:

```
# GitHub Actions
- name: Run Pulumi Up
  env:
    PULUMI_ACCESS_TOKEN: ${{ secrets.PULUMI_ACCESS_TOKEN }}
  run: |
    pulumi login
    pulumi up --yes


# Azure DevOps
- script: |
    pulumi login
    pulumi up --yes
  displayName: 'Run Pulumi Up'
  env:
    PULUMI_ACCESS_TOKEN: $(PULUMI_ACCESS_TOKEN)


# CircleCI
- run: |
    pulumi login
    pulumi up --yes
  environment:
    PULUMI_ACCESS_TOKEN: $PULUMI_ACCESS_TOKEN
```

6.   Once the infrastructure is provisioned, the next stage is to deploy the backend application. The new version of the app is deployed to the green environment as part of the blue-green strategy. This allows testing of the new app without affecting live users. If the deployment succeeds, the system moves on to testing. The following code snippet shows how it's done:

```
# GitHub Actions
- name: Deploy to Azure
  uses: azure/webapps-deploy@v2
  with:
    app-name: ${{ secrets.AZURE_APP_NAME }}
    package: ./build
    slot-name: green
    publish-profile: ${{ secrets.AZURE_PUBLISH_PROFILE }}
```

```
# Azure DevOps
- task: AzureWebApp@1
  inputs:
    azureSubscription: 'My Azure Subscription'
    appName: $(AZURE_APP_NAME)
    package: $(System.DefaultWorkingDirectory)/build
    slot: green

# CircleCI
- run: |
    az webapp deployment source config-zip
--resource-group $AZURE_RESOURCE_GROUP
--name $AZURE_APP_NAME
--slot green
--src ./build.zip
```

7. If all integration tests pass, blue-green deployment begins. Traffic is shifted from blue to green using the az webapp deployment slot swap command. This switch occurs instantly, allowing the new version to go live without downtime. If any errors are detected after the swap, the pipeline rolls back to the previous version by swapping the production slot back to the blue environment. The following code snippet shows how it's done:

```
# GitHub Actions
- name: Swap Blue-Green Environments
  run: |
    az webapp deployment slot swap
      --name ${{ secrets.AZURE_APP_NAME }}
      --resource-group ${{ secrets.AZURE_RESOURCE_GROUP }}
      --slot green
      --target-slot production

# Azure DevOps
- task: AzureCLI@2
  inputs:
    azureSubscription: 'My Azure Subscription'
    scriptType: bash
    scriptLocation: inlineScript
    inlineScript: |
```

```
        az webapp deployment slot swap
--name $(AZURE_APP_NAME)
--resource-group $(AZURE_RESOURCE_GROUP)
--slot green
--target-slot production
# Circle CI
- run: |
    az webapp deployment slot swap
--name $AZURE_APP_NAME
--resource-group $AZURE_RESOURCE_GROUP
--slot green
--target-slot production
```

If a rollback is required, the system swaps the slots back so the blue environment is live. This ensures the system returns to a known stable state.

With this end-to-end process, you have successfully integrated your Pulumi infrastructure deployment step into your CI/CD process.

Managing secrets and secure access

In CI/CD pipelines, managing secrets and secure access is essential to protect sensitive information such as API keys, cloud provider credentials, and service principal tokens. These secrets are critical because they allow the pipeline to authenticate with third-party services, access cloud environments, and deploy infrastructure. Without proper security measures, these secrets could be exposed, leading to serious consequences such as unauthorized access, data breaches, and infrastructure misuse.

The risks associated with exposed secrets are significant. If API keys or cloud credentials are accidentally leaked, attackers could use them to control infrastructure, access sensitive data, or run expensive cloud services at the victim's expense. For example, there have been real-world cases where AWS keys exposed on public GitHub repositories allowed attackers to launch cryptocurrency mining operations using the victim's cloud resources. This highlights the critical need to secure these keys and prevent accidental exposure.

To address these risks, CI/CD platforms such as GitHub Actions, Azure DevOps, and CircleCI provide built-in secret management systems. These platforms offer secure storage mechanisms to store secrets encrypted at rest, ensuring they are only accessible to authorized jobs in the pipeline.

Secure secrets management in GitHub Actions

GitHub Actions provides a secure way to store and access sensitive information such as API keys, cloud provider credentials, and service principal tokens through GitHub Secrets.

To manage secrets, navigate to the **Settings** tab of your GitHub repository, then go to **Secrets and Variables** under **Actions**. Here, you can add new secrets such as PULUMI_ACCESS_TOKEN, AZURE_ CREDENTIALS, AZURE_APP_NAME, and AZURE_RESOURCE_GROUP. Each secret is given a name and value, and once saved, it can only be accessed within GitHub Actions workflows.

To use these secrets in a workflow, reference them with ${{ secrets.NAME }}. Here's a simple example where the Azure login and Pulumi Up steps use secrets for authentication:

```
- name: Login to Azure
  uses: azure/login@v1
  with:
    creds: ${{ secrets.AZURE_CREDENTIALS }}

- name: Run Pulumi Up
  env:
    PULUMI_ACCESS_TOKEN: ${{ secrets.PULUMI_ACCESS_TOKEN }}
  run: |
    pulumi login
    pulumi up --yes
```

When managing secrets in GitHub Actions for your IaC workflows, there are a few best practices that you can follow:

- **Store sensitive information as secrets**: Avoid hardcoding sensitive information such as API keys and tokens in workflow files. Instead, store them as secrets in **Settings** | **Secrets and Variables** | **Actions**. Secrets are encrypted and only accessible during workflow execution.

- **Use secret references in workflows**: Instead of hardcoding credentials in the YAML file, use ${{ secrets.NAME }} to access secrets securely. This prevents sensitive data from being exposed in your repository or logs.

- **Limit access to secrets**: Only users with admin permissions can add, modify, or delete secrets. Restrict repository access to essential personnel and enforce branch protection rules to control which workflows can access secrets.

- **Rotate secrets regularly**: Periodically rotate API keys and tokens to reduce the impact of potential exposure. If a secret is compromised, replace it immediately and remove the old one from GitHub Secrets and cloud providers.

- **Prevent secret exposure in logs**: Be cautious of logging commands that might accidentally print secrets. GitHub masks secrets in logs by default, but avoid commands such as `echo $SECRET` in workflows to prevent accidental exposure.

Secure secrets management in Azure DevOps

Azure DevOps provides a secure way to manage sensitive information using **variable groups** and **pipeline variables**. Secrets stored in variable groups are only accessible during pipeline execution, ensuring that sensitive information is never exposed in YAML files, logs, or source code. This secure method prevents accidental leakage of secrets and limits access to authorized workflows and users.

To create secrets in Azure DevOps, you need to navigate to the **Pipelines** section and access the library. Once inside, you can create a new variable group, which serves as a container for multiple secrets that can be shared across multiple pipelines. This centralization makes it easier to manage secrets for all your CI/CD workflows. When adding secrets to a variable group, you can define key-value pairs, such as `PULUMI_ACCESS_TOKEN`, `AZURE_CLIENT_ID`, `AZURE_CLIENT_SECRET`, and `AZURE_TENANT_ID`. It is critical to check the **Keep this value secret** option, which encrypts the value and prevents it from being viewed later, even by administrators. After creating the variable group, link it to your pipeline, so the secrets become accessible during pipeline execution.

To use these secrets in an Azure DevOps YAML pipeline, you must link the variable group to the pipeline and reference the secrets as environment variables. In the following example, the pipeline references a variable group named `Pulumi-Deployment-Variables`. The Azure login process is handled using the `AzureCLI` task, where the client ID, client secret, and tenant ID are securely accessed as environment variables. Pulumi also logs in using its access token, stored as a secret in the variable group. This method ensures that sensitive data is never directly exposed in YAML files or logs:

```yaml
variables:
  - group: Pulumi-Deployment-Variables

jobs:
  - job: Deploy
    pool:
      vmImage: 'ubuntu-latest'
```

```
    steps:
      - task: AzureCLI@2
        inputs:
          azureSubscription: 'My Azure Subscription'
          scriptType: 'bash'
          scriptLocation: 'inlineScript'
          inlineScript: |
            az login --service-principal
-u $(AZURE_CLIENT_ID)
-p $(AZURE_CLIENT_SECRET)
--tenant $(AZURE_TENANT_ID)

      - script: |
          pulumi login
          pulumi up --yes
        env:
          PULUMI_ACCESS_TOKEN: $(PULUMI_ACCESS_TOKEN)
```

This pipeline links the variable group to the pipeline and references it using the `variables` section. The AzureCLI task logs in to Azure using the stored service principal credentials, accessed securely with the `$(AZURE_CLIENT_ID)`, `$(AZURE_CLIENT_SECRET)`, and `$(AZURE_TENANT_ID)` variables. Once authenticated, the Pulumi CLI logs in using the `$(PULUMI_ACCESS_TOKEN)` variable. This process ensures that sensitive information is securely accessed without being hardcoded or displayed in logs.

When managing secrets in Azure DevOps for your IaC workflows, there are a few best practices that you can follow:

- Use variable groups to centralize and share secrets across multiple pipelines.
- Check the **Keep this value secret** option when adding secrets to variable groups to ensure encryption and prevent viewing of the secret value.
- Access secrets via environment variables in the YAML file using `$(VARIABLE_NAME)` instead of hardcoding them in scripts.
- Rotate secrets periodically to limit the impact of secret exposure. If a secret is compromised, rotate it immediately and update the variable group with the new value.
- Restrict permissions for accessing secrets by limiting access to variable groups and ensuring only essential users and pipelines can access or modify them.

Secure secrets management in CircleCI

CircleCI provides two primary methods for managing secrets: **project environment variables** and **context variables**. Project environment variables are linked to a specific project, while context variables can be shared across multiple projects. Project environment variables are created within the project's settings and are available to any workflow within that project. Context variables, on the other hand, offer a way to reuse the same set of secrets across multiple projects while maintaining secure access control. Both methods ensure that secrets are encrypted and only accessible during job execution, with no direct visibility in logs.

To create secrets in CircleCI, you need to access the project settings. Begin by navigating to the **Project Settings** page for your specific project. From there, you can manage project environment variables by selecting the **Environment Variables** tab. Click the **Add Environment Variable** button and enter the name and value of the secret. Common secrets to store include `PULUMI_ACCESS_TOKEN`, `AZURE_CLIENT_ID`, `AZURE_CLIENT_SECRET`, and `AZURE_TENANT_ID`. Once saved, these secrets are encrypted and can no longer be viewed or modified directly.

For managing secrets that are shared across multiple projects, **contexts** are used. To create a context, go to **Organization Settings** in CircleCI and define a new context. You can add environment variables to this context, which can then be shared with specific jobs or workflows. This approach allows for reusable secret management across multiple projects.

Once secrets have been created, you can reference them in CircleCI YAML configurations. The secrets are injected as environment variables, allowing them to be accessed in command-line scripts. Secrets are referenced using the `$VARIABLE_NAME` syntax. The following is an example of how to log in to Azure and run Pulumi commands using environment variables in CircleCI:

```
version: 2.1

jobs:
  deploy:
    docker:
        - image: circleci/node:latest

    environment:
      PULUMI_ACCESS_TOKEN: $PULUMI_ACCESS_TOKEN
    steps:
      - checkout
      - run: |
          az login --service-principal
```

```
        -u $AZURE_CLIENT_ID
        -p $AZURE_CLIENT_SECRET
        --tenant $AZURE_TENANT_ID
            - run: |
                    pulumi login
                    pulumi up -yes
```

In this configuration, CircleCI uses a `deploy` job with a Node.js container to execute the deployment. The `PULUMI_ACCESS_TOKEN`, `AZURE_CLIENT_ID`, `AZURE_CLIENT_SECRET`, and `AZURE_TENANT_ID` secrets are accessed as environment variables. The first step logs in to Azure using the `az login` command, which relies on the client ID, client secret, and tenant ID. After logging in to Azure, the Pulumi commands run to preview and apply changes to the infrastructure. These commands use `PULUMI_ACCESS_TOKEN` to authenticate with Pulumi's backend.

When managing secrets in CircleCI for your IaC workflows, there are a few best practices that you can follow:

- Use environment variables to store sensitive information such as API keys and cloud credentials.

- Prefer contexts for secrets that need to be shared across multiple CircleCI projects. Contexts allow for centralized secret management and improved reusability.

- Avoid echoing secrets to the console to prevent accidental exposure. Commands such as `echo $VARIABLE_NAME` should be avoided or masked to prevent sensitive information from appearing in logs.

- Rotate secrets regularly to reduce the impact of compromised credentials. If a secret is leaked or suspected of being exposed, rotate it immediately and update it in CircleCI.

- Use **role-based access control (RBAC)** to limit access to context secrets. CircleCI allows you to control which jobs and workflows can access contexts, ensuring that only authorized users and jobs have access.

Handling rollbacks and error management

In the context of CI/CD pipelines, a **rollback** is the process of returning an application or infrastructure to a previous stable version after a failed deployment. It serves as a safety net when something goes wrong, such as failed tests, broken features, or system errors. Error management is crucial in this process because it ensures that issues are detected early and resolved quickly to avoid prolonged downtime. Automated rollbacks are especially important as they allow the system to recover without manual intervention, reducing delays and keeping applications stable for users.

There are several rollback strategies that organizations can use, depending on the context and the system's complexity. **Full rollbacks** revert the entire system to a previous version, often by redeploying a previously known stable build. **Partial rollbacks** focus on reverting specific components of the system, such as rolling back only a microservice or a specific container. Another approach is to use **environment slot swaps**, as seen in **blue-green** or **canary deployments**. In blue-green deployments, two environments (blue and green) exist simultaneously, with one handling live traffic and the other being the staging environment. If the new deployment fails in the green environment, traffic is switched back to the blue environment, providing a seamless rollback experience. Similarly, canary deployments gradually roll out changes to a small percentage of users. If issues are detected during the incremental release, the rollout is paused, and the previous stable version is maintained.

It is important to distinguish between *rollbacks* and *retries*. While a rollback reverts the system to a stable state, a **retry** attempts to re-execute the failed step. Retries are used when the failure is believed to be temporary, such as network timeouts or transient API errors. For example, if a pipeline fails due to a brief network interruption, a retry will attempt to rerun the failed step instead of reverting the entire deployment. Rollbacks, on the other hand, are applied when the issue is persistent or caused by changes in the deployment itself. Both mechanisms have their place, but rollbacks are the safer option when system stability is at risk.

Rollback mechanisms can be categorized into three main types. **Automatic rollbacks** are triggered when a specific condition is met, such as failed health checks, deployment errors, or failed test cases. For instance, an automated system may detect that the production environment is experiencing higher error rates and immediately revert to the last stable version. **Manual rollbacks** require human intervention, often initiated by engineers or DevOps teams when a problem is detected after the deployment has completed. This type of rollback is used when issues are discovered later in production, often through user feedback or system monitoring. **Conditional rollbacks** are based on predefined criteria, such as a health check threshold, application performance metrics, or log-based anomaly detection. If the conditions are met, the rollback is triggered automatically. Conditional rollbacks provide flexibility and customization, allowing teams to define what "failure" means for their specific system, ensuring that rollbacks happen only when necessary.

Rollbacks in CI/CD pipelines occur when specific conditions are met to protect system stability and reduce downtime. One key trigger is test failures. During deployment, unit, integration, and end-to-end tests are run to ensure the new changes work as expected. If any of these tests fail, the system automatically reverts to the previous stable version.

Health check failures are another important trigger. After deployment, health checks monitor the live environment to ensure that the application responds correctly to requests. If the application returns errors such as 500 or 404 status codes instead of the expected 200, an alert is triggered to notify the team, and they can decide whether to roll back or deploy a fix. Deployment failures are another common trigger. If Pulumi encounters issues while creating or updating cloud resources, the pipeline will revert to the previous stable version. Rollbacks can also be triggered by timeouts. If a pipeline step takes too long, the system considers it a failure and initiates a rollback. Custom triggers can also be set, such as rolling back when error rates exceed a certain threshold or when logs detect a specific error pattern.

CI/CD pipelines use error detection to decide when to stop a deployment or trigger a rollback. One way errors are detected is through exit codes. Every command executed in a pipeline returns an exit code, where zero means success and non-zero indicates an error. Test assertions are another method. During testing, if actual results differ from expected results, an error is flagged. Health checks in production are also crucial for detecting issues. After deployment, health checks monitor whether the system is running properly. If health checks fail, alerts are triggered to notify the team, and they can decide whether to roll back or deploy a fix. Logging and monitoring play a key role in detecting errors that aren't obvious. Logs provide detailed information about each step of the pipeline, while monitoring tools track system performance. Errors found in logs or unusual performance trends can trigger alerts, helping teams quickly understand and respond to the problem. When errors are detected, the system can either attempt error recovery or initiate error termination. Recovery involves retrying a failed step, while termination stops the pipeline and often triggers a rollback to a previous version.

Here are some error management techniques:

- **Retry mechanism**: The system attempts to rerun a failed step instead of stopping the entire pipeline. This is useful for handling temporary issues such as network timeouts or transient errors in API calls.

- **Fail-fast strategy**: The pipeline stops immediately when a critical error is detected, preventing unnecessary steps from being executed and allowing faster issue resolution.

- **Graceful shutdowns**: Services are properly stopped or reverted to avoid leftover processes (often called "zombie processes") that could interfere with future deployments.

- **Error logging and alerting**: Logs provide step-by-step details of pipeline execution, while alerting systems notify teams when something goes wrong. This allows for faster root cause analysis and quicker issue resolution.

Best practices for pipeline security and efficiency

Keeping your CI/CD pipeline secure and efficient is essential for protecting sensitive information, ensuring smooth deployments, and speeding up delivery. A secure and efficient pipeline helps avoid data breaches, reduces delays, and ensures fast and stable releases for Pulumi projects. By following certain best practices, teams can create a CI/CD system that is fast, secure, and easy to manage.

A key part of pipeline security is controlling access. Not every user or service needs access to all parts of the pipeline. You can restrict access by using branch protection rules, which only allow changes from certain branches, such as main or release, to trigger important workflows. This prevents unreviewed or unapproved code from triggering sensitive actions, such as deployments. Also, limit who can modify pipeline files or edit secrets. Applying the **least privilege principle** ensures that users and services only have access to what they need and nothing more. Here's an example of how to ensure that a pipeline only runs on changes to specific branches:

```
on:
  push:
    branches:
      - main
      - release
```

This configuration ensures that only changes to the main or release branches will trigger the pipeline. Developers working on feature branches won't accidentally run the production deployment workflows.

To improve pipeline efficiency, avoid running unnecessary steps and try to reuse work that has already been done. One way to do this is by caching Pulumi dependencies. CI/CD platforms such as GitHub Actions, Azure DevOps, and CircleCI allow you to store files (for example, Pulumi CLI binaries, configuration files, and state files) so they don't have to be re-downloaded or rebuilt every time the pipeline runs. Caching reduces build times and speeds up deployments. Here's an example of how to cache the Pulumi CLI in GitHub Actions:

```
jobs:
  build:
    runs-on: ubuntu-latest
    steps:
      - name: Check out repository
        uses: actions/checkout@v3
```

```
    - name: Cache Pulumi CLI
      uses: actions/cache@v3
      with:
        path: ~/.pulumi
        key: ${{ runner.os }}-pulumi-${{ hashFiles('**/Pulumi.yaml') }}
        restore-keys: |
          ${{ runner.os }}-pulumi-

    - name: Install Pulumi CLI
      run: |
        curl -fsSL https://get.pulumi.com | sh
```

This configuration caches the Pulumi CLI binaries so that future runs of the pipeline don't need to re-download Pulumi.

Another way to improve efficiency is to run steps in parallel. If some steps don't depend on each other, they can run at the same time, which shortens the total pipeline duration. For example, running Pulumi previews and Pulumi stack validation at the same time can significantly reduce the total pipeline execution time. Here's an example of how to achieve parallel execution in Azure DevOps:

```
jobs:
- job: Preview
  pool:
    vmImage: 'ubuntu-latest'
  steps:
  - script: |
      pulumi login
      pulumi preview --stack dev

- job: Validate
  pool:
    vmImage: 'ubuntu-latest'
  steps:
  - script: |
      pulumi stack export > stack.json
      jq . stack.json
```

In this example, the `Preview` and `Validate` jobs run in parallel. This speeds up the pipeline since they don't have to wait for each other to finish before moving on to the next step. The `Preview` job runs a Pulumi preview to show what changes will be made, while the `Validate` job exports the Pulumi stack to a JSON file and runs a validation check using `jq`.

Logging and monitoring are also important for security and efficiency. Logs provide a detailed view of everything that happens in the pipeline. If a step fails, logs can show exactly where and why it failed. Logs are also useful for spotting performance issues, such as slow-running tasks or retries. Logs can also be used to track who made changes to the pipeline, when they were made, and why. This is known as auditability, and it helps teams investigate issues when something goes wrong. Here's an example of how to capture logs in CircleCI:

```
jobs:
  build:
    docker:
      - image: circleci/node:latest
    steps:
      - checkout
      - run: |
          echo "Starting Pulumi deployment..."
          pulumi login
          pulumi up --yes
```

The `echo` and `pulumi up` outputs will be captured in the CircleCI job logs. These logs provide insight into what happened during each step and help debug issues when errors occur. By inspecting logs, teams can trace which steps took longer than expected and identify any errors in the deployment process.

To further secure the pipeline, security checks should be built into the workflow. By scanning for vulnerabilities in container images and infrastructure code, teams can catch potential security issues before they reach production. Tools such as Trivy and Snyk can automatically scan for known vulnerabilities before your code goes live. Here's an example of how to run a security scan in GitHub Actions using Trivy:

```
jobs:
  security-scan:
    runs-on: ubuntu-latest
    steps:
      - name: Check out code
```

```
        uses: actions/checkout@v3

    - name: Run Trivy Security Scan
      run: |
        curl -sfL https://raw.githubusercontent.com/aquasecurity/trivy/
main/contrib/install.sh | sh
          trivy filesystem --exit-code 1 --severity HIGH,CRITICAL ./
```

In this example, the Trivy scan identifies known vulnerabilities in the files and container images used in the project. If any critical vulnerabilities are found, the job will fail, preventing deployment.

Summary

In this chapter, we covered how to use Pulumi with CI/CD pipelines to automate infrastructure deployments. You learned how to set up workflows with GitHub Actions, CircleCI, and Azure DevOps, learning step by step how to configure each platform. The process included building and testing application code, previewing changes to infrastructure, and automatically deploying updates using Pulumi. The chapter also showed how to manage secrets securely, with guidance on storing and accessing sensitive information such as API keys and tokens without exposing them. Rollback strategies were discussed, along with ways to detect problems, handle errors, and recover from failures during deployment. The chapter also provided tips on improving pipeline speed and security, such as caching dependencies, running tasks at the same time, and tracking changes to ensure accountability.

In the next chapter, we will explore Pulumi's provider ecosystem.

Questions

1. Why is it necessary to move from local Pulumi CLI execution to CI/CD-based execution for production environments?

2. How does caching Pulumi binaries and dependencies improve pipeline efficiency, and how is it implemented in GitHub Actions?

3. What are the key benefits of running pipeline steps in parallel, and how is parallel execution implemented in Azure DevOps and GitHub Actions?

4. How do rollback strategies, such as blue-green and canary deployments, help mitigate the impact of failed deployments in production?

5. What is the purpose of using branch protection rules in GitHub Actions workflows, and how do they prevent unapproved changes from affecting production?

Unlock this book's exclusive benefits now

Scan this QR code or go to packtpub.com/unlock, then search for this book by name.

Note: *Keep your purchase invoice ready before you start.*

UNLOCK NOW

8

Exploring Pulumi's Provider Ecosystem

There are different kinds of providers in Pulumi, each serving as a link between your code and the services you want to manage. Providers make it possible to control cloud resources, SaaS tools, and even your own internal systems, all from one place. Without them, Pulumi wouldn't be able to connect to the platforms and services that power modern applications.

In this chapter, you'll learn how to use Pulumi's provider ecosystem to manage resources across multiple platforms. We'll start with core cloud providers such as AWS, Azure, Google Cloud, and Kubernetes. You'll see how to install these providers, set them up, and use them to deploy key resources such as servers, storage, and serverless functions.

Next, we'll explore community and custom providers. Community providers help you manage tools such as GitHub, Datadog, and Cloudflare, which are tools you often use alongside cloud platforms. Custom providers go a step further, letting you create your own connectors for services that aren't officially supported. By the end of this section, you'll know how to use these providers and even create one yourself if needed.

By the end of the chapter, you'll have the skills to combine providers in a single Pulumi project, letting you manage resources across clouds and services in one workflow.

In this chapter, we're going to cover the following main topics:

- Introduction to Pulumi providers
- Using core cloud providers
- Exploring community and custom providers

Technical requirements

If you would like to follow along with the examples in this chapter, you will require the following:

- The Pulumi CLI is required for executing commands. You can download it from here: `https://www.pulumi.com/docs/iac/download-install/`.
- Pulumi supports multiple programming languages, but for this chapter, we'll be using JavaScript/TypeScript, which requires Node.js. You can download and install it from the Node.js official site here: `https://nodejs.org/`.

Introduction to Pulumi providers

Pulumi providers are essential components of Pulumi's **infrastructure-as-code** (IaC) system. They act as connectors that allow Pulumi to interact with different platforms, services, and tools. Without providers, Pulumi would not be able to manage infrastructure on cloud platforms such as AWS, Azure, and Google Cloud, nor would it be able to configure resources for services such as GitHub, Cloudflare, and Datadog.

At a high level, providers translate the resource definitions you write in your Pulumi program into API calls that cloud platforms and services understand. Each provider knows how to speak the language of the platform it manages. For example, the AWS provider understands AWS's API calls, while the Azure provider understands Azure's API. This allows you to control infrastructure on multiple platforms from a single Pulumi program.

Why are Pulumi providers important?

Pulumi providers play a central role in making Pulumi a truly multi-cloud, multi-service IaC tool. Here's why they matter:

- **Unified control across platforms:** Providers allow you to manage resources across multiple platforms (such as AWS, Azure, Google Cloud, and Kubernetes) in a single project. This removes the need to learn multiple cloud-specific tools (such as AWS CloudFormation or Azure Resource Manager) and gives you a unified way to manage everything.

- **Multi-service integration**: Providers aren't limited to cloud platforms. Pulumi also has providers for tools such as GitHub, Datadog, PagerDuty, and more. This allows you to configure CI/CD workflows, monitoring dashboards, and incident alerting alongside cloud resources—all from one program.

- **Cross-cloud flexibility**: Providers make it easier to adopt a multi-cloud strategy. If your company uses AWS for some services and Azure for others, you don't need separate workflows for each. With Pulumi, you can provision AWS resources alongside Azure resources, all from the same script.

- **Custom provider support**: Sometimes, you may need to manage a service that isn't officially supported. Pulumi allows you to build custom providers for internal tools or proprietary APIs. This gives you control over everything in your environment, not just the platforms that Pulumi officially supports.

- **Automation**: Providers automate complex workflows such as provisioning cloud instances, configuring security policies, and setting up third-party services. By using Pulumi providers, you avoid the need to manually click through cloud dashboards or use multiple command-line tools for different platforms.

Types of Pulumi providers

Pulumi providers are grouped into distinct types, each serving a specific role in managing infrastructure, DevOps workflows, and cloud-native services. Each type of provider addresses a different part of the infrastructure stack, from cloud compute to SaaS integrations to internal proprietary systems. Here's a closer look at the types of Pulumi providers and how they fit into the bigger picture of infrastructure management.

Core cloud providers

Core cloud providers are the most essential type of providers. They allow Pulumi to control the foundational cloud platforms that power applications and services. These providers connect Pulumi to popular cloud environments such as AWS, Azure, Google Cloud, and Kubernetes.

These providers allow you to create and manage essential cloud resources such as the following:

- Compute (EC2 instances on AWS, virtual machines on Azure, and Compute Engine on GCP)
- Storage (S3 buckets, Azure storage accounts, and Google Cloud Storage)
- Databases (RDS, Azure SQL, and Cloud SQL)
- Networking (VPCs, subnets, firewalls, and load balancers)
- Serverless functions (AWS Lambda, Azure Functions, and Google Cloud Functions)
- Kubernetes clusters (Deployments, Pods, Services, and ConfigMaps)

Each core cloud provider knows how to communicate directly with the cloud provider's API. This means that if you create an S3 bucket using Pulumi, the AWS provider translates your code into the correct AWS API call, makes the request, waits for AWS to create the bucket, and then updates the Pulumi state file to track that the bucket exists. The same process happens with other providers such as Azure, Google Cloud, and Kubernetes.

The following code snippet shows an example of a core cloud provider (AWS):

```
import * as aws from "@pulumi/aws";
const bucket = new aws.s3.Bucket("example-bucket", {
    bucket: "my-unique-bucket-name",
    versioning: {
        enabled: true,
    },
});
```

In this example, Pulumi uses the AWS provider to create an S3 bucket. Pulumi automatically converts this definition into the AWS API request to create the bucket.

SaaS and third-party service providers

This type of provider allows Pulumi to interact with third-party services that are commonly used in DevOps, CI/CD, and application development. These services include source control systems, observability tools, security platforms, and alerting systems. Unlike core cloud providers, these providers focus on managing tools that sit outside of cloud infrastructure but are critical to modern software delivery workflows.

Examples of SaaS and third-party providers include the following:

- **GitHub**: Manage repositories, issues, pull requests, and GitHub Actions workflows
- **GitLab**: Configure projects, pipelines, and users in GitLab
- **Cloudflare**: Control DNS records, caching rules, and **web application firewall** (**WAF**) policies
- **Datadog**: Configure monitoring dashboards, alert rules, and log aggregation for application observability
- **PagerDuty**: Set up incident response workflows and on-call schedules
- **New Relic**: Manage performance monitoring dashboards and alerting policies
- **Sentry**: Control error tracking and issue notifications for applications
- **Slack**: Automate notifications and interactions with Slack channels

With these providers, you can manage not only your cloud resources but also the SaaS services that work alongside your infrastructure.

The following code snippet shows an example of a SaaS Provider (GitHub):

```
import * as github from "@pulumi/github";
const membershipForUserX = new github.Membership("membership_for_user_x",
{});
```

Here, the GitHub provider is used to create a new GitHub membership called `membership_for_user_x`. Pulumi takes this resource definition and calls GitHub's API to create the repository.

Custom providers

While core providers and third-party providers cover most platforms, sometimes you need to manage something unique. This is where custom providers come in. Custom providers are useful in the following situations:

- The platform or tool you want to manage doesn't have an official Pulumi provider
- Your company has internal tools, APIs, or private services that only your team uses
- You want to build a provider specific to your company's proprietary software

Custom providers are created using Pulumi's Provider SDK. They allow you to define how Pulumi should interact with an API, what commands to send, and how to handle responses. Custom providers operate like official providers, but they are tailored for use within a specific team, company, or platform. Here's an example of a custom provider for an internal ticketing system:

```
const ticket = new mycompany.Ticket("incident-ticket", {
    title: "Server Outage",
    description: "The production server is down.",
    priority: "High",
});
```

This custom provider defines a `Ticket` resource. When the Pulumi script is run, the provider makes an API call to the internal ticketing system to create a new ticket.

Using core cloud providers

As organizations adopt multicloud strategies, a unified approach to managing resources across different cloud platforms becomes essential. Without a consistent method to control AWS, Azure, Google Cloud, and other cloud providers, managing infrastructure can become fragmented and complex. Each cloud platform has its own tools, APIs, and workflows, which can create inefficiencies and operational overhead.

Pulumi solves this problem by allowing you to manage multiple cloud providers from a single project and a single code base. With Pulumi's provider system, you can create and control resources across AWS, Azure, and GCP, all within one script. This approach makes it possible to provision cloud infrastructure, storage, and networking resources on multiple platforms at the same time, without juggling multiple IaC tools or IaC projects.

For each cloud, you create a provider instance that specifies where and how Pulumi should interact with that specific cloud. For example, you might have one provider for AWS (us-west-2), another for Azure (East US), and another for GCP (us-central1).

When you define resources, such as an S3 bucket, an Azure storage account, or a GCP Cloud Storage bucket, you explicitly link each resource to its provider. This gives you control over which cloud platform manages which resource and allows you to create AWS, Azure, and GCP resources in one Pulumi project.

The key enabler of this multi-cloud approach is Pulumi's ability to create and manage multiple providers at the same time. Instead of working with three separate tools for three cloud platforms, you work with one tool (Pulumi) to manage everything.

Here are some of the benefits of using core cloud providers in a multi-cloud setup:

- **Unified multi-cloud control**: Manage AWS, Azure, and GCP from a single Pulumi program. No need to juggle different CLI tools, templates, or dashboards.

- **Single source of truth**: Define all cloud infrastructure in one place, reducing the risk of inconsistency between environments.

- **Reduce complexity**: By using Pulumi's programming model, you can write logic (such as loops, conditionals, and shared modules) that work across clouds.

- **Vendor flexibility**: Easily move workloads between AWS, Azure, and GCP by modifying a few configuration details.

- **End-to-end automation**: Deploy all cloud resources in a single automated pipeline.

Now that we've covered why this is important, here's how multi-cloud management works in Pulumi:

- **Create providers for AWS, Azure, and GCP**: Each cloud needs its own provider instance. This is how Pulumi knows where to create resources and which API to call.

- **Link resources to specific providers**: Every AWS resource is linked to the AWS provider, every Azure resource is linked to the Azure provider, and so on. This gives you control over which cloud each resource lives in.

- **Run** `pulumi up`: When you deploy, Pulumi figures out which provider to call for each resource and communicates directly with AWS, Azure, and GCP. It runs the operations concurrently, so all resources are created as efficiently as possible.

This example demonstrates how to create an AWS S3 bucket, an Azure Blob Storage account, and a GCP Cloud Storage bucket, all from a single Pulumi program:

1. Begin by importing the necessary resources:

```
import * as pulumi from "@pulumi/pulumi";
import * as aws from "@pulumi/aws";
import * as azure from "@pulumi/azure-native";
import * as gcp from "@pulumi/gcp";
```

2. Next, create providers for AWS, Azure, and GCP:

```
const awsProvider = new aws.Provider("awsProvider", {
    region: "us-west-2",
});

const azureProvider = new azure.Provider("azureProvider", {
    location: "East US",
});

const gcpProvider = new gcp.Provider("gcpProvider", {
    project: "my-gcp-project",
    region: "us-central1",
});
```

3. Create an AWS S3 bucket using the AWS provider:

```
const awsBucket = new aws.s3.Bucket("awsBucket", {
    bucket: "multi-cloud-aws-bucket",
    versioning: {
        enabled: true,
    },
}, { provider: awsProvider });
```

4. Create an Azure Blob Storage account using the Azure provider:

```
const azureStorageAccount = new azure.storage.
StorageAccount("store", {
    resourceGroupName: "my-resource-group",
    location: "East US",
    sku: {
        name: "Standard_LRS",
    },
    kind: "StorageV2",
}, { provider: azureProvider });
```

5. Create a GCP Storage bucket using the GCP provider:

```
const gcpBucket = new gcp.storage.Bucket("gcpBucket", {
    location: gcpProvider.region,
    name: "multi-cloud-gcp-bucket"H,
}, { provider: gcpProvider });
```

The code creates cloud providers for AWS, Azure, and GCP, each configured with its specific region or project details. It then uses these providers to provision an AWS S3 bucket, an Azure Blob Storage account, and a GCP Cloud Storage bucket, each tied to its respective cloud provider. This allows all three cloud platforms to be managed from a single Pulumi program.

Now that we have established the core cloud providers, let's take a look at some of the other providers you can use.

Exploring community and custom providers

Beyond the official Pulumi providers for popular cloud platforms such as AWS, Azure, and GCP, there are two other types of providers that significantly expand Pulumi's capabilities: community providers and custom providers. **Community providers** are developed and maintained by Pulumi users and contributors through the Pulumiverse ecosystem. These providers allow Pulumi to manage services such as Grafana, Vercel, and Redpanda, which are platforms used for observability, frontend deployments, and data streaming, respectively. By using these community-driven providers, you can automate workflows for these platforms directly within Pulumi projects.

The Pulumiverse ecosystem

The **Pulumiverse ecosystem** is a collection of community-driven providers and libraries that extend Pulumi's support for platforms not officially managed by Pulumi. Notable providers in Pulumiverse include Grafana, which allows you to create and manage dashboards and visualizations; Vercel, which enables the deployment and management of frontend applications; and Redpanda, a Kafka-compatible streaming platform known for its high performance. You can browse available providers through the Pulumiverse GitHub (`https://github.com/pulumiverse`) or the Pulumi Registry (`https://www.pulumi.com/registry/`), making it simple to discover and incorporate them into your Pulumi projects.

For example, you can create a Grafana dashboard using the Pulumiverse Grafana provider like this:

```
import * as grafana from "@pulumiverse/grafana/oss";

const folder = new grafana.Folder("folder", {
title: "Multi-cloud Demo",
});

const dashboardJson = JSON.stringify({
title: "Service Health Dashboard",
    uid:    "service-health",
panels: [],
});

const dashboard = new grafana.Dashboard("dashboard", {
folder:       folder.uid,
    configJson: dashboardJson,
});
```

This code creates a Grafana dashboard called **Service Health Dashboard** with a UTC time zone. Normally, creating dashboards requires manual work in the Grafana UI, but with Pulumi, you can define dashboards in code, making them reusable, version-controlled, and consistent across environments.

In addition to Pulumiverse providers, Pulumi also supports a range of SaaS providers such as Cloudflare, Datadog, and PagerDuty. These providers allow you to manage DNS (Cloudflare), observability dashboards (Datadog), and incident response workflows (PagerDuty) directly from Pulumi projects. By using these SaaS providers, you can automate key operational workflows that go beyond cloud infrastructure, enabling end-to-end automation of infrastructure, monitoring, and incident management. For example, you can configure DNS records in Cloudflare, create alerts in Datadog, or define on-call schedules in PagerDuty, all from within a single Pulumi program.

While community providers such as Grafana, Vercel, and Redpanda help you automate workflows for popular services, custom providers go one step further. **Custom providers** allow companies to manage internal tools, proprietary APIs, or on-premises systems that aren't supported by Pulumiverse or Pulumi's official providers. For instance, if your company has an internal ticketing system or a custom business analytics API, you can create a custom provider to manage and automate those workflows just like you would for a public service.

Custom Pulumi providers

A custom provider is a provider you build yourself when no official or community provider exists for a specific platform, API, or tool. For example, if your company has a work order system with an API to create work items and projects, and you want to automate the provisioning of this system, you can build a custom provider to create, update, and delete tickets as part of your infrastructure deployment process.

A custom provider has several essential components that enable it to interact with an external API. It follows the same principles as Pulumi's official providers for AWS, Azure, and GCP.

Here's how a custom provider works:

- **API integration:** The provider sends HTTP requests to an API (such as a REST API) to create, update, read, and delete resources
- **CRUD functions:** The provider defines methods for **create, read, update, and delete (CRUD)** operations
- **Pulumi's Provider SDK:** Pulumi's Provider SDK allows you to define the schema and logic of your provider
- **Communication with APIs:** Custom providers handle API rate limits, timeouts, and failures

For example, let's imagine a provider for a work order management system. Instead of managing individual work orders, the provider will be responsible for provisioning an instance of the work order tool. This might include configuring its name, region, plan (basic, standard, or enterprise), and enabling email notifications. Once the system is provisioned, users can log in to create, track, and manage their work orders directly in the system. The first step in building a custom provider for this system is to define its schema, which describes the attributes needed to create the system. This is similar to how you define inputs for AWS resources such as S3 buckets or EC2 instances. For our work order system provider, we'll define properties such as the following:

- name: The name of the work order system
- region: The region where the system will be hosted (e.g., us-west, us-east, or europe)
- plan: The type of subscription plan (basic, standard, or enterprise)
- notificationsEnabled: Whether to enable email notifications for system events

Here's an example of the provider schema in **JSON format**:

```
{
  "name": "workorder-tool-provider",
  "version": "0.1.0",
  "resources": {
    "workOrderSystem": {
      "properties": {
        "name": { "type": "string" },
        "region": { "type": "string", "enum": ["us-west", "us-
east", "europe"] },
        "plan": {
"type": "string", "enum": ["basic", "standard", "enterprise"] },
        "notificationsEnabled": { "type": "boolean" }
      },
      "required": ["name", "region", "plan"]
    }
  }
}
```

This schema tells Pulumi that when someone wants to create a work order system, they must provide the name, region, and plan values, while notificationsEnabled is optional. This structure will later be used to validate inputs when users call the provider.

Once the schema is ready, the next step is to define the CRUD logic for the resource. Each CRUD function determines how Pulumi interacts with the provider's API:

- **Create:** The create function sends a request to the API to provision a new system. The API returns a unique ID for the system, which is used to track the system in Pulumi's state file.

- **Read:** The read function retrieves the current state of the resource. It is especially useful in cases where updates to the system are made outside of Pulumi, and you want to reconcile the actual state with the expected state.

- **Update:** The update function is called whenever the user changes properties such as name, region, or plan in the Pulumi program. This function sends an API PUT request to update the resource. The Pulumi diff logic determines which properties have changed and only calls update when necessary.

- **Delete:** The delete function removes the system from the platform. It deprovisions the system and removes it from the external infrastructure.

Here's a full implementation of the CRUD logic for our work order tool provider:

```
export class WorkOrderSystem extends pulumi.dynamic.Resource {
    constructor(name: string, args: WorkOrderSystemArgs, opts?: pulumi.
CustomResourceOptions) {
        super(new WorkOrderSystemProvider(), name, args, opts);
    }
}


class WorkOrderSystemProvider implements pulumi.dynamic.ResourceProvider {
    async create(inputs: WorkOrderSystemArgs) {
        const response = await fetch("https://api.workorderplatform.com/
systems", {
            method: "POST",
            headers: { "Content-Type": "application/json" },
            body: JSON.stringify(inputs)
        });

        const data = await response.json();
        return { id: data.id, outs: data };
    }

    async read(id: string) {
```

```
        const response = await fetch(`https://api.workorderplatform.com/
systems/${id}`, {
            method: "GET",
            headers: { "Content-Type": "application/json" }
        });

        const data = await response.json();
        return { id: id, outs: data };
    }


    async
update(id: string, olds: WorkOrderSystemArgs, news: WorkOrderSystemArgs) {
        await fetch(`https://api.workorderplatform.com/systems/${id}`, {
            method: "PUT",
            headers: { "Content-Type": "application/json" },
            body: JSON.stringify(news)
        });

        return { outs: news };
    }

    async delete(id: string) {
        await fetch(`https://api.workorderplatform.com/systems/${id}`, {
method: "DELETE" });
    }
}

export interface WorkOrderSystemArgs {
    name: string;
    region: string;
    plan: string;
    notificationsEnabled: boolean;
}
```

Once your provider is ready, you can use it like any other Pulumi provider. Here's an example of how to provision our custom work order system with Pulumi:

```
import * as pulumi from "@pulumi/pulumi";
import { WorkOrderSystem } from "./provider";

// Create a new work order system
const workOrderSystem = new WorkOrderSystem("projectManagementSystem", {
    name: "Project Management System",
    region: "us-west",
    plan: "standard",
    notificationsEnabled: true
});
```

What happens when you run `pulumi up`?

- Pulumi calls the `create` method, which sends an API request to `workorderplatform.com` to create the system

- The API returns an ID, and Pulumi stores this ID in the state file

- If you later change the plan from `standard` to `enterprise`, Pulumi detects the change, triggers the `update` function, and sends a `PUT` request to update the system

- If you run `pulumi destroy`, Pulumi calls the `delete` method, which sends a `DELETE` request to remove the system

Once your provider is ready, you can make it available for others. If it's a private provider, you can distribute it as an `npm` package or private repo. However, if you created a provider for a new PaaS tool and you want to make it available for the Pulumi community, you can submit it to Pulumiverse and follow their guidelines for submitting new providers.

Summary

In this chapter, we covered the Pulumi provider ecosystem and its role in managing infrastructure across cloud platforms, SaaS tools, and custom systems. The chapter explored core cloud providers such as AWS, Azure, and GCP, which enable multi-cloud provisioning in a single Pulumi program. It also highlighted SaaS providers such as Cloudflare, Datadog, and PagerDuty, which automate workflows for DNS, monitoring, and incident response.

We introduced community providers from Pulumiverse, focusing on Grafana, Vercel, and Redpanda, which support dashboards, app deployments, and streaming services. The final section focused on custom providers, which allow for the management of internal APIs and proprietary tools. Using a work order tool provider as an example, the chapter explained how to define a schema and implement CRUD logic. This approach enables the creation, packaging, and publishing of providers for both internal and external use.

In the next chapter, we will focus on how to manage your IaC in multiple regions and environments.

Questions

1. Explain the key difference between core cloud providers, SaaS providers, and community providers in Pulumi.

2. How does multi-cloud resource creation in Pulumi ensure that AWS, Azure, and GCP resources are created consistently in a single execution?

3. What is a custom provider, and when would you build one instead of using an official or community provider?

4. How does the process of defining a provider schema affect the attributes available to users when provisioning resources with a custom provider?

5. Explain the role of CRUD logic in a custom provider. Why is it essential to have distinct logic for `create`, `read`, `update`, and `delete` actions?

9

Managing your IaC in Multiple Regions and Environments

As you deploy infrastructure, you probably wouldn't deploy to just one environment and one region. In real-world scenarios, applications often need to be available in different parts of the world to provide faster access for users and stay online even if something goes wrong in one location. At the same time, you'll need separate environments for development, testing, and production to ensure smooth updates and avoid accidental changes to your live system. Managing all of this can get complicated, but **infrastructure as code (IaC)** makes it possible to handle everything in a clear, organized way.

In this chapter, you will learn how to manage IaC across multiple regions and environments, making your infrastructure more reliable, efficient, and easy to maintain. We'll start by looking at how to plan deployments in different regions, where you'll see how to set up infrastructure in multiple locations to improve speed, availability, and disaster recovery. We'll also look at how to manage different environments, such as development, testing, and production. You'll learn how to keep these environments separate so that changes in one environment don't affect the others. We'll also explore how to use configuration files and templates to make it easier to control what happens in each environment.

Finally, we'll focus on automation. Instead of manually setting up each environment, you'll learn how to use tools such as CI/CD pipelines to automatically create, update, and delete environments when needed. This makes it easier to manage infrastructure at scale, reduce mistakes, and save time.

In this chapter, we're going to cover the following main topics:

- Planning for multi-region deployments
- Environment management strategies
- Automating environment setup and management

Technical requirements

If you would like to follow along with the examples in this chapter, you will require the following:

- The Pulumi CLI is required for executing commands. You can download it from here: `https://www.pulumi.com/docs/iac/download-install/`.

- Pulumi supports multiple programming languages, but for this chapter, we'll be using JavaScript/TypeScript, which requires Node.js. You can download and install it from the Node.js official site here: `https://nodejs.org/`.

- We will be using Pulumi ESC to manage shared configurations across different regions, so you will need the ESC CLI. You can get it here: `https://www.pulumi.com/docs/esc/download-install/`.

- Since we'll be deploying resources to Azure, you'll need an Azure account. You can sign up for a free account or use your existing Azure account. For more details, visit the Azure website here: `https://azure.microsoft.com/en-us/pricing/purchase-options/azure-account`.

- The Azure CLI is required to interact with Azure resources from your local machine. You can install the Azure CLI by following the instructions here: `https://learn.microsoft.com/en-us/cli/azure/install-azure-cli`.

- The final section of this chapter is about automation and continuous integration, so you'd need a GitHub account so that you can create a GitHub Actions workflow. You can create an account here: `https://github.com/`.

Planning for multi-region deployments

Modern applications demand speed, reliability, and resilience, which is why deploying infrastructure in a single region is rarely enough. Multi-region deployments solve this by running
infrastructure in multiple geographical locations. This approach ensures continuous availability,
faster response times, and better disaster recovery. If one region experiences an outage due to a
power failure, network issue, or natural disaster, user traffic can be automatically redirected to
another region, minimizing downtime. Additionally, placing infrastructure closer to users reduces
network delays, improving application performance and user experience.

There are several key reasons for adopting multi-region deployments. One of the most important
is to support a global user base. Applications with users worldwide, such as Instagram and Slack,
rely on multi-region deployments to deliver fast, uninterrupted service. For example, a user in
Nigeria will experience faster load times when they connect to a server in Africa or Europe rather
than one in the United States. This reduces latency and ensures a seamless user experience, regardless of where users are located. Without multi-region deployments, apps such as Instagram
would face slower image loads and message delays, frustrating users and increasing the risk of
users abandoning the platform.

Another reason is regulatory compliance. Certain countries have strict data privacy laws that
require user data to stay within their borders. The **General Data Protection Regulation (GDPR)**
in the European Union, for example, limits where personal data can be stored and processed.
Multi-region deployments allow companies to store and process user data in specific regions to
meet legal requirements while still supporting a global user base. For instance, Google Workspace
ensures that customer data from European users can be stored and processed within the European
Union to meet GDPR compliance, even as the service remains accessible globally.

Disaster recovery and business continuity are also major drivers for multi-region deployments.
By deploying infrastructure in multiple regions, companies protect themselves from regional
outages caused by natural disasters or system failures. If one region becomes unavailable, another
region can automatically take over, ensuring that users experience no service disruption. This is
especially important for applications with strict **service-level agreements (SLAs)**, where even
a few minutes of downtime can result in significant financial losses or reputational damage. For
instance, Zoom relies on multi-region deployments to maintain uninterrupted video calls even if
one of its regions faces an outage. Without this strategy, a technical failure in one location could
disrupt business meetings, classes, and large-scale webinars globally.

In addition to these benefits, load balancing and traffic management are easier with multi-region deployments. Instead of placing all the load on one region, traffic can be distributed across multiple regions, preventing any one location from becoming overwhelmed during traffic spikes. This approach ensures better system performance during high-traffic events, such as product launches or major announcements.

Despite these benefits, multi-region deployments come with challenges. Higher costs are a major consideration, as running duplicate infrastructure in multiple regions increases expenses for compute, storage, and networking. Increased complexity is another challenge, as managing multiple regions requires consistent configuration, automation, and monitoring. Data synchronization issues can also be a challenge, especially when databases must remain consistent across regions.

But with the right design, these challenges can be managed. A good design helps control costs, keep regions in sync, and make it easier to manage everything from one place. This makes it possible to build systems that are reliable, fast, and able to support users all over the world.

Key concepts of multi-region design

When designing a multi-region system, one of the first decisions to make is whether to use an active-active or active-passive deployment. These approaches define how traffic is handled across multiple regions and how failovers are managed.

In an **active-active** deployment, all regions are fully operational and actively handle user traffic at the same time. This setup improves performance because users are routed to the closest region, reducing latency. It also provides high availability since, if one region fails, users can still be served by another active region. Active-active deployments are ideal for global applications with users spread across multiple continents, such as social media platforms (e.g., Instagram). Users can be connected to the closest server, resulting in faster load times. However, this design is more expensive since all regions are constantly running, and it requires complex data synchronization to ensure that all regions have consistent information.

On the other hand, an **active-passive** deployment only has one region actively handling user traffic at a time, while the other regions remain on standby. These standby regions remain ready to take over in case of failure but do not process traffic under normal conditions. This approach is often used for disaster recovery. For example, banking applications may use an active-passive design where a primary region serves all customer transactions, while a secondary region is kept on standby, ready to activate if the main region goes down. This setup reduces operational costs since only one region is fully utilized.

Choosing between active-active and active-passive depends on several factors:

- **Cost**: Active-active is more expensive since all regions are running, while active-passive reduces costs by only having one active region
- **Complexity**: Active-active is more complex to set up due to synchronization needs, while active-passive is simpler to manage since only one region is handling traffic at a time
- **Failover time**: Active-active has instant failover since all regions are already running, while active-passive may experience delays during the switchover

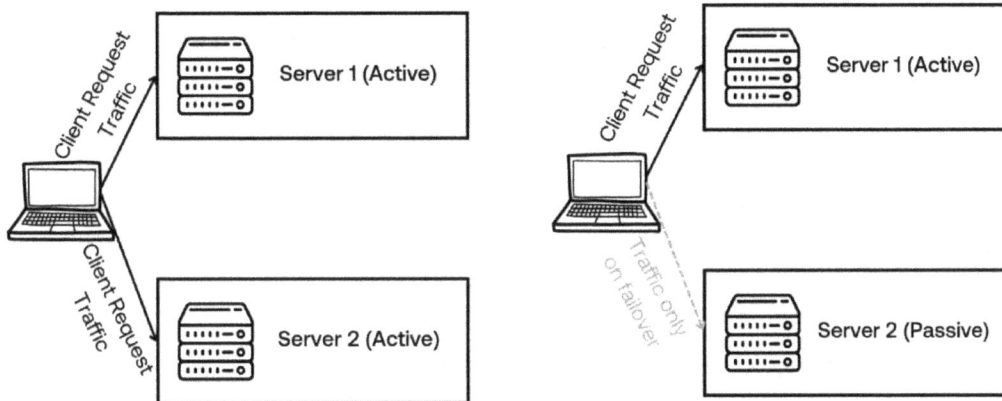

Figure 9.1: Active-active versus active-passive

🔍 **Quick tip**: Need to see a high-resolution version of this image? Open this book in the next-gen Packt Reader or view it in the PDF/ePub copy.

📘 **The next-gen Packt Reader** is included for free with the purchase of this book. Scan the QR code OR go to `packtpub.com/unlock`, then use the search bar to find this book by name. Double-check the edition shown to make sure you get the right one.

Failover ensures that if one region becomes unavailable, traffic is automatically redirected to another region to maintain system availability. This is essential for disaster recovery, allowing applications to stay online even if a region experiences a major outage due to power failures, natural disasters, or network issues.

Azure Traffic Manager supports automated failover using priority-based routing. This method assigns a priority to each region (or endpoint) and routes all traffic to the highest-priority region. If the primary region fails, Traffic Manager automatically redirects traffic to the next region on the priority list. This process is fully automated, ensuring that failover happens instantly without manual intervention. This setup is commonly used in disaster recovery scenarios where one region serves as the primary region, and the other regions act as backups.

For example, consider a system with a primary region in the East US and a backup region in the West US. During normal operation, users are routed to the East US region (priority 1). If that region becomes unavailable, Azure Traffic Manager detects the failure using health checks and automatically redirects user traffic to the West US region (priority 2) until the primary region is restored.

Two key metrics help define how well failover works:

- **Recovery point objective (RPO)**: This defines the maximum acceptable amount of data loss. For example, if the RPO is set to 5 minutes, it means that if a failure occurs, up to 5 minutes of data may be lost.

- **Recovery time objective (RTO)**: This defines how quickly the system should be restored after a failure. For instance, if the RTO is 10 minutes, then users should have full access to the system within 10 minutes of the failure.

Here's a Pulumi TypeScript example of how to create an Azure Traffic Manager profile using priority-based routing. This profile will automatically route traffic to the primary endpoint first. If the primary endpoint fails, it will route traffic to the secondary endpoint:

```typescript
import * as azure from "@pulumi/azure-native";
const trafficManagerProfileName = "tm001";

const trafficManager = new azure.network.
Profile(trafficManagerProfileName, {
    resourceGroupName: "my-test-rg",
    trafficRoutingMethod: "Priority",
    dnsConfig: { relativeName: "tm001", ttl: 30 },
    monitorConfig: { protocol:"HTTP", port:80, path:"/" },
});
```

```
const primaryEndpoint = new azure.network.Endpoint("primary", {
    profileName: trafficManager.name,
    resourceGroupName: "my-test-rg",
    endpointType: "ExternalEndpoints",
    target: "example-primary.mywebsite.com",
    priority: 1,
}, { dependsOn: [trafficManager] });

const secondaryEndpoint = new azure.network.Endpoint("secondary", {
    profileName: trafficManager.name,
    resourceGroupName: "my-test-rg",
    endpointType: "ExternalEndpoints",
    target: "example-secondary.mywebsite.com",
    priority: 2,
}, { dependsOn: [trafficManager] });
```

Let's look at how it works:

- **Traffic Manager profile**: Uses priority-based routing, meaning traffic goes to the endpoint with the highest priority value (1 is higher priority than 2)
- **Primary endpoint**: The endpoint has a priority value of 1, so all user traffic is sent here first
- **Secondary endpoint**: The endpoint has a priority value of 2, so it will only receive traffic if the primary endpoint becomes unhealthy

With this setup, failover happens automatically if the primary endpoint fails, and traffic is redirected to the secondary endpoint.

Beyond managing failovers, you can also use Traffic Manager for load balancing. Load balancing ensures that traffic is distributed across multiple regions, improving performance and availability. Instead of directing all users to a single region, traffic is spread to multiple regions, reducing the load on any single server. If one region fails, load balancing allows traffic to be redirected to the next available region.

Azure provides Azure Traffic Manager to manage load balancing across multiple regions. By using performance-based routing, Traffic Manager directs users to the region with the best response time. This ensures that users are connected to the fastest, most available region.

Here's how to create a Traffic Manager profile with performance-based routing using Pulumi:

```
import * as azure from "@pulumi/azure-native";
const tm = new azure.network.Profile("tm001", {
    resourceGroupName: " my-test-rg",
    trafficRoutingMethod: "Performance",
    dnsConfig: { relativeName: " tm001", ttl: 30 },
    monitorConfig: { protocol:"HTTP", port:80, path:"/" },
});
```

The preceding code snippet creates an Azure Traffic Manager profile that uses performance-based routing to send users to the region with the fastest response time. Traffic Manager continuously monitors the health of each endpoint by sending HTTP requests to check whether they are responsive. If an endpoint becomes unhealthy, Traffic Manager automatically redirects users to the next fastest available region. This ensures that users are always connected to a healthy, responsive region, improving both performance and availability.

Designing a multi-region architecture

Designing a multi-region architecture requires thoughtful planning to ensure high performance, availability, and security. It involves selecting the right regions, managing resources efficiently, and securing inter-region communication. Using Pulumi makes this process easier with the use of stacks, parameterized templates, environment-specific configurations, and parent-child stack models. These tools enable shared configurations, region-specific overrides, and reusable infrastructure logic.

If you have Pulumi Cloud and you're not self-hosting, you can also use ESC for this. Pulumi's **ESC** (which stands for **Environments, Secrets, and Configuration**) provides an enhanced way to manage shared environment configurations and secrets in a structured way. By using ESC, you can centralize shared environment variables, manage sensitive information such as API keys, and control configurations specific to production, staging, or development environments. ESC allows these values to be easily accessed and modified without embedding them in the code. We will cover ESC in more detail in *Chapter 11*, but before then, this chapter will show how you can use ESC to achieve multi-region configurations.

Choosing the right cloud regions to deploy in is essential for multi-region design. Major cloud providers have data centers worldwide, but not all regions have the same capabilities, costs, or compliance guarantees.

Here are some key factors to consider:

- To reduce latency, you should deploy your infrastructure in regions close to your users. For example, if you have users in Southeast Asia, using Azure Southeast Asia (Singapore) ensures faster access compared to the US or European regions.

- Certain countries have data sovereignty laws that require user data to be stored in specific regions. For example, to comply with GDPR for European customers, you might deploy to Azure West Europe.

- Different regions have different prices for compute, storage, and bandwidth. For instance, cloud costs in Mumbai may be cheaper than in Tokyo. Balancing cost and performance is important when choosing regions.

- To give your users the fastest experience, you should route them to the closest available region. Multi-region architectures support this by allowing you to place resources in locations such as West US, East US, and Southeast Asia, each serving users from the nearest location.

- Having at least one secondary region ensures availability even if the primary region fails. Some architectures also use a tertiary region as an additional failover for disaster recovery.

What are primary, secondary, and tertiary regions?

Primary regions handle normal traffic and serve as the main endpoint for users. Secondary regions act as a failover for disaster recovery. If the primary region fails, the system automatically redirects traffic to the secondary region. Tertiary regions provide additional redundancy for applications with very high availability requirements.

Managing resources across multiple regions can become challenging, but Pulumi simplifies this with stacks and configurations. You can use something I like to call the parent-child stack model, and this paradigm follows the principle of inheritance in object-oriented programming. This model allows you to create a shared configuration at the base (parent) level and specific configurations for each region (child) stack. With the addition of Pulumi's ESC, you can centralize and control shared configuration values across environments and stacks.

Parent-child stack model

The parent-child stack model is a concept similar to inheritance in object-oriented programming:

- **Parent stack**: Contains shared logic and configuration. It acts as a "base" where shared values are stored, such as app names, shared resource groups, or global secrets.
- **Child stacks**: Each child stack represents a specific region (e.g., West US, Southeast Asia, etc.) and inherits configuration from the parent. It can override shared values and add its own custom logic, such as region-specific virtual machine sizes.

This is what your directory structure may look like if you decide to adopt this model in your Pulumi projects:

```
|-- ./templates
|-- Pulumi.yaml
|-- Pulumi.prod.yaml(Parent stack - shared configurations)
|-- Pulumi.prod-wu2.yaml (Child stack for West US 2)
|-- Pulumi.prod-sea.yaml (Child stack for Southeast Asia)
|-- index.ts (Main Pulumi script for defining resources)
```

Let's imagine that the parent stack had the following configurations:

```
config:
  app: "myapp"
  environment: "prod"
  sharedResourceGroupName: "prod-shared-resources"
  loggingEnabled: true
```

Let's also imagine that the child stack for westus2 had the following configurations:

```
config:
  region: "West US 2"
  vmSize: "Standard_D2s_v3"
  customEndpoint: "westus2.website.com"
```

Let's also imagine that the child stack for southeastasia had the following configurations:

```
config:
  region: "Southeast Asia"
  vmSize: "Standard_D4s_v3"
  customEndpoint: "southeastasia.website.com"
```

With this setup, `Pulumi.prod.yaml` holds shared values for the production environment, while the `Pulumi.prod-wu2.yaml` and `Pulumi.prod-sea.yaml` child stacks define region-specific values. These child stacks can "inherit" shared properties such as app, environment, and sharedResourceGroupName while defining their own regional properties such as region and vmSize. To do this, they can use stack references. A stack reference allows one stack to access the outputs of another stack. The parent stack can output shared configurations, and child stacks can reference these outputs.

The following code snippet is the code for the parent stack's `index.ts` file. It defines the shared configurations and exports them so they can be accessed by child stacks:

```
import * as pulumi from "@pulumi/pulumi";
const config = new pulumi.Config();

const appName = config.require("app");
const environment = config.require("environment");
const sharedResourceGroupName = config.require("sharedResourceGroupName");
const loggingEnabled = config.require("loggingEnabled");

export const outputs = {
    appName,
    environment,
    sharedResourceGroupName,
    loggingEnabled,
};
```

The following code snippet is the code for the child stacks (`westus2` and `southeastasia`). Child stacks reference the parent stack's shared configurations and define their own regional-specific logic:

```
import * as pulumi from "@pulumi/pulumi";
import * as azure from "@pulumi/azure-native";

const parentStack = new pulumi.StackReference("org-name/project-name/prod");

const appName = parentStack.getOutput("appName");
const environment = parentStack.getOutput("environment");
const sharedResourceGroupName = parentStack.
```

```
getOutput("sharedResourceGroupName");
const loggingEnabled = parentStack.getOutput("loggingEnabled");

const config = new pulumi.Config();
const region = config.require("region");
const vmSize = config.require("vmSize");
const customEndpoint = config.require("customEndpoint");

const resourceGroup = new azure.resources.ResourceGroup(`${appName}-rg`, {
    location: region,
});

const vm = new azure.compute.VirtualMachine(`${appName}-vm`, {
    resourceGroupName: resourceGroup.name,
    location: region,
    size: vmSize,
    networkInterfaceIds: [],
    osProfile: {
        adminUsername: "adminuser",
        computerName: `${appName}-vm`,
    },
});

export const outputs = {
    region,
    vmSize,
    customEndpoint,
};
```

In the preceding code snippet, the child stack follows the parent-child stack model to inherit shared configurations from the parent stack while also defining region-specific configurations. The child stack references the parent stack using `pulumi.StackReference`, allowing it to access shared configurations such as `appName`, `environment`, and `sharedResourceGroupName`. These shared values are exported by the parent stack and made available for reuse in each child stack, enabling consistent and maintainable infrastructure deployments.

Each child stack defines its own region-specific configurations, such as region, vmSize, and customEndpoint. While the parent stack provides shared values common to all regions, the child stack specifies unique details required for the specific region. For instance, the child stack for West US 2 may define its region as West US 2 with a Standard_D2s_v3 virtual machine, while the child stack for Southeast Asia defines its region as Southeast Asia and uses a Standard_D4s_v3 virtual machine. These region-specific configurations ensure that the infrastructure can be tailored to meet the unique needs of each deployment region.

This entire setup promotes code reuse and consistency. By centralizing shared logic in the parent stack, you avoid duplicating code in each child stack. Each child stack can access shared values using parentStack.getOutput(), ensuring that if shared values such as appName or sharedResourceGroupName change in the parent, all child stacks automatically receive the updated values. This approach allows for flexibility, as region-specific details are kept separate from shared logic, and it significantly reduces manual effort when updates are needed across multiple regions.

Pulumi ESC

When managing multi-region deployments, it's important to have a clean separation between shared configurations and region-specific configurations. Pulumi's ESC also provides a structured way to handle this. Shared configurations that apply to all production regions (such as West US 2 and Southeast Asia) can be managed through Pulumi ESC, while region-specific configurations are stored in the standard stack configuration files. This approach reduces duplication, centralizes shared values, and makes it easier to manage sensitive data and reusable configuration logic.

Pulumi has a dedicated ESC CLI (separate from the Pulumi CLI) for managing ESC-related commands. The first step is to create an environment. This environment will store shared configurations and secrets that apply across multiple regions. For example, to create a production environment for the myproject project, you can run the following command:

```
esc env init myorg/myproject/prod
```

This creates an environment called prod for the myorg/myproject project. The prod environment will act as a global context where you can store configuration values, secrets, and shared logic for all production regions (such as West US 2 and Southeast Asia). After creating the environment, you can store shared configurations in it.

The command to store configurations in the ESC environment is as follows:

```
esc env set myorg/myproject/prod shared.appName "myapp"
esc env set myorg/myproject/prod shared.environment "prod"
esc env set myorg/myproject/prod shared.sharedResourceGroupName "prod-
shared"
esc env set myorg/myproject/prod shared.loggingEnabled "true"
```

These values are now centrally stored in the ESC environment and can be accessed by any stack that imports the myorg/myproject/prod environment. This allows shared values to be defined once and accessed by all production stacks, reducing duplication and centralizing management.

To access the shared configurations in Pulumi.prod-wu2.yaml (West US 2) and Pulumi.prod-sea.yaml (Southeast Asia), you need to import the ESC environment into the configuration files. This is done using the imports key. For example, the configuration for the West US 2 child stack might look like this:

```
imports:
  - myproject/prod
config:
  region: "West US 2"
  vmSize: "Standard_D2s_v3"
  customEndpoint: "westus2.website.com"
```

In this configuration, myproject/prod is imported, allowing the child stack to access shared values defined in the prod ESC environment. In addition to the shared configurations, the child stack also defines region-specific configurations such as region, vmSize, and customEndpoint. These region-specific configurations are only applicable to the West US 2 stack.

For the Southeast Asia region, you can create a Pulumi.prod-sea.yaml file with its own region-specific configurations. This file also imports the myproject/prod environment to access shared values while maintaining its own unique settings. The configuration might look like this:

```
imports:
  - myproject/prod
config:
  region: "Southeast Asia"
  vmSize: "Standard_D4s_v3"
  customEndpoint: "southeastasia.website.com"
```

With this approach, the Pulumi.prod-wu2.yaml and Pulumi.prod-sea.yaml stacks both inherit shared configurations (such as appName and sharedResourceGroupName) from myproject/prod. They also define their own region-specific configurations, allowing for the flexibility to handle differences between regions.

To access shared and region-specific configurations in your index.ts file, you can use Pulumi's Config object to retrieve shared values from the imported ESC environment as well as region-specific values defined in the stack. Here's an example of how to retrieve both shared and region-specific values in the Pulumi code:

```typescript
import * as pulumi from "@pulumi/pulumi";
import * as azure from "@pulumi/azure-native";

const config = new pulumi.Config();
const appName = config.require("shared.appName");
const environment = config.require("shared.environment");
const sharedResourceGroupName = config.require("shared.
sharedResourceGroupName");
const loggingEnabled = config.require("shared.loggingEnabled");

const region = config.require("region");
const vmSize = config.require("vmSize");
const customEndpoint = config.require("customEndpoint");

const resourceGroup = new azure.resources.ResourceGroup(`${appName}-rg`, {
    location: region,
});

const vm = new azure.compute.VirtualMachine(`${appName}-vm`, {
    resourceGroupName: resourceGroup.name,
    location: region,
    size: vmSize,
    networkInterfaceIds: [],
    osProfile: {
        adminUsername: "adminuser",
        computerName: `${appName}-vm`,
    },
```

```
});

export const outputs = {
    appName,
    region,
    vmSize,
    customEndpoint,
};
```

There are many things you can do with Pulumi ESC, and this is just one of them. Centralizing shared configurations and managing secrets with ESC makes it easier to maintain consistent and secure multi-region deployments.

Best practices for multi-region deployments

When working with multi-region deployments, it's easy to get caught up in the complexity of managing resources across different regions. Without a clear strategy, you may end up with duplicated logic, increased costs, and unpredictable rollouts. Following best practices helps keep everything clean, consistent, and cost-effective. Here are some practices you should keep in mind.

Minimize region-specific customizations

One of the most important things you can do is limit how much you customize deployments for each region. The more differences you have between regions, the harder it becomes to maintain and debug. Instead, use the same IaC templates for all regions and pass in region-specific parameters. For example, instead of hardcoding virtual machine sizes for each region, you can store them in configuration files or Pulumi ESC environments. This makes it easy to deploy updates consistently across all regions.

To achieve this, you can create one Pulumi script (such as index.ts) and reuse it for all regions by providing the region-specific details in the stack configuration files (Pulumi.prod-wu2.yaml, Pulumi.prod-sea.yaml, etc.). This approach is similar to using functions with parameters in programming, where the function stays the same, but the input changes depending on the situation.

Use blue/green or canary deployments for safer rollouts

Deploying updates across multiple regions can be risky if done all at once. Instead of applying changes everywhere at the same time, you can use blue/green deployments or canary deployments. Both methods reduce the risk of downtime and allow for quick rollbacks in case of issues.

With a blue/green deployment, you have two environments: blue (the current environment) and green (the new environment). The update is made to the green environment, and once it's verified, you switch traffic from blue to green. If issues arise, you can instantly switch back to blue. This method works well for major infrastructure changes.

Canary deployments take a more gradual approach. Instead of switching all traffic at once, you route traffic to the new environment in small percentages (such as 5%, 10%, 25%, and so on) while monitoring its performance. If everything works as expected, you continue to increase the percentage until 100% of traffic is on the new version. If something goes wrong, you can stop the rollout and revert traffic back to the previous environment. This method works best when changes are smaller but still have the potential to impact users.

Enable monitoring and observability for every region

You can't fix what you can't see. When you have applications running in multiple regions, you need to know what's happening in each one. Monitoring and observability are crucial for this. Without visibility into each region's performance, you might not even realize there's a problem until users report it.

Tools such as Azure Monitor, Amazon CloudWatch, and Prometheus help you track key metrics such as CPU usage, memory, and request failures. By aggregating data from all regions into a single dashboard, you can compare region performance side-by-side. If the Southeast Asia region suddenly shows higher latency than West US 2, you'll have immediate visibility into the issue.

It's also important to set up alerts so your team is notified as soon as issues arise. Alerts can be sent to PagerDuty, Slack, or via email, ensuring that someone on the team is always aware of issues. Distributed tracing is another useful practice for tracking requests as they move through different regions. It allows you to pinpoint slow steps in the request flow and determine which region is causing delays.

Cost optimizations for multi-region deployments

Multi-region deployments aren't cheap, especially when you have active infrastructure running in multiple locations. The more regions you deploy to, the more you pay for compute, storage, and data transfer. Without proper cost management, your cloud bill can spiral out of control.

If you want to track and control costs, use cost management tools such as AWS Cost Explorer or Azure Cost Management. These tools break down where your costs are coming from, which allows you to identify which regions are the most expensive. You can also set spending alerts so you know whether your usage goes beyond a set budget. For example, if your normal monthly cost is $1,000 and suddenly it jumps to $2,000, you'll be notified right away.

Environment management strategies

Beyond creating multiple regions in production, it's still recommended to have multiple environments such as development, staging, and production. Each environment serves a different purpose. For example, the development environment is where engineers can test features and experiment without worrying about breaking anything. Staging is used to replicate production as closely as possible, acting as a final testing ground before updates go live. Production, of course, is where your actual users interact with your application, so it must remain stable and secure.

Mismanaging these environments can lead to serious problems. Accidentally deploying untested features from development to production could cause downtime, data loss, or a poor user experience. Overlapping resources, such as shared databases or networks, can lead to unexpected bugs or disruptions. Without clear boundaries between environments, it becomes harder to debug, test, and safely roll out updates.

With Pulumi stacks, you can create a stack as an environment, such as `Pulumi.dev.yaml`, to hold your development configurations. The same applies to other environments, such as staging and production. This approach lets you isolate environments while reusing shared logic across all of them. For example, your development stack might use smaller, cost-efficient virtual machines and minimal monitoring, while your production stack is configured with larger machines, monitoring, and global failover setups. Each environment has its unique configuration but shares the same code logic.

Stacks also make it straightforward to spin up new environments for testing or deployment. Let's say you need to test a feature in an isolated setting. You can simply copy your Pulumi code, create a new stack configuration file (such as `Pulumi.test.yaml`), and deploy it as a temporary test environment.

The ability to reuse the same code with different parameters means you can create new environments in minutes, not hours or days. This is especially valuable in agile workflows, where developers frequently need to test changes or deploy experimental features without affecting ongoing work in development or staging.

Pulumi's programming model supports this design by linking each stack to its own configuration and state. These configurations are stored in YAML files, which Pulumi uses to generate environment-specific infrastructure. For instance, `Pulumi.dev.yaml` might specify parameters such as region, machine size, and logging preferences, while `Pulumi.prod.yaml` contains settings optimized for production. The Pulumi code dynamically reads these parameters, ensuring that the same script can deploy to multiple environments without duplication.

Here's an example of how these configurations might look:

```yaml
# Pulumi.dev.yaml
config:
  environment: "development"
  region: "West US 2"
  vmSize: "Standard_B2s"
  enableMonitoring: false

# Pulumi.prod.yaml
config:
  environment: "production"
  region: "East US"
  vmSize: "Standard_D4s_v3"
  enableMonitoring: true
```

The corresponding Pulumi code reads these configurations dynamically:

```typescript
import * as pulumi from "@pulumi/pulumi";
import * as azure from "@pulumi/azure-native";

const config = new pulumi.Config();
const environment = config.require("environment");
const region = config.require("region");
const vmSize = config.require("vmSize");
const enableMonitoring = config.requireBoolean("enableMonitoring");

const resourceGroup = new azure.resources.ResourceGroup(`${environment}-rg`, {
    location: region,
});

const vm = new azure.compute.VirtualMachine(`${environment}-vm`, {
    resourceGroupName: resourceGroup.name,
    location: region,
    size: vmSize,
    osProfile: {
        adminUsername: "adminuser",
        computerName: `${environment}-vm`,
```

```
    },
});

if (enableMonitoring) {
    const monitor = new azure.monitor.DiagnosticSetting(`${environment}-
monitor`, {
        resourceUri: resourceGroup.id,
        logs: [{ category: "Administrative", enabled: true }],
    });
}
```

Let's say you need a temporary test environment. All you need to do is create a new stack called test by running the following:

```
pulumi stack init test
```

This creates a new stack that you can configure independently. Next, define test-specific parameters in your Pulumi.test.yaml configuration file to specify settings unique to this environment, as in this example:

```
config:
  environment: "test"
  region: "Central US"
  vmSize: "Standard_B2s"
  enableMonitoring: false
```

Once your configuration is in place, deploy the environment using the pulumi up command.

Proper environment management involves isolating resources to prevent unintended interactions. Each environment should have its own dedicated resources, such as virtual networks, resource groups, or databases. This ensures that testing in development or staging doesn't accidentally impact production. Pulumi supports resource isolation by linking resources to environment-specific parameters in stack configurations.

For example, a development stack could create its own resource group:

```
const resourceGroup = new azure.resources.ResourceGroup(
`${environment}-rg`, {
    location: region,
});
```

The same script can create an entirely separate resource group for production, thanks to the environment-specific parameters in `Pulumi.prod.yaml`.

Using Pulumi with CI/CD pipelines ensures that your deployments remain consistent across all environments. With tools such as GitHub Actions or Azure DevOps, you can automate deployments based on specific triggers and enforce rules for each environment. For example, you might configure the pipeline to deploy to development automatically whenever a pull request is opened. Once the code is approved and merged into the `main` branch, it gets deployed to staging for further testing. Finally, production deployment might require a manual approval step to ensure everything is ready. This process ensures that changes are thoroughly tested and reviewed before they reach the live environment, reducing the risk of downtime or bugs.

> Example use case: feature rollout
>
> Let's say you're adding a new feature to an e-commerce platform. A developer opens a pull request with their changes, which triggers a deployment to the development environment using a small, cost-efficient setup. The team tests the feature, validates it, and approves the pull request. Once merged, the feature is automatically deployed to staging, an environment that closely matches production. Here, the QA team runs final checks, and only after staging passes verification does the pipeline require manual approval for the production deployment. The feature is then rolled out to customers in a controlled and predictable way.

Automating environment setup and management

Managing multiple environments manually can quickly become error-prone and time-consuming, especially as the number of environments or the complexity of the infrastructure grows. Automating environment setup and management not only saves time but also ensures consistency and reliability across development, staging, and production.

For instance, you can configure pipelines to deploy a specific environment automatically when certain triggers occur, as in this example:

- **Development**: Deploy when a pull request is created
- **Staging**: Deploy when code is merged into the `main` branch
- **Production**: Deploy after a manual approval step

The following is a GitHub Actions pipeline that manages deployments for two environments: development and production. The development step runs automatically on **pull request** (**PR**) builds, staging runs when changes are merged into the main branch, and production runs only after staging completes successfully and a manual approval is provided:

```yaml
name: Deploy Environments
on:
  pull_request:
    branches:
      - '*'
  push:
    branches:
      - main
jobs:
  dev:
    name: Deploy to Development
    runs-on: ubuntu-latest
    if: github.event_name == 'pull_request'
    steps:
      - name: Check out repository
        uses: actions/checkout@v2
      - name: Set up Pulumi
        uses: pulumi/actions@v3
        with:
          command: up
          stack-name: dev
          work-dir: ./infrastructure
  production:
    name: Deploy to Production
    runs-on: ubuntu-latest
    needs: dev
    steps:
      - name: Manual approval
        uses: manual-approval-job
      - name: Check out repository
        uses: actions/checkout@v2
      - name: Set up Pulumi
        uses: pulumi/actions@v3
```

```
      with:
        command: up
        stack-name: production
        work-dir: ./infrastructure
```

We've covered spinning up infrastructure for testing and production. How about tearing down infrastructure for testing? Cleaning up resources after testing is just as important as creating them, especially to avoid unnecessary costs and keep your environment tidy. You can automate this process using two methods: a cleanup pipeline job triggered by specific events and a scheduled cron job that runs periodically to remove unused test resources.

The first method involves adding a cleanup step to your CI/CD pipeline. This step automatically destroys the development environment when a PR is closed or merged. For example, you could configure your pipeline to run the following Pulumi job:

```
jobs:
  cleanup:
    name: Clean up Development Environment
    runs-on: ubuntu-latest
    if: github.event.action == 'closed' || github.event.action == 'merged'
    steps:
      - name: Check out repository
        uses: actions/checkout@v2

      - name: Set up Pulumi
        uses: pulumi/actions@v3
        with:
          command: destroy
          stack-name: dev
          work-dir: ./infrastructure
          refresh: true
          yes: true
```

This cleanup job is triggered when a PR is merged or closed, ensuring that test resources are removed immediately after they are no longer needed. This method works well for PR-driven workflows where each PR creates its own test environment. By tearing down the infrastructure promptly, you minimize resource usage and costs while maintaining a clean development stack.

The second method uses a scheduled `cron` job to remove unused test resources regularly. This is particularly useful for catching resources that were not cleaned up due to incomplete workflows or abandoned test environments. For instance, you can schedule a `cron` job to run daily and destroy any lingering resources in the development environment:

```
name: Scheduled Cleanup

on:
  schedule:
    - cron: "0 2 * * *" # Runs daily at 2:00 AM

jobs:
  cleanup:
    name: Clean up Test Resources
    runs-on: ubuntu-latest
    steps:
      - name: Check out repository
        uses: actions/checkout@v2

      - name: Set up Pulumi
        uses: pulumi/actions@v3
        with:
          command: destroy
          stack-name: dev
          work-dir: ./infrastructure
          refresh: true
          yes: true
```

This job ensures that any test resources left behind after the pipeline cleanup are automatically removed within 24 hours. Running the `cron` job daily keeps your infrastructure lean, reduces operational clutter, and ensures that no resources are accidentally left consuming your budget.

Summary

In this chapter, we covered how to effectively manage IaC in multiple regions and environments. We began by exploring the importance of multi-region deployments for global user bases, disaster recovery, and regulatory compliance, followed by a discussion on designing architectures such as active-active and active-passive setups.

The chapter introduced practical strategies such as the parent-child stack model and Pulumi ESC to centralize shared configurations while allowing region-specific overrides. We also detailed best practices, including minimizing region-specific customizations, using blue/green or canary deployments, and enabling observability and cost optimization. Finally, we covered automating environment setup and life cycle management using Pulumi and CI/CD pipelines.

In the next chapter, we will cover managing multi-cloud and hybrid scenarios.

Questions

1. What are the primary benefits of managing IaC in multiple regions and environments?

2. Describe the difference between active-active and active-passive architectures in multi-region setups.

3. How do tools such as Pulumi ESC facilitate managing shared configurations across multiple environments?

4. What are the advantages of using a parent-child stack model for managing infrastructure across regions?

5. How can you use Pulumi to automate the tearing down of unused resources in test environments?

6. Why is it important to minimize hardcoding in IaC templates when managing multiple regions?

7. What best practices can help maintain consistency across multiple environments when using Pulumi?

8. How can you ensure reliable failover mechanisms in a multi-region architecture?

10

Managing Multi-Cloud and Hybrid Scenarios

Beyond multi-environment and multi-region deployments, there is also the possibility that you might need to handle infrastructure across multiple cloud providers or even combine cloud and on-premises systems. These scenarios are becoming more common as organizations seek to balance flexibility, cost, and resilience while avoiding being tied to a single cloud provider.

The appeal of multi-cloud and hybrid setups is clear. They provide options to choose the best tools and services from different platforms, distribute workloads to improve performance, and minimize risk by avoiding over-reliance on a single provider. Hybrid scenarios take this a step further by blending on-premises systems with cloud environments, which can be crucial for industries with strict data residency or regulatory requirements.

But let's not sugarcoat it; managing these environments is complex. Each cloud provider has its own set of rules, tools, and unique features, making it challenging to maintain consistency across platforms. This chapter dives deep into these challenges and provides practical strategies to overcome them. Using Pulumi, we'll explore how to orchestrate resources across multiple cloud platforms with precision and control.

In this chapter, we're going to cover the following main topics:

- Understanding multi-cloud and hybrid architectures
- Designing cross-platform network configurations
- Data integration and management across clouds
- Security and compliance in multi-cloud environments

Technical requirements

If you would like to follow along with the examples in this chapter, you will require the following:

- The Pulumi CLI is required for executing commands. You can download it from here: `https://www.pulumi.com/docs/iac/download-install/`.

- Pulumi supports multiple programming languages, but for this chapter, we'll be using JavaScript/TypeScript, which requires Node.js. You can download and install it from the Node.js official site here: `https://nodejs.org/`.

- Since we'll be deploying some resources to Azure, you'll need an Azure account. You can sign up for a free account or use your existing Azure account. For more details, visit the Azure website here: `https://azure.microsoft.com/en-us/pricing/purchase-options/azure-account`.

- The Azure CLI is required to interact with Azure resources from your local machine. You can install the Azure CLI by following the instructions here: `https://learn.microsoft.com/en-us/cli/azure/install-azure-cli`.

- Since we'll be deploying some resources to AWS, you'll need an AWS account. You can sign up for a free account or use your existing AWS account. For more details, visit the AWS website here: `https://aws.amazon.com/`.

- The AWS CLI is required to interact with AWS resources from your local machine. You can install the AWS CLI by following the instructions here: `https://aws.amazon.com/cli/`.

Understanding multi-cloud and hybrid architectures

Managing infrastructure is no longer just about choosing one cloud provider or sticking to on-premises servers. Organizations today have more complex needs that often require using multiple clouds or blending on-premises systems with cloud environments. Let's break this down and explore how these strategies work in real-world scenarios.

Multi-cloud means using more than one cloud provider to meet your business needs. For example, a company might store data in one cloud (e.g., AWS), run applications in another (e.g., Azure), and use a third for specialized services such as AI or analytics (e.g., Google Cloud). The main idea is to take advantage of the best features from different providers while avoiding being locked into just one.

A **hybrid cloud** combines on-premises infrastructure with cloud environments. This allows organizations to keep some systems and data in their own data centers while still benefiting from the scalability and flexibility of the cloud. It's useful for companies with sensitive data or regulatory requirements that make it hard to move everything to the cloud.

Use case examples

Let's look at two hypothetical companies, Snapstagram and Doora AI, to see how multi-cloud and hybrid strategies can be applied.

Snapstagram

Snapstagram is a fast-growing social media platform that lets users share photos and short videos. To handle its massive user base, Snapstagram uses a multi-cloud strategy.

Why multi-cloud? Snapstagram stores its user data in Cloud A because of its reliable and affordable storage services. Meanwhile, it uses Cloud B for video streaming since it offers better performance for media delivery. Finally, Snapstagram uses Cloud C's advanced AI tools to suggest content to users based on their preferences. By combining the strengths of these providers, Snapstagram's platform stays fast, scalable, and engaging.

Doora AI

Doora AI is an AI platform that offers personalized insights to businesses using machine learning. Since some of its clients work in healthcare and finance, they need to keep sensitive data on-premises for compliance reasons. However, Doora AI also requires the scalability of the cloud to train large AI models.

Why hybrid cloud? Doora AI processes sensitive customer data on its private servers to meet strict security and compliance requirements. Once the data is anonymized, it uploads the cleaned datasets to a public cloud for large-scale training of AI models. This setup lets Doora AI maintain high levels of security without giving up the power of the cloud.

Both Snapstagram and Doora AI have very different needs, but they've found solutions that work best for their situations. As we move forward, you'll learn about things to consider when designing systems like these and making the most of both worlds.

Motivations behind multi-cloud strategies

One big reason companies choose a multi-cloud strategy is to avoid vendor lock-in. When you rely too much on one cloud provider, you're stuck with their pricing, tools, and limitations. This can make it harder to negotiate better deals or adapt to new technologies. As a new platform, Snapstagram might need flexibility to keep up with trends and user demands, and being locked into a single provider could slow them down. By using multiple clouds, they have the freedom to switch services or providers if something better comes along.

Another advantage is the ability to pick the best tools for the job. Each cloud provider has its strengths. For example, Snapstagram stores its photos and videos in a provider with excellent storage and retrieval capabilities, while using a different cloud that excels at streaming content to deliver smooth video playback. And for AI-driven features such as personalized recommendations, Snapstagram works with a third provider that offers very good machine learning tools.

Multi-cloud also improves resilience and disaster recovery. If one provider experiences an outage, Snapstagram's operations won't grind to a halt because other parts of the platform are still running on different clouds. This approach distributes risk and keeps the platform reliable for its users. For example, even if the provider managing their AI tools goes down, users can still upload and view content because those functions are handled by separate systems. This kind of redundancy is critical for maintaining trust with users in an always-online world.

Motivations behind hybrid architectures

Hybrid architectures are often driven by the need to handle sensitive data while still benefiting from the cloud's scalability. Many industries, such as healthcare and finance, have strict regulations about where data can be stored or processed. We created a hypothetical company called Doora AI earlier, which works with clients in these sectors. For companies like them, keeping sensitive data on their private servers is essential to ensure compliance with laws and regulations. However, instead of limiting their capabilities to on-premises resources, Doora AI uses the cloud for tasks such as large-scale AI model training, where sensitive data has already been anonymized. This hybrid approach allows them to stay compliant while leveraging the cloud for what it does best.

Another reason organizations adopt hybrid setups is to support a gradual migration to the cloud. Moving all systems to the cloud in one go is risky, costly, and often unrealistic for companies with complex operations or legacy systems. Hybrid architectures let businesses transition workloads over time, testing and adapting at their own pace.

Hybrid systems also allow organizations to extend the capabilities of their on-premises infrastructure. Private data centers are often limited by physical constraints, such as the amount of compute power or storage they can handle. Instead of investing heavily in expanding their own servers, Doora AI could use the cloud to scale up quickly when needed. For example, during periods of high demand for AI insights, they can temporarily offload some of the processing work to the cloud while keeping regular operations running on their private systems. This gives them the ability to scale on demand without overcommitting resources.

Another important motivation for hybrid architectures is maintaining operational continuity during disruptions. With a hybrid approach, businesses can create redundancy between on-premises and cloud systems. If an unexpected issue affects one environment, such as hardware failure in their private data center or a temporary outage in their cloud provider, the other environment can step in to keep critical services running. For Doora AI, this redundancy ensures that their clients can continue accessing insights and tools, even when one part of the infrastructure is temporarily unavailable.

Hybrid architectures also provide flexibility for experimenting with new technologies while minimizing risks. For companies such as Doora AI, integrating emerging AI tools from the cloud becomes easier because they can test these technologies in the cloud without impacting their on-premises systems. This ability to explore innovation while maintaining control over sensitive operations ensures that companies such as Doora AI can remain at the forefront of the AI industry without compromising their clients' trust.

Designing multi-cloud and hybrid cloud architectures

Designing multi-cloud and hybrid architectures requires careful planning. These setups can make your applications flexible and resilient, but can also introduce complexity if not done properly. To address these challenges, you need to prioritize consistency, interoperability, visibility, and performance. Let's look at each area and explore how tools such as Pulumi, using TypeScript, can help simplify the process.

Standardization is key

Without standardization, maintaining consistent workflows across platforms becomes a nightmare. Because Pulumi takes the approach to infrastructure as software, you can create reusable abstractions that ensure consistency, regardless of the cloud provider. Imagine you want to design a serverless infrastructure, but abstract away the underlying differences for developers.

Using Pulumi, you could create a `ServerlessApp` class that takes in properties such as `cloud`, `runtime`, and `handler`. Based on the `cloud` property, it provisions resources in AWS or Azure, ensuring that resource names follow a consistent format. Let's build this step by step:

1. First, we define an interface for the class properties:

    ```
    interface ServerlessAppProps {
        name: string;
        cloud: "AWS" | "Azure";
        runtime: string;
        handler: string;
    }
    ```

    💡 **Quick tip**: Enhance your coding experience with the **AI Code Explainer** and **Quick Copy** features. Open this book in the next-gen Packt Reader. Click the **Copy** button

    (1) to quickly copy code into your coding environment, or click the **Explain** button

    (2) to get the AI assistant to explain a block of code to you.

    ```
                                              Copy      Explain
    function calculate(a, b) {
        return {sum: a + b};                    1          2
    };
    ```

    📖 **The next-gen Packt Reader** is included for free with the purchase of this book. Scan the QR code OR visit packtpub.com/unlock, then use the search bar to find this book by name. Double-check the edition shown to make sure you get the right one.

The `ServerlessAppProps` interface ensures that the input to the class is structured and enforces consistency. It includes the application name, the target cloud (either `AWS` or `Azure`), and function-specific details such as `runtime` and `handler`.

2. Now, we move on to creating the class. The following code snippet does this and also standardizes resource names:

```
class ServerlessApp {
    constructor(props: ServerlessAppProps) {
        const standardizedName = `${props.name}-serverless-app`;
}
```

This naming convention (`<name>-serverless-app`) ensures that resources across clouds are named in the same format, making it easier to identify and manage them.

3. Next, we handle the AWS-specific implementation:

```
if (props.cloud === "AWS") {
    new aws.lambda.Function(standardizedName, {
        runtime: props.runtime,
        handler: props.handler,
        code: new pulumi.asset.AssetArchive({
            ".": new pulumi.asset.FileArchive("./code"),
        }),
        role: aws.iam.getRole({ name: "lambda-exec-role" }).
then((role) => role.arn),
    });
}
```

Here, the `ServerlessApp` class provisions an AWS Lambda function. It uses the standardized name, along with the runtime and handler details passed to the constructor. The function's code is packaged from a local directory (`./code`), and an IAM role (`lambda-exec-role`) is assigned for execution.

4. For Azure, we include a different block of logic:

```
else if (props.cloud === "Azure") {
    new azure.web.WebApp(standardizedName, {
        resourceGroupName: "example-resource-group",
        serverFarmId: azure.appservice.getAppServicePlan({
            name: "example-plan",
```

```
            resourceGroupName: "example-resource-group",
        }).then((plan) => plan.id),
        siteConfig: {
            appSettings: [
                { name: "FUNCTIONS_WORKER_RUNTIME", value: props.
    runtime },
                { name: "WEBSITE_RUN_FROM_PACKAGE", value: "1" },
            ],
        },
    });
}
```

This block provisions an Azure function app. It sets the runtime and integrates it with an existing App Service Plan. The use of `appSettings` ensures that the function app's environment is configured correctly.

5. Finally, we add error handling for unsupported cloud providers:

```
else {
    throw new Error(`Unsupported cloud: ${props.cloud}`);
}
```

This ensures that the class handles invalid input gracefully and prevents misconfigurations.

When you bring it all together, using this class is simple:

```
const app = new ServerlessApp({
    name: "my-app",
    cloud: "AWS",
    runtime: "nodejs14.x",
    handler: "index.handler",
});
```

When standardization is not an afterthought in your IaC code, it changes how you build and manage infrastructure. It makes your deployments predictable, your resources consistent, and your teams more productive. In multi-cloud and hybrid environments, where different providers have their own tools and rules, standardization helps keep things simple and organized. It reduces mistakes, saves time, and ensures that your systems can grow without becoming chaotic.

Beyond naming conventions and abstraction, here are three examples of how you can enforce standardization in your multi-cloud IaC.

Tagging resources consistently

Adding the same tags (such as environment, owner, or project) to all your resources helps you organize and track them better, as in this example:

```
const defaultTags = { environment: "production", owner: "team-xyz" };
```

For AWS, you can use this:

```
const awsBucket = new aws.s3.Bucket("myBucket", {
    tags: { ...defaultTags, service: "storage" },
});
```

For Azure, you can use this:

```
const azureStorage = new azure.storage.StorageAccount("myStorage", {
    tags: { ...defaultTags, service: "storage" },
});
```

Centralized configuration

Use shared configuration files or environment variables to define settings such as regions or instance sizes. This ensures that all resources follow the same setup. The following code snippet shows how you can retrieve configuration for your infrastructure:

```
const config = new pulumi.Config();
const region = config.require("region");
const instanceType = config.get("instanceType") || "t2.micro";
```

Reusable components

Instead of writing the same code repeatedly, you can create a single module or class that handles a specific task, such as setting up a network or creating a storage bucket. This saves time and ensures that all your resources follow the same standards. If something needs to change, such as a new best practice or policy, you only update the component, and everything using it stays up to date. It also reduces errors since the component can include tested configurations that work reliably.

Planning for interoperability

Interoperability is about ensuring that systems in different environments can communicate and work together effectively. In multi-cloud and hybrid setups, resources often need to exchange data or coordinate processes across providers, making seamless connections crucial.

For example, you might use an AWS database for its robust data storage options while running backend processing with Azure Functions. To make this work, you can save the AWS database connection string in the app settings of the Azure function, enabling it to securely access the database without hardcoding sensitive information.

Here's how you could achieve this with Pulumi:

1. First, create an AWS RDS database and retrieve its connection string, as shown here:

    ```
    import * as aws from "@pulumi/aws";

    // Create an RDS instance in AWS
    const db = new aws.rds.Instance("myDatabase", {
        engine: "mysql",
        instanceClass: "db.t2.micro",
        allocatedStorage: 20,
        dbName: "mydb",
        username: "admin",
        password: "password123",
        publiclyAccessible: true,
    });

    // Export the connection string
    export const dbConnectionString = pulumi.interpolate`mysql://${db.
    username}:${db.password}@${db.endpoint}/mydb`;
    ```

2. Next, pass the database connection string to an Azure function's app settings:

    ```
    import * as azure from "@pulumi/azure-native";

    // Create an Azure Function App
    const appServicePlan = new azure.web.
    AppServicePlan("myAppServicePlan", {
        resourceGroupName: "example-resource-group",
        sku: { tier: "Dynamic", name: "Y1" },
    });

    const functionApp = new azure.web.WebApp("myFunctionApp", {
        resourceGroupName: "example-resource-group",
        serverFarmId: appServicePlan.id,
    ```

```
    siteConfig: {
        appSettings: [
            {
    name: "FUNCTIONS_WORKER_RUNTIME",
    value: "node" },
            {
    name: "AWS_DB_CONNECTION",
    value: dbConnectionString
},
        ],
    },
});
```

This setup allows your Azure function to securely interact with the AWS database. You've enabled the Azure compute layer to connect to and leverage the storage capabilities of AWS, showcasing real interoperability.

Beyond connecting resources, interoperability also involves managing security, ensuring low-latency communication, and defining clear protocols. For instance, in the preceding example, you can configure network rules to allow secure communication between the Azure function and the AWS database while restricting public access.

Centralized monitoring and observability

Monitoring and observability are critical for managing multi-cloud setups effectively. When you have resources running in both AWS and Azure, it's important to have a clear picture of how everything is performing and where potential issues might arise. Without centralized monitoring, diagnosing problems or tracking performance across different clouds can become overwhelming.

A good way to handle this is by using the native tools provided by each cloud platform, such as Amazon CloudWatch and Azure Monitor, to collect logs and metrics. These tools can track resource usage, errors, and other vital information for the services running in their respective environments. For example, Amazon CloudWatch can monitor the CPU usage of EC2 instances, while Azure Monitor can track memory usage and logs from virtual machines.

To make observability effective, you can send the collected data to a unified monitoring platform such as Datadog, Grafana, or Elastic. This gives you a single dashboard where you can view performance metrics and logs from both AWS and Azure in one place. It allows you to compare trends, set up alerts, and quickly identify problems no matter which cloud is involved.

To monitor resources in AWS, connect CloudWatch to Grafana. You need to provide the necessary AWS credentials and Regions:

```
const cloudWatchDataSource = new grafana.oss.DataSource(
"cloudWatchSource", {
    name: "AWS CloudWatch",
    type: "cloudwatch",
    url: "",
    access: "proxy",
    jsonDataEncoded: JSON.stringify({
        defaultRegion: "us-east-1",
        authType: "keys",
    }),
    secureJsonDataEncoded: JSON.stringify({
        accessKey: "your-aws-access-key",
        secretKey: "your-aws-secret-key",
    }),
});
```

To monitor Azure resources, connect Azure Monitor to Grafana using Azure credentials:

```
const azureMonitorDataSource = new grafana.oss.DataSource(
"azureMonitorSource", {
    name: "Azure Monitor",
    type: "grafana-azure-monitor-datasource",
    access: "proxy",
    jsonDataEncoded: JSON.stringify({
        cloudName: "azuremonitor",
        tenantId: "your-azure-tenant-id",
        clientId: "your-azure-client-id",
        subscriptionId: "your-azure-subscription-id",
    }),
    secureJsonDataEncoded: JSON.stringify({
        clientSecret: "your-azure-client-secret",
    }),
});
```

Once the data sources are set up, you can define Grafana dashboards to visualize metrics from both AWS and Azure. Here's an example of a simple dashboard combining data from CloudWatch and Azure Monitor:

```
const dashboard = new grafana.Dashboard("multiCloudDashboard", {
    configJson: JSON.stringify({
        title: "Multi-Cloud Metrics",
        panels: [
          {
              datasource: cloudWatchDataSource.name,
              type: "graph",
              title: "AWS EC2 CPU Usage",
              // ... more code to configure your AWS CloudWatch Data Source
          },
          {
              datasource: azureMonitorDataSource.name,
              type: "graph",
              title: "Azure VM Memory Usage",
              // ... more code to configure your Azure Monitor Data Source
          },
        ]
    })
});
```

Centralizing monitoring and observability also helps with scalability. As your infrastructure grows across multiple clouds, a unified view ensures that your team doesn't have to juggle separate tools or dashboards for each provider. Instead, they can focus on making sure that your entire system is reliable.

Scalability and performance

In a multi-cloud setup, scalability and performance are key to handling increasing demand while keeping applications fast and reliable. A practical example is deploying serverless functions in both AWS Lambda and Azure Function App and using Azure Traffic Manager to load balance traffic between them. This approach allows you to scale serverless compute automatically and direct requests to the best-performing or nearest cloud.

AWS Lambda and Azure Function Apps automatically scale based on the number of incoming requests. Deploying the same function logic to both clouds keeps functionality and performance consistent.

Azure Traffic Manager acts as a DNS-based load balancer, routing traffic based on policies such as priority, geographic location, or performance. For example, it can send traffic to AWS Lambda in one region and to Azure Function Apps in another, reducing latency for users.

This setup adapts dynamically. If one cloud experiences high traffic or an outage, Traffic Manager redirects requests to the other, keeping services uninterrupted.

In the next section, you will see how to configure cross-platform networking.

Designing cross-platform network configurations

In multi-cloud and hybrid cloud architectures, networks from different providers may need to communicate or interact. For example, you might have an application hosted in Azure that needs to pull data from a database in AWS, or users accessing services from both clouds. To make this possible, your network configurations must support seamless communication across these boundaries. There are two ways to do this: by maintaining consistent IP addressing and by managing how traffic flows between application instances.

Implementing consistent IP addressing and DNS across clouds

One of the most important aspects of cross-cloud networking is maintaining consistent IP addressing and DNS naming conventions. Each cloud provider has its own way of managing networks, but when you connect them, overlapping IP ranges or inconsistent DNS names can cause conflicts. For example, if an Amazon VPC uses the same CIDR block as an Azure virtual network, communication between the two will fail. To avoid this, you need to assign unique IP ranges to each network.

In your Pulumi code, you can define and manage IP ranges and DNS names as part of your infrastructure. You can standardize configurations across both clouds, reducing the risk of conflicts. Here's how this might look in practice:

- **Define unique CIDR ranges:** Assign separate, non-overlapping CIDR blocks for each cloud, as in this example:

    - **Amazon VPC:** `10.0.0.0/16`
    - **Azure Virtual Network:** `10.1.0.0/16`

- **Shared DNS resolution**: Set up DNS configurations that allow services in one cloud to resolve the domain names of services in the other. For example, you can use Amazon Route 53 to manage a shared DNS zone or integrate Azure's DNS service for a common namespace.

Using Pulumi, you can write code that manages these configurations consistently across clouds:

- **Amazon VPC**:

```
const awsVpc = new aws.ec2.Vpc("awsVpc", {
    cidrBlock: "10.0.0.0/16",
});
```

- **Azure Virtual Network**:

```
const azureVnet = new azure.network.VirtualNetwork("azureVnet", {
    addressSpace: { addressPrefixes: ["10.1.0.0/16"] },
    resourceGroupName: "example-resource-group",
    location: "East US",
});
```

- **Shared DNS zone in AWS**:

```
const dnsZone = new aws.route53.Zone("sharedDnsZone", {
    name: "multicloud.example.com",
});
```

With standardized IP ranges and shared DNS resolution, services in AWS and Azure can discover and communicate with each other without conflicts.

Configuring load balancing and traffic routing

Once networks are connected, the next step is to manage how traffic flows between them. Tools such as Azure Traffic Manager or Amazon Route 53 can route traffic based on factors such as performance, geographic location, or failover requirements, as shown here:

- **Performance-based routing**: Traffic is sent to the cloud provider with the lowest latency for the user
- **Geographic routing**: Users are directed to the nearest data center, whether it's in AWS or Azure
- **Failover routing**: If one provider experiences downtime, traffic is automatically routed to the other

Pulumi can help automate this setup. For instance, you can use Azure Traffic Manager to distribute traffic across serverless functions in AWS Lambda and Azure Functions:

- **Traffic Manager profile:**

```
const trafficManager = new azure.network.TrafficManagerProfile(
"trafficManager", {
    resourceGroupName: "example-resource-group",
    location: "global",
    dnsConfig: {
        relativeName: "multicloud-traffic",
        ttl: 30,
    },
    trafficRoutingMethod: "Performance",
    monitorConfig: {
        protocol: "HTTPS",
        port: 443,
        path: "/health",
    },
});
```

- **AWS endpoint:**

```
const awsEndpoint = new azure.network.TrafficManagerEndpoint(
"awsEndpoint", {
    profileName: trafficManager.name,
    resourceGroupName: "example-resource-group",
    type: "ExternalEndpoints",
    target: "aws-lambda-url.amazonaws.com",
    weight: 1,
});
```

- **Azure endpoint:**

```
const azureEndpoint = new azure.network.TrafficManagerEndpoint(
"azureEndpoint", {
    profileName: trafficManager.name,
    resourceGroupName: "example-resource-group",
    type: "ExternalEndpoints",
```

```
            target: "azure-function-url.azurewebsites.net",
            weight: 1,
    });
```

This configuration distributes requests based on performance, sending traffic to the fastest end-point. If one endpoint becomes unavailable, Traffic Manager automatically directs traffic to the healthy one. This means that as long as at least one instance of the application is up, users will always get responses from a healthy endpoint.

Data integration and management across clouds

Imagine your users in Asia use your services through Azure, and your users in Europe use your services through AWS. However, one of your Asia users goes to Europe for vacation and isn't able to log in because their data is only present in data centers in Asia. This is a common problem when data isn't synchronized across cloud providers. To avoid situations like this, you need a strategy for keeping data consistent between multiple clouds.

One effective method is database replication. For example, you can use AWS **Database Migration Service (DMS)** to replicate data from an Azure SQL Database to an Amazon RDS instance, or vice versa. Replication can happen in near-real time, meaning any update made in one database is quickly reflected in the other. Another option is scheduled syncs, where tools such as Azure Data Factory are used to periodically copy and update data between clouds. These approaches ensure that no matter where your users are, their data is always available. Using Azure Data Factory pipelines, you can schedule regular syncs or even set up near-real-time replication. These pipelines act as bridges, so that your data stays aligned regardless of the cloud it resides in.

To set up these connections, you need linked services in Azure Data Factory, which act as connectors to your data sources. For example, to synchronize data from an Amazon RDS PostgreSQL database to Azure SQL Database, you can create linked services for both data sources. The following linked service connects Azure Data Factory to an Amazon RDS database:

```
const linkedServiceAmazonRds = new azure_native.datafactory.
LinkedService("linkedServiceAmazonRds", {
    factoryName: "myDataFactory",
    resourceGroupName: "myResourceGroup",
    linkedServiceName: "AmazonRdsService",

    ...

});
```

The following linked service connects Azure Data Factory to Azure SQL Database:

```
const linkedServiceAzureSql = new azure_native.datafactory.LinkedService(
"linkedServiceAzureSql", {
    factoryName: "myDataFactory",
    resourceGroupName: "myResourceGroup",
    linkedServiceName: "AzureSqlService",

    ...
});
```

The first linked service connects Azure Data Factory to an Amazon RDS PostgreSQL database. It includes basic details such as the factory name (`myDataFactory`), resource group (`myResourceGroup`), and a unique name for the service (`AmazonRdsService`). This setup allows Azure Data Factory to communicate with the RDS database in AWS, so it can read or process data. Although the specific properties aren't shown, it would include details such as the database endpoint, name, and secure credentials stored in Azure Key Vault.

The second linked service connects Azure Data Factory to Azure SQL Database. It also includes the factory name (`myDataFactory`), resource group (`myResourceGroup`), and a unique service name (`AzureSqlService`). This linked service allows Azure Data Factory to send data to Azure SQL Database. The missing details would usually include the database connection string and secure authentication information.

However, as you replicate data, it's critical to ensure you are not violating any compliance, regulatory, or data residency laws. For instance, certain regulations, such as GDPR in Europe or HIPAA in the United States, require data to remain within specific geographic regions or follow strict encryption and privacy standards. Before implementing cross-cloud replication, you need to confirm that moving or syncing data across borders complies with these laws. This might mean restricting replication for certain datasets or ensuring encrypted connections and storage.

While these tools make synchronization easier, there are challenges to think about. Latency is a key issue. Data might not always update instantly, which can cause delays. This might not be a big deal for less critical data, but for something like login information, even a few seconds of delay can lead to a poor user experience. Data integrity is another concern. If the same piece of data is updated in both systems at the same time, you'll need a way to handle conflicts, such as prioritizing one update over the other or merging changes intelligently.

Another factor is the volume of data being synced. Small updates are manageable, but syncing large datasets between clouds can strain bandwidth and increase costs. Tools such as DMS and Data Factory often have features to filter and move only the most important data, helping you manage these challenges. Since these are cloud services from the cloud providers (AWS and Azure), we can use Pulumi (as displayed previously) to configure the infrastructure and set up our multi-cloud data management. Beyond syncing databases, another powerful way to handle cross-cloud data is by building data pipelines. These pipelines enable you to move, process, and analyze data seamlessly between clouds in both real-time and batch modes. Tools such as **Apache Kafka, AWS Kinesis**, and **Azure Event Hubs** are excellent choices for creating robust data pipelines that work across clouds.

Real-time data streaming

Real-time data streaming pipelines are essential for use cases such as analytics, fraud detection, or live data synchronization. For example, imagine your application collects real-time transaction data from users globally. You might use AWS Kinesis to ingest the data in AWS and then forward it to Azure Event Hubs for further processing in Azure. The streaming data could then trigger Azure Functions for analysis or storage in Azure SQL Database.

Kafka can also act as a multi-cloud bridge, enabling producers and consumers to exchange data in real time across AWS and Azure. By running Kafka clusters in both clouds and synchronizing topics, you can ensure that all systems receive the same data with minimal delay.

Batch processing

Batch pipelines are ideal for scenarios like nightly data synchronization or ETL (Extract, Transform, Load) workflows. For example, you can extract large volumes of data from AWS S3, transform it using Apache Spark running in Azure, and then load the processed data back into Azure Blob Storage or an Azure database for reporting.

Using tools like **Azure Data Factory** or **AWS Glue**, you can automate these workflows across clouds. These tools support integration with a variety of data sources, allowing you to set up pipelines that process data at scheduled intervals or based on triggers.

Using Pulumi to Automate Pipeline Deployment

Pulumi makes it easy to automate the deployment of cross-cloud data pipeline components. For instance, you can create Kafka topics in AWS, configure event hubs in Azure, and link them into a unified pipeline. Here's an example:

```
import * as aws from "@pulumi/aws";
import * as azure from "@pulumi/azure-native";
import * as kafka from "@pulumi/kafka";
```

Following is an example of AWS Kinesis Stream:

```
const kinesisStream = new aws.kinesis.Stream("kinesisStream", {
    shardCount: 1
});
```

Following is an example of Azure Service Bus namespace:

```
const servicebusNamespace = new azure.servicebus.Namespace("servicebus", {
    location: "East US",
    resourceGroupName: "myResourceGroup"
    sku: "Standard"
});
```

Following is an example of Kafka topic:

```
const kafkaTopic = new kafka.Topic("kafkaTopic", {
    name: "multi-cloud-data",
    partitions: 3,
    replicationFactor: 2
});
```

In this example, we could use the following:

- AWS Kinesis Stream to ingest real-time data from applications in AWS
- Azure Service Bus to receive processed data from Kinesis for further analysis or storage in Azure
- An Apache Kafka topic as a central data exchange point, allowing both clouds to produce and consume data

In the next section, we will discuss security and compliance in multi-cloud environments.

Security and compliance in multi-cloud environments

Managing identities and permissions in a multi-cloud setup can be challenging, but it is critical for securing your resources. Each cloud provider offers tools to handle this: AWS uses IAM, and Azure uses Entra ID. In AWS, IAM lets you define who can access what by creating policies for users, roles, or services. In Azure, Entra ID helps manage identities and permissions using **role-based access control** (**RBAC**), which assigns roles to users or applications at different levels, such as a single resource or an entire subscription.

When working across both AWS and Azure, federated authentication and role mapping are essential. For example, you can configure Entra ID as your central **identity provider** (**IdP**) and set up AWS IAM to trust it. This allows users to log in with one account and securely access resources in both clouds. You can also do the reverse by using AWS Identity Center to manage access to both AWS and Azure. This approach avoids creating separate accounts in each cloud and keeps permissions consistent.

By tying identity management together across clouds, you create a secure foundation for controlling access. However, managing identities is only part of the picture—data itself must also be protected. This brings us to the next critical aspect: data protection strategies.

Protecting data is one of the most critical aspects of securing a multi-cloud environment. In a setup where data moves between AWS and Azure, you need to ensure that it is secure at all stages—when it's stored (at rest) and when it's being transferred (in transit). Cloud providers have tools such as AWS **Key Management Service** (**KMS**) and Azure Key Vault to handle encryption, and secure transport mechanisms such as HTTPS and VPNs help protect data during transfers. Additionally, sensitive configurations, such as database credentials or API keys, must be stored securely using tools such as AWS Secrets Manager or Azure Key Vault.

Encrypting data at rest

Encryption at rest ensures that even if someone gains unauthorized access to the underlying storage, they cannot read the data without the proper keys. Azure Storage integrates seamlessly with Azure Key Vault to handle encryption keys securely. The following is an example of configuring a storage account with **customer-managed keys** (**CMKs**) from Azure Key Vault using Pulumi:

```
const keyVault = new azure.keyvault.Vault("myKeyVault", {
    resourceGroupName: "myResourceGroup",
    location: "East US",
    properties: {
```

```
            sku: { family: "A", name: "standard" },
            tenantId: "your-tenant-id",
            accessPolicies: [{
                tenantId: "your-tenant-id",
                objectId: "your-object-id",
                permissions: {
                    keys: ["get", "create", "list"],
                },
            }],
        },
    });


const key = new azure.keyvault.Key("storageEncryptionKey", {
    keyName: "storageEncryptionKey",
    resourceGroupName: "myResourceGroup",
    vaultName: keyVault.name,
    properties: {
        kty: "RSA",
        keySize: 2048,
    },
});


const storageAccount = new azure.storage.StorageAccount(
"myStorageAccount", {
    resourceGroupName: "myResourceGroup",
    location: "East US",
    sku: { name: "Standard_LRS" },
    kind: "StorageV2",
    encryption: {
        keySource: "Microsoft.Keyvault",
        keyVaultProperties: {
            keyName: key.name,
            keyVaultUri: keyVault.properties.vaultUri,
        },
    },
});
```

Here, Azure Key Vault manages the encryption keys for the storage account, providing a higher level of control and security compared to platform-managed keys.

Encrypting data in transit

When data is in transit, encryption ensures that it cannot be intercepted by attackers. The most common method is using HTTPS to secure communication between clients and services. HTTPS encrypts the data using SSL/TLS certificates, which can be managed using cloud-native tools such as Azure App Service certificates.

The following is an example of configuring HTTPS for Azure App Service:

```
// Create an App Service Plan
const appServicePlan = new azure.web.AppServicePlan("myAppServicePlan", {
    resourceGroupName: "myResourceGroup",
    location: "East US",
    sku: {
        tier: "Standard",
        size: "S1",
    },
});

// Create an App Service
const appService = new azure.web.WebApp("myWebApp", {
    resourceGroupName: "myResourceGroup",
    serverFarmId: appServicePlan.id,
    httpsOnly: true,
});

// Upload an SSL Certificate to Secure the App
const certificate = new azure.web.Certificate("mySSLCertificate", {
    resourceGroupName: "myResourceGroup",
    location: "East US",
    pfxBlob: "BASE64_ENCODED_CERTIFICATE_CONTENT",
    password: "CERTIFICATE_PASSWORD",
    serverFarmId: appServicePlan.id,
});

// Bind the Certificate to the App Service
```

```
const sslBinding = new azure.web.WebAppHostNameBinding ("sslBinding", {
    resourceGroupName: "myResourceGroup",
    siteName: appService.name,
    hostName: appService.defaultHostName,
    sslState: "SniEnabled",
    thumbprint: certificate.thumbprint,
});
```

This setup makes sure your Azure App Service uses HTTPS to protect all data sent between users and the server. While encryption is a key part of securing multi-cloud environments, security doesn't stop there. To fully safeguard your systems, it's also important to think about how compliance requirements are met across different cloud providers.

In a multi-cloud setup, following rules such as GDPR, HIPAA, or CCPA is essential to avoid fines and protect your users' data. These regulations often require you to store and handle sensitive data in specific ways, such as keeping data in certain regions or using encryption. Managing compliance across multiple clouds can be tricky because each cloud provider has its own tools and processes.

Instead of checking everything manually, automating compliance is a smarter approach. Pulumi Policy as Code lets you write rules in code that ensure your resources meet compliance requirements. For example, you can create a policy that checks whether all storage accounts in Azure and S3 buckets in Amazon are encrypted. If a resource doesn't follow the rule, the system will block it automatically. We will cover Policy as Code in more detail in *Chapter 14*; however, here's how a policy might look with Pulumi:

```
import * as policy from "@pulumi/policy";
const ensureStorageEncryption = new policy.PolicyPack(
"storage-encryption", {
    policies: [
        {
            name: "require-storage-encryption",
            description: "Ensure all storage accounts and S3 buckets are
            encrypted",
            enforcementLevel: "mandatory",
            validateResource: (args, reportViolation) => {
                if (args.type === "azure-native:storage:StorageAccount"
                && !args.props.encryption) {
                    reportViolation("Azure Storage Accounts must have
                    encryption enabled.");
```

```
                    }
                    if (args.type === "aws:s3/bucket:Bucket" &&
                    !args.props.serverSideEncryptionConfiguration) {
                        reportViolation("AWS S3 Buckets must have
                        server-side encryption enabled.");
                    }
                },
            },
        ],
    });
```

This rule makes sure all your storage resources are encrypted before they are created, so you don't accidentally deploy something that breaks compliance.

By using tools such as these, you can automatically check that your cloud setup is compliant with the necessary rules, and this saves you a lot of trouble later.

Summary

In this chapter, we looked at how to manage multi-cloud and hybrid environments, focusing on making systems flexible, reliable, and secure. We discussed how to design multi-cloud setups to use the best tools from different providers and hybrid architectures that combine on-premises systems with the cloud. We went over how to standardize deployments with Pulumi, ensure that systems in different clouds can work together, and use tools such as Grafana to monitor everything in one place. We also talked about strategies for sharing and syncing data, such as real-time streaming and database replication, and covered security tips such as encrypting data and setting up automated compliance checks. These ideas provide a solid starting point for handling the challenges of working across multiple cloud platforms.

In the next chapter, we will cover advanced Pulumi features.

Questions

1. How can Pulumi simplify the deployment of consistent infrastructure across multiple cloud providers?

2. What are the advantages of using Pulumi to enforce naming conventions and standardization in multi-cloud setups?

3. How does shared DNS resolution improve interoperability in multi-cloud architectures?

4. What factors should be considered when setting up real-time data pipelines between AWS and Azure?

5. What Pulumi features can simplify compliance enforcement across multiple clouds?

Part 4

Advanced Features, Best Practices and Hands-On Examples

The fourth and final part of the book brings together Pulumi's most advanced capabilities with proven best practices for building reliable, maintainable, and secure infrastructure at scale. It moves beyond day-to-day usage and focuses on the techniques that make infrastructure code production ready.

You will begin with advanced Pulumi features that enhance flexibility and efficiency, then learn how to structure projects for maintainability, scalability, and ease of collaboration. This includes applying design patterns, managing dependencies, and organizing code for long term success.

From there, you will focus on testing and debugging, gaining the skills to verify infrastructure changes before deployment and troubleshoot issues with confidence. You will also implement Policy as Code to enforce compliance and security rules across your environments.

The part concludes with guidance on migrating from other tools to Pulumi, followed by practical exercises that walk through building a complete infrastructure solution from scratch to production.

By the time you come to the end of this part, you will have the knowledge and practical experience to design, implement, and operate high quality infrastructure solutions with Pulumi in any environment.

This part of the book includes the following chapters:

- *Chapter 11, Advanced Pulumi Features*
- *Chapter 12, Writing Maintainable, Testable, and Scalable Code in Pulumi*
- *Chapter 13, Testing and Debugging Your Pulumi IaC*
- *Chapter 14, Implementing Policy as Code*
- *Chapter 15, Migrating From Other Tools to Pulumi*
- *Chapter 16, Tests and Exercises on Infrastructure Automation with Pulumi*

11

Advanced Pulumi Features

In earlier chapters, we covered Pulumi as a tool for managing infrastructure, setting it up in different environments, and using it in various scenarios. But Pulumi is more than just a tool for writing infrastructure code. In this chapter, we'll explore some of its more advanced features that make managing and automating cloud resources even more powerful.

We'll start by looking at Pulumi ESC, a feature that helps you organize environments, securely handle secrets, and manage configurations in one place. From there, we'll look at Pulumi AI, a tool designed to boost your productivity by helping you build and manage infrastructure more efficiently. The chapter also introduces the Automation API, which enables you to automate workflows and complex tasks. Finally, we'll cover dynamic ways to manage configurations, so your infrastructure can adapt to changing needs.

These advanced capabilities work together to help you build smarter and more adaptable infrastructure with Pulumi. By the end of this chapter, you'll be ready to use them to solve real-world challenges with confidence.

In this chapter, we're going to cover the following main topics:

- Mastering Pulumi ESC: Environments, Secrets, and Configuration
- Building your projects using Pulumi AI
- Automation API: scripting and workflow automation
- Dynamic configuration management techniques

Technical requirements

If you would like to follow along with the examples in this chapter, you will require the following:

- The Pulumi CLI is required for executing commands. You can download it from here: `https://www.pulumi.com/docs/iac/download-install/`.

- The Pulumi ESC CLI is required for executing ESC commands. You can download it from here: `https://www.pulumi.com/docs/esc/download-install/`.

- Pulumi supports multiple programming languages, but for this chapter, we'll be using JavaScript/TypeScript, which requires Node.js. You can download and install it from the Node.js official site here: `https://nodejs.org/`.

Mastering Pulumi ESC: Environments, Secrets, and Configuration

In a real-world application, you'd probably be juggling multiple regions and environments simultaneously. For example, your development and staging environments might be deployed to West Europe and East Europe regions, while a canary environment spans three regions, and your production environment runs across six or more regions. Some of these environments might share configurations, such as common API endpoints or shared database schemas, since certain aspects won't change, especially between development and staging or between canary and production. Managing these individually can quickly become overwhelming, with duplicated settings, inconsistencies, and increased risk of errors creeping into your workflow.

Pulumi **ESC** (which stands for **Environments, Secrets, and Configuration**) offers a practical solution to this complexity by centralizing and streamlining the management of configurations and secrets. With ESC, you can define reusable collections of configuration values and secrets called **environments**, making it easier to maintain consistency while accommodating the unique needs of each deployment setup. Let's look at the key concepts of ESC.

Key concepts of Pulumi ESC

When talking about Pulumi ESC, there are four key concepts to note, and they are environments, sources, targets, and centralized management.

Environments

Environments in Pulumi ESC are organized collections of configurations and secrets that are used for specific deployments, such as development, staging, or production. These environments aren't isolated; they can be reused and combined, which means you can share common settings across environments while still customizing what makes each one unique. This makes managing multiple setups much easier.

Environments can include both static and dynamic configurations. Static configurations are fixed settings, such as an app name or a database URL, that don't change often. Dynamic configurations are more flexible and come from external sources, such as secret managers or APIs. For example, instead of storing a password in a file, ESC can fetch it securely from a secret manager when needed. This makes dynamic configurations a great option for handling sensitive or temporary data, such as API keys or short-term access tokens.

Let's say your staging and production environments both need to connect to the same external API. Instead of defining this API URL in two places, you can store it in a shared base environment. Staging and production can then inherit this shared setting but use their own database credentials or region-specific overrides. This way, you avoid repeating yourself while still tailoring the configuration for each environment.

Sources

Pulumi ESC supports static configurations defined as key-value pairs in YAML files. These are straightforward and ideal for things such as default settings or constant values, such as a service name or a timeout duration.

Dynamic sources allow ESC to securely fetch configurations and secrets from external systems. For example, ESC can retrieve credentials from AWS Secrets Manager or Azure Key Vault when they are needed, instead of storing them in a file. This makes it easy to keep secrets up to date without manually updating files.

ESC also works with **OpenID Connect (OIDC)** to generate temporary credentials. These short-lived credentials are more secure because they expire after a set time. For example, during a deployment, ESC can request a token from AWS that only works for one hour. This means your infrastructure only uses secure, time-limited access, reducing the risk of credentials being misused.

Targets

Once your configurations and secrets are ready, ESC sends them to the right place. It can output them as environment variables for your app, save them in configuration files, or make them available through APIs. This flexibility allows ESC to fit into many workflows.

ESC is especially useful in automated pipelines and for local development. For example, during a CI/CD process, ESC can provide secrets as environment variables. This ensures that your pipeline has the right credentials at the right time. Similarly, in local development, you can use ESC to pull configurations securely, avoiding the need to hardcode sensitive data into your code.

Centralized management

Pulumi ESC keeps all your environments, configurations, and secrets in one place, making them easier to manage and secure. It uses **role-based access control (RBAC)** to ensure that only authorized people or teams can access specific environments or secrets. For example, you can restrict production secrets to senior engineers while letting junior developers access only the staging environment.

Versioning helps track changes to environments. Every update creates a new version, so you can label specific ones (e.g., `staging-v2` or `prod-release`) and roll back if something breaks. This is especially helpful for testing and deployment workflows, where different versions might be running simultaneously.

Suppose your company has two teams: a billing team managing payment processor secrets and a communications team handling email and SMS configurations. RBAC ensures that each team only has access to its own configurations, preventing accidental access to unrelated secrets.

Setting up Pulumi ESC

To begin using Pulumi ESC, you'll first need to install the ESC **command-line interface (CLI)**. The CLI is open source and freely available for various operating systems. For macOS users, the recommended installation method is via Homebrew. You can install it by running the following command in your terminal:

```
brew update && brew install pulumi/tap/esc
```

This command updates Homebrew and installs the ESC CLI from Pulumi's tap. After installation, verify that the CLI is correctly installed by checking its version with the following command:

```
esc version
```

This should display the installed version of the ESC CLI, confirming a successful installation.

For Windows users, you can download the ESC binary from `https://www.pulumi.com/docs/esc/download-install/` or run the following installation script in your command line:

```
@"%SystemRoot%\System32\WindowsPowerShell\v1.0\powershell.
exe" -NoProfile -InputFormat None -ExecutionPolicy Bypass
-Command "[Net.ServicePointManager]::SecurityProtocol = [Net.
SecurityProtocolType]::Tls12; iex ((New-Object System.Net.WebClient).
DownloadString('https://get.pulumi.com/esc/install.ps1'))" && SET
"PATH=%PATH%;%USERPROFILE%\.pulumi\bin"
```

This will install the `esc.exe` CLI to `%USERPROFILE%\.pulumi\bin` and add it to your path. You can then verify the installation by running the following:

```
esc version
```

This command should output the version number of the installed ESC CLI.

Now, you're ready to begin properly. Follow these steps:

1. Once the CLI is installed, the next step is to log in to Pulumi Cloud, which ESC uses to manage environments and secrets. Initiate the login process with the following:

   ```
   esc login
   ```

   This command prompts you to authenticate with Pulumi Cloud, either through a web browser or by providing an access token. Upon successful authentication, you'll see a confirmation message indicating that you're logged in.

2. Now that you're logged into ESC, it's time to use its functionality to manage configurations and secrets in environments. Let's imagine you were building a food delivery application with multiple environments. For instance, you have a development environment for testing new features, a staging environment for integrating with third-party services, and a production environment running across multiple regions. Let's say the organization you created is named `foodie-tech`, and your project is `delivery-app`. You'd structure your environments to clearly belong to both the organization and the project. For example, to initialize the development environment, you will run the following command:

   ```
   esc env init foodie-tech/delivery-app/development
   ```

   This command creates the development environment under the `delivery-app` project within the `foodie-tech` organization.

3. To confirm the environment was created successfully, list all the available environments:

    ```
    esc env ls
    ```

    You should see foodie-tech/delivery-app/development listed.

4. Now, let's add a configuration for the development database. Suppose your app needs a PostgreSQL database connection string:

    ```
    esc env set foodie-tech/delivery-app/development database_url
    "postgres://dev_user:dev_password@localhost:5432/dev_db"
    ```

5. To verify the value, you can retrieve it like this:

    ```
    esc env get foodie-tech/delivery-app/development database_url
    ```

    This ensures that database_url is stored correctly and ready for use.

6. Next, suppose the development environment also requires an API key for a third-party geolocation service. You can add it using the following:

    ```
    esc env set foodie-tech/delivery-app/development geolocation_api_key
    "dev_geo_key_123"
    ```

7. You can also decide to add more configurations to your environment as needed. For example, in the development environment, you might include a VM size for testing, and any other configuration you like:

    ```
    esc env set foodie-tech/delivery-app/development vm_size "Standard_
    D2s_v3"
    ```

8. Once these configurations are set, you can import the environment into your Pulumi stack configuration file to use it. This is done using the imports key in the YAML file. For example, your Pulumi.dev-wu2.yaml file for the West US 2 development stack might look like this:

    ```yaml
    imports:
      - foodie-tech/delivery-app/development
    config:
      keyvaultName: "westus-kv"
      region: "West US 2"
      custom_endpoint: "westus2.dev.delivery-app.com"
    ```

9. If you have another development stack in a different region, such as Southeast Asia, you can create a similar configuration file while still importing the shared development environment:

```
imports:
  - foodie-tech/delivery-app/development
config:
  region: "Southeast Asia"
  keyvaultName: "sea-kv"
  custom_endpoint: "sea.dev.delivery-app.com"
```

10. In your Pulumi program, you can access these configurations easily. Here's how to retrieve them in a TypeScript Pulumi program:

```
const config = new pulumi.Config();

// Access shared configurations from the imported environment
const databaseUrl = config.require("database_url");
const geoApiKey = config.require("geolocation_api_key");
const vmSize = config.require("vm_size");

// Access region-
specific configurations from the stack configuration
const region = config.require("region");
const customEndpoint = config.require("custom_endpoint");

// ... Use them for your IaC
```

This setup allows you to maintain shared configurations in the `foodie-tech/delivery-app/development` environment and customize them for specific regions or deployment needs. With ESC, you're able to share and reuse common configurations and secrets across different environments in a way that can scale as your IaC continues to grow.

Building your projects using Pulumi AI

Imagine you're setting up the infrastructure for a new web app. You need a load balancer, a group of VMs that can scale as needed, and a database. If you're experienced with Pulumi, you might start writing configuration files and code in your preferred language. But if you're new or pressed for time, Pulumi AI can help by generating the code for you based on a simple description.

For example, you could type something like this:

```
I need an Azure App Service connected to a MySQL database, with logging
turned on and scaled for medium traffic.
```

Pulumi AI takes this input and generates the infrastructure code for you. *Figure 11.1* shows an example of what you might see as a response to your prompt.

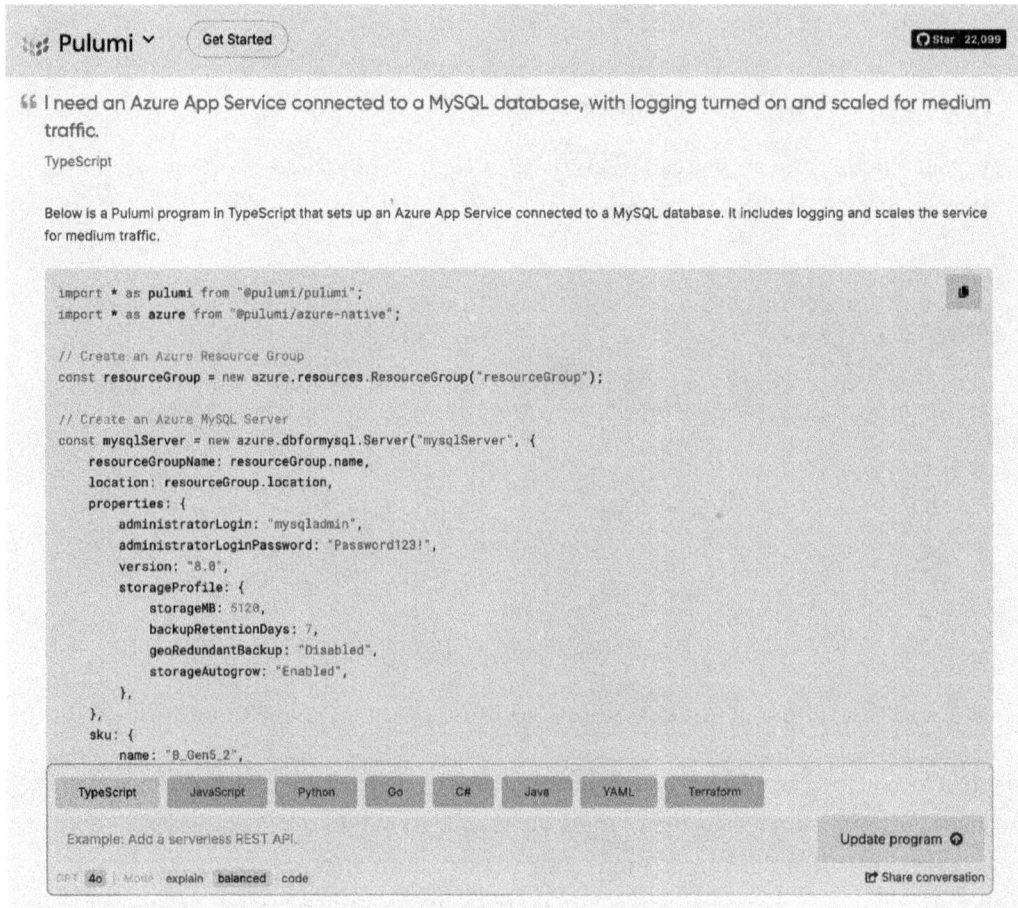

Figure 11.1: Pulumi AI

This makes the process of building infrastructure much easier. Instead of spending time searching for how to do things, you can focus on the overall design of your app while Pulumi AI fills in the details.

For people who are new to Pulumi, this is also a great way to learn. You can see how a simple description turns into working code and pick up best practices along the way. Over time, you'll get more confident writing code yourself, even for more complex setups.

Pulumi AI doesn't just help you get started; it's also useful when you need to add new features or make changes to an existing setup. To get started with Pulumi AI, you can visit the official website and try it for yourself: `https://www.pulumi.com/ai`.

Pulumi also has AI answers, which is a curated collection of commonly asked **infrastructure-as-code (IaC)** questions that Pulumi AI has received. These questions are anonymized and organized into an archive, making it a valuable resource for anyone building cloud infrastructure with Pulumi. You can find some answers here: `https://www.pulumi.com/ai/answers`.

Automation API: scripting and workflow automation

Pulumi's Automation API is a tool that lets you control your infrastructure directly through code. Instead of using the Pulumi CLI, you can write programs that create, update, or manage cloud resources as part of your application or scripts. It allows you to handle infrastructure tasks such as deployments, updates, or tests dynamically, all within your own code base. Automation API has a few key concepts and terms, and they are workspaces, stacks, local programs, and inline programs.

Workspace

`Workspace` is the execution context where Pulumi operations run. It includes the Pulumi project, the program to execute, and one or more stacks. Workspaces are responsible for managing the environment, such as installing plugins, configuring runtime settings, and handling stack configurations.

`LocalWorkspace` is the default `Workspace` implementation that uses local `Pulumi.yaml` and `Pulumi.[stack].yaml` files for project and stack configuration. It closely mirrors the behavior of the Pulumi CLI. Modifying the project or stack settings through the API automatically updates the corresponding YAML files.

`RemoteWorkspace` is used for Pulumi deployments, where the program is stored in a remote Git repository. This is ideal for use cases where infrastructure operations need to run remotely, such as in centralized CI/CD systems or managed services.

Stack

A **stack** represents an isolated, independently configurable instance of a Pulumi program. It allows you to manage the full Pulumi life cycle, such as deploying, previewing changes, refreshing state, or destroying resources, and to set and retrieve configuration values. Stacks are commonly used to represent different environments (for example, development, staging, and production) or feature branches.

`RemoteStack` is similar to a standard stack, but operates within `RemoteWorkspace`. It provides life cycle methods such as `up`, `preview`, and `destroy`, but these operations are executed remotely.

Local program versus inline program

Local programs are traditional Pulumi programs with a dedicated directory, a `Pulumi.yaml` file, and supporting program files. They are often driven by the CLI, but Automation API can also execute them, making it possible to script their behavior programmatically.

Inline programs are defined as functions within your Automation API code. They don't require a separate directory or `Pulumi.yaml` file. This approach is lightweight and well-suited for dynamic scenarios where the Pulumi logic is part of a larger application or service.

Use cases for Automation API

Automation API is versatile and supports several practical use cases:

- **CI/CD workflows**: Automate infrastructure changes by embedding Pulumi directly into your CI/CD pipelines. For example, deploy new infrastructure whenever a new version of your application is built.

- **Integration testing**: Spin up isolated environments programmatically to test application code against realistic infrastructure setups.

- **Application-centric deployments**: Combine infrastructure operations with application deployments, such as provisioning a database and running migrations in a single script.

- **Custom tools and CLIs**: Build higher-level tools, custom dashboards, or internal developer platforms that simplify infrastructure management for non-technical teams.

- **Infrastructure-as-a-service APIs**: Use the API behind a REST interface, enabling teams to request infrastructure on demand through a simple HTTP call.

Here's a real example of how Pulumi's Automation API can be used to programmatically deploy Azure resources. This script creates an Azure resource group and a storage account using an inline program:

```javascript
import * as automation from "@pulumi/pulumi/automation";
import * as azure from "@pulumi/azure-native";
async function createInfrastructure() {
    // Create or select a Pulumi stack
    const stack = await automation.LocalWorkspace.createOrSelectStack({
        stackName: "dev",
        projectName: "automation-api-example",
        program: async () => {
            // Define the infrastructure programmatically
            const resourceGroup = new azure.resources.ResourceGroup(
            "example-rg");

            const storageAccount = new azure.storage.StorageAccount(
            "examplestorage", {
                resourceGroupName: resourceGroup.name,
                sku: {
                    name: "Standard_LRS",
                },
                kind: "StorageV2",
            });

            return {
                resourceGroupName: resourceGroup.name,
                storageAccountName: storageAccount.name,
            };
        },
    });

    console.log("Setting up stack configuration...");
    await stack.setConfig("azure:location", { value: "WestUS" });

    console.log("Refreshing stack...");
    await stack.refresh({ onOutput: console.log });

    console.log("Deploying infrastructure...");
```

```
    const result = await stack.up({ onOutput: console.log });

    console.log("Deployment complete! Outputs:");
    console.log(result.outputs);
}

// Execute the function
createInfrastructure().catch((err) => {
    console.error("Error deploying infrastructure:", err);
});
```

In this example, the script starts by creating or selecting a Pulumi stack, which represents an isolated environment for your infrastructure, such as development, staging, or production. The stack setup is tied to an inline program that defines the infrastructure resources directly within the code. Here, an Azure resource group and a storage account are provisioned as part of the program.

Before deployment, the script sets the Azure region dynamically using `stack.setConfig`. This flexibility allows configurations to be adjusted at runtime based on the deployment requirements. After setting up the configurations, the `stack.refresh` method ensures that the current state of the resources is synced with Pulumi's understanding of the infrastructure.

The deployment process is initiated with `stack.up`, which provisions the defined resources. The script captures and logs the outputs of the deployment, such as the names of the created resource group and storage account. These outputs can then be used in other parts of your application or pipeline.

This script is a good fit for CI/CD workflows, where infrastructure needs to be provisioned as part of an automated deployment process. It can also be adapted for use in event-driven workflows, such as automatically creating resources when specific application events occur.

Dynamic configuration management techniques

Dynamic configuration values change, and not as a result of the state of your infrastructure project changing. Different things, such as environment-specific requirements, runtime application needs, or deployment contexts, can trigger changes to those values. As you build out your infrastructure, some of your configuration values will be dynamic, and you're going to manage them that way. A technique for managing this is Pulumi ESC, something we discussed in the earlier sections of this chapter.

You can change the value of some configurations without opening a new pull request to make the update, and the next time your IaC scripts need to run, the most current values will be used. There are some other techniques for managing dynamic configurations: secrets references such as Azure Key Vault, and configuration management in CI/CD pipelines.

Azure Key Vault

One effective way to manage dynamic configurations is by integrating secrets references from services such as Azure Key Vault. Secrets such as API keys, database credentials, and storage account keys are sensitive and need to be managed securely. Using Azure Key Vault, you can store these secrets and dynamically reference them in your infrastructure or applications. For instance, when deploying Azure App Service, you can configure it to pull secrets from Azure Key Vault at runtime using Key Vault references. This ensures that sensitive data remains secure and up to date without being hardcoded into your configuration files.

The following Pulumi code dynamically configures the App Service with a Key Vault reference:

```
const keyVault = new azure.keyvault.Vault("exampleKeyVault", {
    properties: {
        sku: { family: "A", name: "standard" },
        tenantId: azure.authorization.getClientConfig().then(
            cfg => cfg.tenantId),
        accessPolicies: [{
            objectId: azure.authorization.getClientConfig().then(
                cfg => cfg.objectId),
            tenantId: azure.authorization.getClientConfig().then(
                cfg => cfg.tenantId),
            permissions: { secrets: ["get", "list"] },
        }],
    },
});

const storageKeySecret = new azure.keyvault.Secret("storageKeySecret", {
    vaultName: keyVault.name,
    properties: {
        value: "SuperSecretStorageKey",
    },
```

```
    });

    // Configure an App Service with Key Vault references
    const appService = new azure.web.WebApp("exampleAppService", {
        siteConfig: {
            appSettings: [
                {
                    name: "AzureStorageKey",
                    value: `@Microsoft.KeyVault(SecretUri=
                        ${storageKeySecret.properties.secretUriWithVersion})`,
                },
            ],
        },
    });
```

This code ensures that the App Service retrieves the storage key securely at runtime using the @
Microsoft.KeyVault syntax. This setup is reflected in the application settings, as shown in the
following figure, where secrets are dynamically referenced through Key Vault, providing both
security and ease of management. *Figure 11.2* shows what it will look like in the Azure portal.

Application settings

Application settings are encrypted at rest and transmitted over an encrypted channel. You can choose to disp
below. Application Settings are exposed as environment variables for access by your application at runtime. l

+ New application setting   👁 Show values   ✏ Advanced edit   ▽ Filter

Name	Value	Source
APPINSIGHTS_INSTRUMENTATIONKEY	👁 Hidden value. Click show values button ⦂	App Config
AzureStorageAccountName	👁 Hidden value. Click show values button ⦂	⊘ Key vault Reference
AzureStorageKey	👁 Hidden value. Click show values button ⦂	⊘ Key vault Reference
AzureWebJobsStorage	👁 Hidden value. Click show values button ⦂	⊘ Key vault Reference
DemoSetting	👁 Hidden value. Click show values button ⦂	App Config

Figure 11.2: Key Vault reference

Azure Key Vault isn't the only situation where you need to think about dynamic configurations.

CI/CD pipelines

Dynamic configurations are also critical in CI/CD pipelines, where inputs such as artifact paths, environment-specific settings, or build metadata need to be passed during runtime. For example, when deploying an application binary built during a pipeline run, you need to pass the path to that binary dynamically into your Pulumi configuration. In a CI/CD pipeline, this might look like setting the artifact path during the build step and passing it as a Pulumi configuration value during deployment. This allows Pulumi to use the correct file path dynamically without requiring manual intervention or code changes. Here's how you can set this up in an Azure DevOps pipeline:

```
trigger:
  - main
pool:
  vmImage: "ubuntu-latest"
steps:
  # Step 1: Install Pulumi and dependencies
  - task: UsePythonVersion@1
    displayName: "Install Python"
    inputs:
      versionSpec: "3.x"
      addToPath: true
  - task: Bash@3
    displayName: "Build Application"
    inputs:
      targetType: "inline"
      script: |
        mkdir -p $(Build.ArtifactStagingDirectory)/build
        echo "Hello, Pulumi!" > $(Build.ArtifactStagingDirectory)/build
          /app.txt
  - task: PublishPipelineArtifact@1
    displayName: "Publish Build Artifact"
    inputs:
      targetPath: "$(Build.ArtifactStagingDirectory)/build"
      artifact: "build"

  # Step 2: Pulumi Login, Configure, and Deploy in one task
  - task: Bash@3
    displayName: "Pulumi Login, Configure, and Deploy"
```

```
inputs:
  targetType: "inline"
  script: |
    # Add Pulumi to PATH
    curl -fsSL https://get.pulumi.com | sh
    export PATH=$PATH:$HOME/.pulumi/bin

    # Log in to Pulumi
    pulumi login --cloud-url https://app.pulumi.com

    # Set the artifact path in Pulumi configuration
    pulumi config set artifactPath "$(Build.ArtifactStagingDirectory)
      /build/app.txt"

    # Deploy infrastructure
    pulumi up --stack dev --yes
env:
  PULUMI_ACCESS_TOKEN: "$(PulumiAccessToken)"
```

The pipeline begins by installing Pulumi and ensuring the necessary tools are available. Next, it builds the application and saves the resulting artifact in the $(Build.ArtifactStagingDirectory)/ build directory. This artifact is then published as part of the pipeline's outputs, ensuring that it can be referenced in subsequent steps. Pulumi login is handled securely using the pulumi login command with the access token passed through the PULUMI_ACCESS_TOKEN environment variable.

Once authenticated, the path to the artifact is dynamically set as a Pulumi configuration using the pulumi config set command. This ensures that the deployment references the correct build artifact without manual updates to the Pulumi stack configuration files. Finally, pulumi up is executed to deploy the infrastructure, using the configuration values set earlier. This pipeline dynamically ties the build artifacts to the infrastructure deployment process, making it highly automated and efficient for deploying infrastructure and application code.

Summary

In this chapter, we covered advanced Pulumi features that help you manage infrastructure more effectively. We started with Pulumi ESC, which allows you to handle environments, secrets, and configurations in a centralized and reusable way. Then, we explored Pulumi AI, which helps you write infrastructure code and find answers to common questions.

We also introduced Automation API, showing how it lets you control deployments and workflows directly in your code. Finally, we discussed dynamic configuration management, focusing on using Pulumi ESC, Azure Key Vault for secure secrets, and managing configuration values in CI/CD pipelines. These features make it easier to manage cloud infrastructure in real-world scenarios.

In the next chapter, we will cover writing maintainable, testable, and scalable code in Pulumi.

Questions

1. What is Pulumi ESC, and how does it help with managing environments, secrets, and configurations?

2. How does Pulumi AI assist in generating infrastructure code?

3. What is the difference between an inline Pulumi program and a local Pulumi program?

4. How does Automation API differ from the Pulumi CLI in terms of infrastructure management?

5. What are the key features of the Pulumi Automation API's LocalWorkspace class?

6. What are the steps to dynamically configure artifact paths in a CI/CD pipeline using Pulumi?

7. What are some common use cases for Pulumi's Automation API?

12

Writing Maintainable, Testable, and Scalable Code in Pulumi

Pulumi's approach to infrastructure as software means that developers can use programming principles and patterns to organize their infrastructure code in a way that makes it easier to understand, maintain, and scale. In this chapter, you will learn how to structure Pulumi projects using modular design, making your code reusable and easier to manage as your infrastructure grows.

You will see how principles such as **Don't Repeat Yourself** (**DRY**) and SOLID can be applied to create cleaner and more reliable infrastructure code. This chapter will also explain the importance of consistent naming and documentation to keep projects clear and easy for teams to work on together. Finally, you will learn how to write tests for your infrastructure code to catch problems early and ensure high-quality deployments. By the end, you'll know how to create Pulumi projects that are both efficient and built to last.

In this chapter, we're going to cover the following main topics:

- Modularity and code reusability
- Applying traditional programming paradigms to IaC
- Consistent naming and documentation practices

Technical requirements

If you would like to follow along with the examples in this chapter, you will require the following:

- The Pulumi CLI is required for executing commands. You can download it here: `https://www.pulumi.com/docs/iac/download-install/`.

- Pulumi supports multiple programming languages, but for this chapter, we'll be using JavaScript/TypeScript, which requires Node.js. You can download and install it from the Node.js official site: `https://nodejs.org/`.

Modularity and code reusability

Modularity in **Infrastructure as Code (IaC)** means breaking your infrastructure setup into smaller, manageable pieces. Instead of writing one large block of code for everything, you separate parts of the infrastructure into smaller components that can work together. Each of these pieces handles a specific task, making it easier to work with and understand.

Breaking infrastructure into reusable components is important because it keeps your code clean and organized. If a part of the infrastructure needs to change or be updated, you only need to work on that specific part instead of going through everything. This saves time and reduces mistakes.

Modularity also makes it easy to manage your project as it grows. When you reuse the same components in different parts of the infrastructure, it's faster to build new features. It also makes it easier for teams to work together, as everyone can focus on specific parts of the project without getting overwhelmed by the entire system.

A well-thought-out structure helps developers work more efficiently and makes it easier to debug or extend the project over time. There are two common approaches to organizing Pulumi projects: the single-project layout and the multi-project layout.

In a single-project layout, all resources are defined in one project. This approach is ideal for smaller projects or when managing a single environment. For example, your project might be organized like this:

```
iac-project/
├── Pulumi.yaml
├── Pulumi.dev.yaml
├── Pulumi.prod.yaml
├── index.ts
├── resources/
```

```
|    ├── network.ts
|    ├── storage.ts
|    └── compute.ts
```

Here, the index.ts file serves as the entry point for the project, where you import and use resources defined in the resources directory. Different environments, such as development and production, are managed using Pulumi.dev.yaml and Pulumi.prod.yaml.

For larger projects, a multi-project layout is more appropriate. This structure splits the infrastructure into multiple Pulumi projects, making it easier to manage different components or delegate work across teams. An example layout might look like this:

```
pulumi-infra/
├── auth-service/
|    ├── Pulumi.yaml
|    ├── Pulumi.dev.yaml
|    ├── Pulumi.prod.yaml
|    ├── index.ts
|    └── resources/
|         ├── network.ts
|         └── storage.ts
├── payments-service/
|    ├── Pulumi.yaml
|    ├── Pulumi.dev.yaml
|    ├── Pulumi.prod.yaml
|    ├── index.ts
|    └── resources/
|         ├── storage.ts
|         ├── compute.ts
|         └── security.ts
└── shared/
     ├── Pulumi.yaml
     ├── utils.ts
     └── monitoring/
          ├── logging.ts
          ├── alerts.ts
          └── metrics.ts
```

In this structure, each service, such as `auth-service` and `payments-service`, is self-contained and includes everything it needs for its infrastructure. Shared code, such as utilities or monitoring configurations, lives in a dedicated shared folder, and it's reusable across multiple services.

Organizing resources into logical groups is another key aspect of modularity. For example, a network group might define resources such as virtual networks, subnets, and public IP addresses, while a compute group might include virtual machines and scale sets. Here's an example of how you might define multiple resources in a `network.ts` file using Azure resources:

```typescript
// network.ts
import * as azure from "@pulumi/azure-native";


export const virtualNetwork = new azure.network.VirtualNetwork("my-
vnet", {
    location: "WestUS",
    addressSpace: { addressPrefixes: ["10.0.0.0/16"] },
    resourceGroupName: "my-resource-group",
});


export const subnet = new azure.network.Subnet("my-subnet", {
    addressPrefix: "10.0.1.0/24",
    virtualNetworkName: virtualNetwork.name,
    resourceGroupName: "my-resource-group",
});


export const publicIp = new azure.network.PublicIPAddress("my-public-
ip", {
    dnsSettings: {
        domainNameLabel: "dnslbl",
    },
    location: "westus",
    publicIpAddressName: "my-ip",
    resourceGroupName: " my-resource-group",
});
```

In the `compute.ts` file, you could define resources such as virtual machines and scale sets:

```typescript
// compute.ts
import * as azure from "@pulumi/azure-native";
import { subnet } from "./network";

export const virtualMachine = new azure.compute.VirtualMachine("my-vm", {
    location: "WestUS",
    resourceGroupName: "my-resource-group",
    networkProfile: {
        networkInterfaces: [{
            id: subnet.id,
            primary: true,
        }],
    },
    osProfile: {
        adminUsername: "adminuser",
        adminPassword: "secure-password",
        computerName: "my-compute",
    },
    hardwareProfile: {
        vmSize: "Standard_B2ms",
    },
});

export const scaleSet = new azure.compute.VirtualMachineScaleSet("my-
scale-set", {
    location: "WestUS",
    resourceGroupName: "my-resource-group",
    sku: {
        name: "Standard B2ms",
        capacity: 2,
    },
    virtualMachineProfile: {
        storageProfile: {
            imageReference: {
                offer: "UbuntuServer",
                publisher: "Canonical",
```

```
                sku: "18.04-LTS",
                version: "latest",
            },
        },
        osProfile: {
            adminUsername: "adminuser",
            adminPassword: "secure-password",
        },
        networkProfile: {
            networkInterfaceConfigurations: [{
                name: "my-nic",
                primary: true,
                ipConfigurations: [{
                    name: "my-ipconfig",
                    subnet: { id: subnet.id },
                }],
            }],
        },
    },
});
```

In your `index.ts` file, you would then bring all of these resources together:

```
import { virtualNetwork, subnet, publicIp } from "./resources/network";
import { virtualMachine, scaleSet } from "./resources/compute";
export { virtualNetwork, subnet, publicIp, virtualMachine, scaleSet };
```

Separating concerns by grouping resources into logical files and directories keeps your project organized and makes the code easier to navigate.

Applying traditional programming paradigms to IaC

As we treat infrastructure like software, using common programming ideas can help make our code easier to manage and understand. Principles such as DRY, SOLID, and design patterns can reduce repeated code, keep things organized, and make it easier to grow your Pulumi projects. This section looks at how these ideas can be used to write clear and simple IaC.

Understanding DRY and its application in IaC

The DRY principle is a key idea in programming that focuses on reducing repetition in code. In IaC, repetition often happens when similar resources or configurations are defined multiple times across different parts of the project. Following DRY helps create cleaner and more efficient code by grouping common patterns into reusable components or modules.

In Pulumi, applying DRY means identifying repetitive parts of your infrastructure code and refactoring them into shared functions, classes, or even separate modules. This makes your code easier to maintain because changes only need to be made in one place. For example, if you find yourself creating similar virtual networks for different environments, you can write a reusable function to handle that setup.

Here's an example where DRY is applied to avoid repeating code to create a virtual network and its subnet:

Without DRY (repetitive code)

```
const devVnet = new azure.network.VirtualNetwork("dev-vnet", {
    location: "WestUS",
    addressSpace: { addressPrefixes: ["10.0.0.0/16"] },
    resourceGroupName: "dev-rg",
});

const devSubnet = new azure.network.Subnet("dev-subnet", {
    addressPrefix: "10.0.1.0/24",
    virtualNetworkName: devVnet.name,
    resourceGroupName: "dev-rg",
});

const prodVnet = new azure.network.VirtualNetwork("prod-vnet", {
    location: "WestUS",
    addressSpace: { addressPrefixes: ["10.1.0.0/16"] },
    resourceGroupName: "prod-rg",
});

const prodSubnet = new azure.network.Subnet("prod-subnet", {
```

```
        addressPrefix: "10.1.1.0/24",
        virtualNetworkName: prodVnet.name,
        resourceGroupName: "prod-rg",
});
```

In this example, the code for creating virtual networks and subnets is repeated for both the dev and prod environments. This not only clutters the code but also makes updates tedious.

With DRY (reusable function)

```
function createNetwork(name: string, addressSpace: string, subnetPrefix:
string, resourceGroupName: string) {
    const vnet = new azure.network.VirtualNetwork(`${name}-vnet`, {
        location: "WestUS",
        addressSpace: { addressPrefixes: [addressSpace] },
        resourceGroupName,
    });

    const subnet = new azure.network.Subnet(`${name}-subnet`, {
        addressPrefix: subnetPrefix,
        virtualNetworkName: vnet.name,
        resourceGroupName,
    });

    return { vnet, subnet };
}

const devNetwork = createNetwork(
"dev", "10.0.0.0/16", "10.0.1.0/24", "dev-rg");
const prodNetwork = createNetwork(
"prod", "10.1.0.0/16", "10.1.1.0/24", "prod-rg");
```

With this approach, the repetitive code is replaced by a reusable function, createNetwork. You only need to call the function with the required parameters to set up networks for different environments. If you need to change something (e.g., adding a new tag or updating a property), you can update it once in the function, and all instances will automatically reflect the change.

By following DRY, your infrastructure code becomes easier to read and maintain. It also reduces the chance of errors, as there's less duplication.

Using SOLID principles to improve infrastructure code

The SOLID principles are a set of five guidelines that help developers create better-organized and more flexible code. Originally meant for object-oriented programming, these principles can also be applied to IaC to make your Pulumi projects easier to maintain and scale. Let's look at how each principle works and how it relates to IaC.

Single responsibility principle

The **single responsibility principle** states that each class or function should handle one specific responsibility. For IaC, this means creating components that focus on distinct tasks, such as managing virtual networks or subnets, instead of mixing multiple responsibilities in one place.

The following code snippet shows a class, `AzureNetworkManager`, that focuses on networking tasks, such as creating virtual networks and subnets. Each method is designed to handle a single task, keeping the logic modular and easy to maintain.

```
import * as azure from "@pulumi/azure-native";
```

Here's a class that handles different networking tasks:

```
class AzureNetworkManager {
    createVirtualNetwork(
    name: string, resourceGroupName: string, cidr: string) {
        return new azure.network.VirtualNetwork(name, {
            resourceGroupName,
            location: "WestUS",
            addressSpace: { addressPrefixes: [cidr] },
        });
    }

    createSubnet(
    name: string, vnetName: string, resourceGroupName: string,
    cidr: string) {
        return new azure.network.Subnet(name, {
            virtualNetworkName: vnetName,
            resourceGroupName,
            addressPrefix: cidr,
        });
    }
}
```

You can use `AzureNetworkManager` to handle tasks:

```
const networkManager = new AzureNetworkManager();
const vnet = networkManager.createVirtualNetwork(
    "prod-vnet", "prod-rg", "10.0.0.0/16");
const appSubnet = networkManager.createSubnet(
    "app-subnet", vnet.name, "prod-rg", "10.0.1.0/24");
const dbSubnet = networkManager.createSubnet(
    "db-subnet", vnet.name, "prod-rg", "10.0.2.0/24");
```

Here, we separate responsibilities into methods such as `createVirtualNetwork` and `createSubnet`. As a result, the class remains modular, and each method is easy to maintain and test independently.

Open-closed principle

The **open-closed principle** means that code should be open to extensions but closed to modifications. For IaC, this means building abstractions that allow for additional configurations or features without changing the original logic.

The following code snippet shows how `AzureNetworkManager` uses a configuration object to handle dynamic network requirements. This allows new features, such as additional subnets or properties, to be added without modifying the existing logic.

```
interface NetworkConfig {
    name: string;
    resourceGroupName: string;
    location: string;
    addressPrefixes: string[];
    subnets: { name: string; addressPrefix: string }[];
}
```

Here's a class to create networks with dynamic configurations:

```
class AzureNetworkManager {
    createNetwork(config: NetworkConfig) {
        const vnet = new azure.network.VirtualNetwork(config.name, {
            resourceGroupName: config.resourceGroupName,
            location: config.location,
            addressSpace: { addressPrefixes: config.addressPrefixes },
```

```
        });

        const subnets = config.subnets.map(subnet =>
            new azure.network.Subnet(`${config.name}-${subnet.name}`, {
                virtualNetworkName: vnet.name,
                resourceGroupName: config.resourceGroupName,
                addressPrefix: subnet.addressPrefix,
            }),
        );

        return { vnet, subnets };
    }
}

const networkConfig: NetworkConfig = {
    name: "prod-vnet",
    resourceGroupName: "prod-rg",
    location: "WestUS",
    addressPrefixes: ["10.0.0.0/16"],
    subnets: [
        { name: "subnet1", addressPrefix: "10.0.1.0/24" },
        { name: "subnet2", addressPrefix: "10.0.2.0/24" },
    ],
};

const networkManager = new AzureNetworkManager();
const resources = networkManager.createNetwork(networkConfig);
```

This approach ensures that new configurations or features (e.g., additional subnets) can be added without modifying the core logic.

Liskov substitution principle

The **Liskov substitution principle** states that objects of a parent class or interface should be replaceable by objects of a subclass without affecting the program. In IaC, this is useful when dealing with multiple providers or resource types.

The following code snippet shows how a common `NetworkProvider` interface enables different providers, such as Azure, to implement the same method for creating networks. This abstraction makes it easy to swap out providers without changing the core logic.

```
// Define a common interface for network providers
interface NetworkProvider {
    createNetwork(config: NetworkConfig): { vnet: any; subnets: any[] };
}

// Implement Azure as a provider
class AzureNetworkProvider implements NetworkProvider {
    createNetwork(config: NetworkConfig) {
        const vnet = new azure.network.VirtualNetwork(config.name, {

            ...

        });

        const subnets = config.subnets.map(subnet =>
            new azure.network.Subnet(`${config.name}-${subnet.name}`, {

                ...

            }),
        );
        return { vnet, subnets };
    }
}

// Use the interface to deploy a network
function deployNetwork(provider: NetworkProvider, config: NetworkConfig) {
    return provider.createNetwork(config);
}

const azureProvider = new AzureNetworkProvider();
const resources = deployNetwork(azureProvider, networkConfig);
```

With this abstraction, switching to a different provider (e.g., AWS) only requires creating a new implementation of the `NetworkProvider` interface.

Interface segregation principle

The **interface segregation principle** ensures that components only implement the functionality they actually need. In IaC, this means creating specific interfaces for distinct tasks rather than forcing a single class to handle unrelated operations.

The following code snippet demonstrates how networking responsibilities, such as managing virtual networks, subnets, and security groups, are split into targeted interfaces. A single class implements these interfaces, keeping the design modular and focused.

```
// Interfaces for distinct networking tasks
interface VirtualNetworkManager {
    createVirtualNetwork(
    name: string, resourceGroupName: string, cidr: string): any;
}
interface SubnetManager {
    addSubnet(
    vnetName: string, resourceGroupName: string, name: string,
    cidr: string): any;
}
interface SecurityGroupManager {
    createSecurityGroup(name: string, resourceGroupName: string): any;
}

// A class implementing all networking interfaces
class AzureNetworkManager implements VirtualNetworkManager, SubnetManager,
SecurityGroupManager {
    createVirtualNetwork(name: string, resourceGroupName: string, cidr:
string) {
        return new azure.network.VirtualNetwork(name, {
            resourceGroupName,
            location: "WestUS",
            addressSpace: { addressPrefixes: [cidr] },
        });
    }

    addSubnet(vnetName: string, resourceGroupName: string, name: string,
    cidr: string) {
        return new azure.network.Subnet(name, {
```

```
            virtualNetworkName: vnetName,
            resourceGroupName,
            addressPrefix: cidr,
        });
    }

    createSecurityGroup(name: string, resourceGroupName: string) {
        return new azure.network.NetworkSecurityGroup(name, {
            resourceGroupName,
            location: "WestUS",
        });
    }
}

// Using the manager class
const networkManager = new AzureNetworkManager();
const vnet = networkManager.createVirtualNetwork(
    "prod-vnet", "prod-rg", "10.0.0.0/16");
const subnet = networkManager.addSubnet(
    vnet.name, "prod-rg", "app-subnet", "10.0.1.0/24");
const nsg = networkManager.createSecurityGroup("prod-nsg", "prod-rg");
```

This design ensures that responsibilities are clear, interfaces are focused, and the class remains easy to extend or modify without becoming bloated.

Dependency inversion principle

The **dependency inversion principle** ensures that high-level modules don't depend on low-level modules; instead, both should rely on abstractions. In IaC, this means your core deployment logic should depend on interfaces or abstractions, not concrete implementations, so the system remains flexible and easy to extend.

The following code snippet demonstrates how a DeploymentStrategy interface abstracts deployment logic. This allows you to swap implementations, such as deploying networks or storage, without changing the main deployment flow.

```
// Define an abstraction for deployment
interface DeploymentStrategy {
    deploy(): void;
}
```

```typescript
// A strategy for deploying networks
class NetworkDeployment implements DeploymentStrategy {
    constructor(private config: NetworkConfig, private
provider: NetworkProvider) {}
    deploy() {
        const resources = this.provider.createNetwork(this.config);
        console.log("Deployed Network:", resources.vnet.name);
    }
}

// Another strategy for deploying storage
class StorageDeployment implements DeploymentStrategy {
    constructor(private config: StorageConfig,
        private provider: StorageProvider) {}
    deploy() {
        const storageAccount = this.provider.createStorage(this.config);
        console.log("Deployed Storage Account:", storageAccount.name);
    }
}

// Use the abstraction in the main program
function executeDeployment(strategy: DeploymentStrategy) {
    strategy.deploy();
}

// Create configurations and providers
const networkStrategy = new NetworkDeployment(
    networkConfig, azureProvider);
const storageStrategy = new StorageDeployment(
    storageConfig, azureStorageProvider);

// Execute deployments
executeDeployment(networkStrategy);
executeDeployment(storageStrategy);
```

In the code snippet, the `DeploymentStrategy` interface defines a common abstraction for deployments. The `NetworkDeployment` class implements this interface for provisioning networks, while `StorageDeployment` handles storage accounts. The `executeDeployment` function depends only on the `DeploymentStrategy` abstraction, allowing it to work with any deployment strategy. If a new type of resource, such as databases, needs to be added, you only need to create a new implementation of `DeploymentStrategy`, without altering the main logic.

This decoupling provides flexibility and scalability. For example, switching from Azure to AWS for storage doesn't require changes to the high-level deployment process; only the low-level storage implementation needs to be replaced.

Applying Gang of Four Design patterns to IaC

The **Gang of Four (GoF)** design patterns are a set of 23 classic solutions for common software design problems. They are common solutions for organizing code in a way that is reusable and easy to work with. These patterns are very helpful in IaC projects, where the infrastructure can get complicated quickly. Patterns such as Factory Method, Builder, and Singleton can make it easier to manage resources, reduce repetition, and handle complex setups step by step.

These patterns are especially useful when building **Internal Developer Platforms (IDPs)**. IDPs often need flexible, reusable infrastructure components that teams can adapt to their needs. Using GoF patterns helps create clean, consistent, and modular infrastructure code that simplifies this process.

Using the Factory Method pattern

The **Factory Method pattern** is useful when you need to create resources dynamically based on input, such as the environment or configuration. This helps standardize resource creation while allowing flexibility for different requirements.

The following code snippet demonstrates using the Factory Method pattern to create storage accounts based on the target environment:

```
import * as azure from "@pulumi/azure-native";

// Base class for storage factories
abstract class StorageFactory {
    abstract getSku(): azure.types.input.storage.SkuName;
    abstract getLocation(): string;
    createStorageAccount(name: string, resourceGroupName: string) {
```

```
            return new azure.storage.StorageAccount(name, {
                resourceGroupName,
                location: this.getLocation(),
                sku: { name: this.getSku() },
                kind: "StorageV2",
            });
        }
    }

    // Factory for development storage accounts
    class DevStorageFactory extends StorageFactory {
        getSku() {
            return "Standard_LRS";
        }

        getLocation() {
            return "WestUS";
        }
    }

    // Factory for production storage accounts
    class ProdStorageFactory extends StorageFactory {
        getSku() {
            return "Standard_GRS";
        }

        getLocation() {
            return "EastUS";
        }
    }

    // Function to decide which factory to use based on environment
    function getStorageFactory(environment: string): StorageFactory {
        if (environment === "dev") return new DevStorageFactory();
        if (environment === "prod") return new ProdStorageFactory();
        throw new Error(`Unknown environment: ${environment}`);
    }
```

```
// Create a storage account for the "dev" environment
const factory = getStorageFactory("dev");
const storageAccount = factory.createStorageAccount(
    "devstorage", "dev-rg"
);
```

This pattern lets you dynamically create resources for different environments without duplicating code.

Using the Builder pattern

The **Builder pattern** is ideal for creating resources that need multiple configurations. It breaks down the creation process into steps, making it easy to customize and reuse.

The following code snippet shows how the Builder pattern can create a web app with a configurable app service plan and settings:

```
class WebAppBuilder {
    private name: string;
    private resourceGroupName: string;
    private planId: string = "";
    private appSettings: { name: string; value: string }[] = [];

    constructor(name: string, resourceGroupName: string) {
        this.name = name;
        this.resourceGroupName = resourceGroupName;
    }

    setAppServicePlan(planId: string) {
        this.planId = planId;
        return this;
    }

    addAppSetting(key: string, value: string) {
        this.appSettings.push({ name: key, value: value });
        return this;
    }

    build() {
```

```
        return new azure.web.WebApp(this.name, {
            resourceGroupName: this.resourceGroupName,
            serverFarmId: this.planId,
            siteConfig: { appSettings: this.appSettings },
            location: "WestUS",
        });
    }
}


// Build a web app step by step
const webApp = new WebAppBuilder("dev-webapp", "dev-rg")
    .setAppServicePlan("/subscriptions/subId/resourceGroups/dev-rg/
providers/Microsoft.Web/serverfarms/dev-plan")
    .addAppSetting("ENVIRONMENT", "Development")
    .addAppSetting("API_URL", "https://dev.api.example.com")
    .build();
```

The Builder pattern makes creating configurable resources easier to read and maintain, which is especially useful in IDPs where developers may need custom setups for their applications.

Using the Singleton pattern

The **Singleton pattern** ensures that a single instance of a resource is created, which is useful for shared resources such as monitoring workspaces or logging setups.

The following code snippet demonstrates how the Singleton pattern manages a shared App Insights instance:

```
class AppInsights {
    private static instance: azure.insights.Component;

    static getInstance(resourceGroupName: string, location: string) {
        if (!AppInsights.instance) {
            AppInsights.instance = new azure.insights.Component("shared-
app-insights", {
                resourceGroupName,
                location,
                applicationType: "web",
            });
        }
```

```
        return AppInsights.instance;
    }
}


// Ensure only one App Insights instance exists
const appInsights = AppInsights.getInstance("shared-rg", "WestUS");
```

This ensures that all teams or environments using the IDP share the same App Insights instance, which avoids duplication and reduces costs.

While this book can't possibly show all the different ways to use the GoF patterns in your IaC, this is supposed to open your mind to the possibilities of applying software design principles to infrastructure management. These patterns are not just theoretical; they give you solutions to real-world challenges such as managing shared resources, handling configuration complexity, and adapting to different team or environment needs.

Using patterns such as Factory Method, Builder, and Singleton encourages consistency and scalability in your code base, which becomes critical as your projects grow in size and complexity. Beyond simplifying resource provisioning, they foster collaboration within teams by making your infrastructure code modular and understandable. For example, Factory Method can enable teams to easily switch environments or resource types without rewriting core logic, while the Builder pattern can standardize how configurations are created across multiple teams or services.

Moreover, these patterns can be extended far beyond what is covered here. You might use the Observer pattern to trigger alerts when certain infrastructure changes occur or the Strategy pattern to define different deployment methods for different application types. The goal is to spark your creativity so you can take these foundational ideas and adapt them to your unique use cases, whether you're building an IDP, a cloud-native application, or automating infrastructure at scale.

Ensuring infrastructure validity with basic assertions

Before deploying any infrastructure, it's important to validate configurations to ensure they meet your requirements. Basic assertions provide a simple way to catch common misconfigurations early in the development process. These checks allow you to confirm that critical parameters, such as resource locations or settings, are correctly configured before any infrastructure is provisioned. By performing these validations, you can save time and prevent costly mistakes that might otherwise only appear during deployment.

Basic assertions are especially useful when dealing with user-provided inputs, such as configuration files or environment variables. Instead of allowing invalid values to proceed to resource creation, assertions flag these issues early and provide clear feedback for corrections. For instance, you can verify that a storage account is configured to use the correct redundancy level or that it will be deployed to an approved region.

The following code demonstrates how to validate inputs for a storage account, using an array of acceptable values to enforce standards for configuration parameters:

```javascript
// Define acceptable values for validation
const allowedLocations = ["WestUS", "EastUS"];
const allowedSkus = ["Standard_LRS", "Standard_GRS"];

// Input parameters for storage account configuration
const config = new pulumi.Config();
const location = config.require("location");
const sku = config.require("sku");

// Assertions to validate inputs against allowed values
if (!allowedLocations.includes(location)) {
    throw new Error(`Invalid location: ${location}. Allowed locations
are:        ${allowedLocations.join(", ")}.`);
}

if (!allowedSkus.includes(sku)) {
    throw new Error(`Invalid SKU: ${sku}. Allowed SKUs are:
        ${allowedSkus.join(", ")}.`);
}

// Define the storage account only after inputs pass validation
const storageAccount = new azure.storage.
StorageAccount("validatedStorage,{
    resourceGroupName: "my-rg",
    location,
    sku: { name: sku },
    kind: "StorageV2",
});
```

In this example, the `allowedLocations` and `allowedSkus` arrays define the permissible values for the location and redundancy level of the storage account. The program retrieves these inputs using Pulumi's Config module and validates them against the allowed values. If an input doesn't match the expected values, the program provides a clear error message and halts execution. This ensures that only valid configurations proceed to resource creation.

The use of arrays for validation makes it easy to adapt to new requirements. For instance, adding a new location or SKU is as simple as updating the respective array. This approach provides flexibility while maintaining control over infrastructure configurations.

Basic assertions like these are an excellent starting point for ensuring infrastructure validity, but they are not sufficient for validating complex scenarios or interactions between resources. To address these needs, unit and integration testing come into play. Unit tests allow you to isolate specific parts of your infrastructure code, verifying that logic generates the correct resource definitions. Integration tests take this further by simulating real-world deployment scenarios, ensuring that resources interact correctly and perform as expected in a live environment.

While we've done a basic introduction here, the next chapter will cover testing in much more detail. It will guide you through setting up and automating unit and integration tests, running them in CI/CD pipelines, and debugging issues when they arise.

Consistent naming and documentation practices

The easiest way to help other developers find things in a large project is by naming classes, methods, and resources clearly and consistently. It sounds simple, but proper naming is one of the most effective ways to make infrastructure projects easier to understand and work with. When names are clear and follow a predictable pattern, teams can quickly identify resources, know what they are for, and avoid mistakes.

Consistent naming conventions improve collaboration and readability because they give everyone a shared understanding of how resources are named. For example, using a pattern such as `{environment}-{resource-type}-{name}` makes it obvious what a resource is, what it does, and where it belongs. A name such as `prod-app-db` instantly tells you this is a database for the production environment, while `dev-app-web` clearly points to a web app in the development environment. Without naming conventions like these, resources can become hard to track, especially in large projects with multiple environments and many contributors.

Bad naming habits can lead to big problems. For instance, if resource names don't follow a clear pattern, it can be hard to find the right resource when troubleshooting an issue. You might accidentally delete the wrong resource or waste time trying to figure out what something does. Inconsistent names also make onboarding new team members more difficult because they have to spend extra time learning how the project is organized. These problems grow worse as the project gets bigger and more people work on it.

Good naming conventions, on the other hand, keep your project organized and save time. Developers can trust that names make sense and follow the same rules everywhere. This is especially helpful in Pulumi projects, where infrastructure code defines many different resources. Clear names allow teams to scale their projects without worrying about losing track of what each resource does or where it belongs.

Establishing a naming convention

A good naming convention is built on three key principles: clarity, predictability, and adherence to standards. These principles ensure that resource names are easy to understand, follow a consistent structure, and align with any organizational or team-specific guidelines. When naming conventions are clear and predictable, they reduce confusion, improve collaboration, and make managing infrastructure simpler, even in large Pulumi projects.

Clarity means using names that accurately describe the resource's purpose and context. A clear name immediately tells you what the resource is, what it's used for, and where it belongs. For example, a storage account named `prod-storage-logs` clearly indicates that it is a storage account in the production environment used for logs. Compare this to a vague name such as `storage1`, which provides no useful information and could easily lead to mistakes.

Predictability ensures that naming follows a consistent format or pattern across the project. For Pulumi projects, a common pattern is `{environment}-{resource-type}-{name}`. This structure helps standardize naming while allowing enough flexibility to describe different types of resources. Here are some examples:

- `dev-app-web` refers to a web app in the development environment
- `prod-db-main` refers to the main database in production
- `test-storage-backups` refers to a storage account for backups in a testing environment

Using such patterns makes it easy to guess or deduce the name of a resource even if you've never worked with it before, saving time and reducing errors.

Adherence to standards ensures that your naming conventions align with broader organizational policies or cloud provider constraints. For example, Azure imposes limits on resource name lengths and allows only certain characters. Naming conventions should consider these restrictions while remaining consistent. For instance, a team might adopt a rule such as limiting names to 24 characters and using hyphens (-) as separators to comply with Azure's guidelines.

Prefixes and suffixes are especially important for differentiating between environments, regions, or versions:

- Using prefixes such as `prod-` or `dev-` makes it immediately clear which environment a resource belongs to, avoiding accidental changes to production resources
- Suffixes can help distinguish resources in different regions, such as `prod-app-web-us` for a US-based web app versus `prod-app-web-eu` for one in Europe
- Including versioning in names can make it easier to manage updates, such as `prod-app-v1` and `prod-app-v2`

Managing naming conventions manually for every resource in a project can quickly become error-prone and tedious, especially in large-scale infrastructure projects. Automating naming conventions not only ensures consistency but also helps maintain clean, organized code. Instead of creating separate naming logic for each resource, you can use a single utility function to generate all required resource names in one step. This simplifies resource management and ensures uniformity across teams and environments.

In a multi-team setup, including the project name, environment, and optionally the region in resource names is crucial. It prevents conflicts in shared environments and makes it easy to identify team-owned resources. A centralized utility, such as `generateResourceNames`, can automate this process, generating names for all required resources while adhering to organizational standards.

Here's an example of a utility function that generates consistent names for resources such as resource groups, storage accounts, key vaults, and traffic manager profiles:

```
// resource-name-generator.ts
export function generateResourceNames({
    project,
    environment,
    region,
}: {
    project: string;
    environment: string;
```

```
        region?: string;
    }): {
        resourceGroupName: string;
        storageAccountName: string;
        appName: string;
        trafficManagerName: string;
        keyVaultName: string;
    } {
        const baseName = `${project}-${environment}`;
        const regionSuffix = region ? `-${region}` : "";

        return {
            resourceGroupName: `${baseName}-rg${regionSuffix}`,
            storageAccountName: `${baseName}-storage${regionSuffix}`,
            appName: `${baseName}-app${regionSuffix}`,
            trafficManagerName: `${baseName}-tm${regionSuffix}`,
            keyVaultName: `${baseName}-kv${regionSuffix}`,
        };
    }
```

This function dynamically generates names based on the provided project, environment, and optional region. The returned object contains consistent names for various resources. Here's how you can use this utility in a Pulumi project:

```
import * as azure from "@pulumi/azure-native";
import { generateResourceNames } from "./resource-name-generator";

// Define parameters for naming
const project = "devex";
const environment = "prod";
const region = "us";

// Generate names for resources
const resourceNames = generateResourceNames({ project, environment, region
});

// Create a resource group
const resourceGroup = new azure.resources.ResourceGroup(resourceNames.
```

```
resourceGroupName, {
    location: "WestUS",
});

// Create a storage account
const storageAccount = new azure.storage.StorageAccount(resourceNames.
storageAccountName, {
    resourceGroupName: resourceGroup.name,
    location: resourceGroup.location,
    sku: { name: "Standard_LRS" },
    kind: "StorageV2",
});

// Create a key vault
const keyVault = new azure.keyvault.Vault(resourceNames.keyVaultName, {
    resourceGroupName: resourceGroup.name,
    location: resourceGroup.location,
    properties: {
        sku: { name: "standard" },
        tenantId: "your-tenant-id",
    },
});

// Create a traffic manager profile
const trafficManager = new azure.network.
TrafficManagerProfile(resourceNames.trafficManagerName, {
    resourceGroupName: resourceGroup.name,
    location: resourceGroup.location,
    trafficRoutingMethod: "Performance",
});
```

For a project named devex in the prod environment and us region, the generated names would
be as follows:

```
{
    "resourceGroupName": "teamA-prod-rg-us",
    "storageAccountName": "teamA-prod-storage-us",
    "appName": "teamA-prod-app-us",
```

```
        "trafficManagerName": "teamA-prod-tm-us",
        "keyVaultName": "teamA-prod-kv-us"
  }
```

This approach makes things clearer because the names show useful information about the project, environment, and purpose of each resource. In big organizations where many teams share the same environments, automated naming helps keep everything organized and easy to follow.

The role of good documentation

Documentation is one of the most important parts of any Pulumi project. It helps developers understand the project, especially when new team members join or when the project is handed over to another team. Without clear documentation, it can take a lot of time to figure out why certain decisions were made or how the project is structured.

Good documentation explains both *what* the code does and *why* it was done that way. For example, you should document the purpose of each resource, the naming rules you are following, and how the files are organized. If a specific region or redundancy setting was chosen, documenting the reason makes it easier for others to understand the project's requirements and avoid making changes that might cause problems. Documentation also helps developers quickly find what they need, making it easier to work together.

Over time, as a project grows, documentation becomes even more useful. It serves as a guide for making updates, fixing issues, or scaling the system. When teams change, having clear documentation ensures that new contributors can easily pick up where others left off.

To make documentation effective, it should include both an overview of the project and details where necessary. A README file can provide high-level information, while inline comments can explain specific parts of the code.

Using README files

Every project folder should have a **README** file that explains what the folder is for and what resources it manages. A README is like a quick guide for anyone working on the project.

Here's a simple outline for a Pulumi project README:

- **Project overview**: A short description of the project, its purpose, and the infrastructure it manages
- **Resource naming rules**: The naming conventions used in the project, with examples
- **File structure**: A description of the folders and files, and what they contain

- **Configuration details**: Information on required settings such as environment variables or Pulumi stack configurations
- **How to deploy**: Step-by-step instructions for running Pulumi and deploying the resources
- **Troubleshooting**: A section for common issues and how to fix them

Inline comments

Inline comments in your Pulumi code are also important. They explain why certain choices were made or how things work. Here are some examples:

- Document why a specific region was chosen for a resource
- Highlight connections between resources, such as why two resources need to be in the same resource group
- Explain any settings that aren't obvious, such as custom configurations

Here's an example of using inline comments:

```
import * as azure from "@pulumi/azure-native";

// Create the main resource group for the project
// This is where all resources for "teamA" will be organized
const resourceGroup = new azure.resources.ResourceGroup("teamA-rg", {
    location: "WestUS", // Selected for better performance for our users
                        //    in the US
});


// Create a storage account for log data
// Using Standard_LRS to keep storage costs low
const storageAccount = new azure.storage.StorageAccount("teamA-storage", {
    resourceGroupName: resourceGroup.name,
    location: resourceGroup.location,
    sku: { name: "Standard_LRS" },
    kind: "StorageV2",
});
```

Consistent naming and clear documentation are key to keeping Pulumi projects organized and easy to work with. Predictable names make it simple to understand what resources are for, while good documentation explains the reasoning behind decisions and provides a guide for navigating the project. They reduce confusion and help teams collaborate more effectively.

These practices also bring long-term benefits. They make debugging faster, as developers can quickly find and identify resources. As projects grow, they ensure that infrastructure remains structured and manageable, even with many resources or contributors.

Summary

In this chapter, we covered how to apply essential programming principles and practices to Pulumi projects to create infrastructure code that is modular, maintainable, and scalable. We discussed how to structure code with modular design and reusable components, using principles such as DRY and SOLID to reduce complexity and repetition. We looked at simple strategies such as basic assertions to catch errors early and how consistent naming and clear documentation make projects more organized and easier to navigate.

In the next chapter, we will cover testing and debugging your Pulumi IaC.

Questions

1. What is the primary benefit of modularizing Pulumi projects, and how can it improve code reuse?

2. Explain how the DRY principle applies to Pulumi infrastructure code. Can you provide an example?

3. How can SOLID principles, such as single responsibility and dependency inversion, be applied in Pulumi projects?

4. What is the purpose of using design patterns such as Factory Method or Builder in Pulumi projects?

5. What are the core components of a good naming convention for infrastructure resources?

13

Testing and Debugging Your Pulumi IaC

Testing helps us confirm that our **Infrastructure as Code (IaC)** works as expected. Just like we test application code, it's important to test our infrastructure to catch mistakes early, set things up securely, and make sure everything performs well in the cloud.

In this chapter, we'll cover why testing Pulumi programs matters and how to do it step by step. You'll learn about different types of testing, such as unit testing to check your code's logic without deploying it, and integration testing to check how everything works together once it's deployed. These methods help find and fix problems so you can trust your infrastructure.

We'll also explain how to set up tests in CI/CD pipelines so they run on their own whenever you make changes. Lastly, we'll cover how to debug Pulumi programs and solve problems when something goes wrong. By the end of this chapter, you'll know how to test and debug Pulumi projects in simple and practical ways, and this will help make your infrastructure work smoothly and as planned.

In this chapter, we're going to cover the following main topics:

- Introduction to testing in Pulumi
- Unit testing your Pulumi code
- Integration testing for Pulumi
- Automating tests in CI/CD pipelines
- Debugging Pulumi programs

Technical requirements

If you would like to follow along with the examples in this chapter, you will require the following:

- The Pulumi CLI is required for executing commands. You can download it here: `https://www.pulumi.com/docs/iac/download-install/`.

- Pulumi supports multiple programming languages, but for this chapter, we'll be using JavaScript/TypeScript, which requires Node.js. You can download and install it from the Node.js official site here: `https://nodejs.org/`.

Introduction to testing in Pulumi

It's not recommended to create infrastructure and deploy it in production without running some validations first. Without testing, there's a higher risk of making mistakes such as setting up resources incorrectly, exposing sensitive data, or using configurations that slow things down or cost more money. These issues might not seem obvious at first, but can lead to bigger problems such as security breaches, downtime, or unexpected costs.

Testing helps avoid these risks by catching errors early, before they affect production systems. It also ensures that your application behaves exactly as it should when running on the deployed infrastructure. For example, testing can confirm that a database is configured properly and is accessible only to the application, or that a load balancer routes traffic to the correct servers. Testing isn't just about verifying the infrastructure; it's also about validating that the application works as intended when it runs on that infrastructure.

By running tests during development, you can check that all components, both the infrastructure and the application, interact correctly. This helps uncover issues such as missing permissions, incorrect networking setups, or resource limitations that could break the application once it's deployed. Testing both the infrastructure and the application together gives you confidence that the system as a whole will work smoothly when it goes live.

With Pulumi, there are different things you can do to test your infrastructure, depending on what you need to validate. Let's look at three key approaches: unit testing, integration testing, and property testing.

Unit testing

Unit testing focuses on testing the logic of your Pulumi code in isolation, without deploying any resources to the cloud. With Pulumi's programming capabilities, you can write unit tests using your favorite testing frameworks, such as Mocha for JavaScript/TypeScript or pytest for Python. These tests rely on mocking cloud resources to simulate how they are created and configured.

Integration testing

Integration testing takes things a step further by deploying the infrastructure and verifying that it behaves as expected in a real environment.

For example, you might deploy a virtual network, a virtual machine, and an Azure SQL database. Once deployed, you can write and run tests to verify that the virtual machine has connectivity to the database, the network security rules allow traffic as expected, and the database is accepting connections with the correct authentication method.

Integration testing can also include running application-specific checks, such as ensuring an API deployed to Azure App Service can query the database and return the expected results. These tests give you confidence that both the infrastructure and the applications deployed on it function properly together.

Property testing

Property testing is about validating specific properties of the resources you create. These tests ensure that your infrastructure adheres to policies, standards, and best practices. For example, you can use Pulumi to verify that all virtual machines in Azure are deployed with managed disks, that storage accounts use private endpoints, or that **Azure Kubernetes Service** (**AKS**) clusters enforce **role-based access control** (**RBAC**).

While property testing ensures compliance at a detailed level, it also forms the basis for higher-level validation methods such as **Policy as Code**, which will be explored in *Chapter 14*. Policy as Code allows you to enforce rules across your infrastructure automatically, and this ensures that every resource deployed meets your organization's requirements.

With these fundamentals in mind, you're ready to dive deeper into testing strategies that will help you handle larger, more dynamic environments and address the challenges of real-world cloud deployments. Let's explore how to take your Pulumi testing practices to the next level.

Unit testing your Pulumi code

To write unit tests for your infrastructure, you need to validate the logic of your Pulumi code without deploying actual resources. Now, let's focus on a critical part of unit testing in Pulumi: mocking cloud resources.

Mocking is a technique used in unit testing to simulate the behavior of real systems without directly interacting with them. This means you can test your code's logic without creating actual resources in Azure or any other cloud environment. Mocking is essential because it speeds up testing, avoids costs, and provides a controlled environment for checking the correctness of your code.

Pulumi provides built-in support for mocking cloud resources using `pulumi.runtime.Mocks` and makes it easy to simulate the resources your program creates. For example, if your Pulumi program defines an Azure storage account, a mock can mimic the behavior of the storage account during the test. You can use mocks to verify specific properties, such as whether encryption is enabled or the storage tier is set correctly.

Working with mocks in Pulumi

You can work with mocks in Pulumi in the following three steps:

1. You define a mock class or function that simulates the behavior of your resources. For instance, if your Pulumi program creates any kind of resource (e.g., an Azure storage account), you can define a mock that returns specific properties.

```
import * as pulumi from "@pulumi/pulumi";
Class IaCMocks implements pulumi.runtime.Mocks {
    newResource(type: string, name: string, inputs: pulumi.
Inputs): { id: string; state: pulumi.Outputs } {
        return {
            id: `${name}-mock-id`, // Simulate resource ID
            state: { ...inputs }, // Pass through the inputs as the
state
        };
    }

    call(args: pulumi.runtime.MockCallArgs): Record<string, any> {
        return {};
    }
}
```

2. After creating your mocks, the next step would be to inject your mocks into the testing framework. When your Pulumi code runs, it interacts with the mocks instead of real cloud services. You can do this with the following line of code:

```
pulumi.runtime.setMocks(new IaCMocks());
```

> ♀ **Quick tip:** Enhance your coding experience with the **AI Code Explainer** and **Quick Copy** features. Open this book in the next-gen Packt Reader. Click the **Copy** button
>
> **(1)** to quickly copy code into your coding environment, or click the **Explain** button
>
> **(2)** to get the AI assistant to explain a block of code to you.

```
                                                    Copy      Explain

function calculate(a, b) {                           ①          ②
    return {sum: a + b};
};
```

> 🔖 **The next-gen Packt Reader** is included for free with the purchase of this book. Scan the QR code OR visit packtpub.com/unlock, then use the search bar to find this book by name. Double-check the edition shown to make sure you get the right one.

3. After writing your IaC code, defining your mocks and injecting them, you can now write tests to validate the logic of your Pulumi code using a testing framework such as Mocha and assertion libraries such as Chai. Here's an example of testing a Pulumi program that creates an Azure storage account:

```
import * as pulumi from "@pulumi/pulumi";
import { expect } from "chai";
import * as myProgram from "./index"; // Replace with your Pulumi
                                      // program file path


describe("Azure Storage Account", () => {
    before(() => {
        pulumi.runtime.setMocks(new IaCMocks());
```

```
});

it("should create a storage account with HTTPS-only enabled",
async () => {
    const httpsOnly = await myProgram.httpsOnly;
    expect(httpsOnly).to.be.true; // Assert HTTPS-only is
                                  // enabled
});

it("should have a specific name", async () => {
    const name = await myProgram.storageAccountName;
    expect(name).to.include("mystorageaccount"); // Assert the
                                                 // name contains
                                                 // "mystorageaccount"
});
});
```

The code for the corresponding Pulumi program is shown here:

```
import * as azure from "@pulumi/azure";
const storageAccount = new azure.storage.
Account("mystorageaccount", {
    resourceGroupName: "my-resource-group",
    location: "West Europe",
    accountTier: "Standard",
    accountReplicationType: "LRS",
    enableHttpsTrafficOnly: true,
});

export const storageAccountName = storageAccount.name;
export const httpsOnly = storageAccount.enableHttpsTrafficOnly;
```

This shows you what's possible with unit testing in Pulumi. However, there's a limit to the impact that this kind of testing can have on your overall **Infrastructure as Code (IaC)** workflow. While unit testing is great for validating the logic of your Pulumi programs and catching early-stage errors, it doesn't cover everything. The next section will discuss some of these limitations in detail.

Limitations of unit testing

Unit testing focuses on testing your code in isolation, using mocks to stand in for real cloud resources. While this is helpful, there are some things it can't handle:

- Unit tests don't check how resources interact once deployed. For example, suppose your Pulumi program creates an Azure function app and an Azure SQL database. A unit test can verify that both resources are defined and configured properly, but it won't test whether the function app has the correct permissions to connect to the database. This means you can't confirm that a GET request to your API will correctly query the database and return the expected results. These kinds of end-to-end interactions need to be validated to conclude that the infrastructure and application work well together and it's safe to do live deployments.

- Mocks are useful for testing your code, but they don't act exactly like real cloud services. For instance, a mock of an Azure storage account might pass all your tests, but during a real deployment, you could run into issues such as unsupported settings or conflicts with existing resources. These problems won't show up in unit tests.

- Unit tests don't account for real-world changes, like what happens during a network failure or how resources behave under heavy load. For example, testing whether a load balancer handles traffic correctly during a failover isn't something a unit test can do. These scenarios need to be tested in a deployed environment.

- Unit tests don't ensure that your resources follow organizational policies or best practices. For example, if your organization requires all databases to have encryption enabled or all function apps to use managed identities for secure access, unit tests won't validate these rules. Property testing or policy as code is better suited for these kinds of checks.

To test more scenarios holistically, you need to go beyond unit tests and validate how your infrastructure behaves in a real environment. The next section will focus on integration testing, where you'll deploy resources and ensure that they interact correctly to support real-world use cases, such as serving API requests and handling data securely.

Integration testing for Pulumi

Imagine you're building a social media application and you want to verify that the chat feature works as expected when you deploy new infrastructure. This isn't just about ensuring that your servers, databases, and APIs exist; it's about confirming that they are created correctly, configured properly, and function together as intended in a real-world environment.

This is where integration testing comes in. For this, you'd need to test that the application is live, that messages can be exchanged between two users, that data is stored and retrieved accurately, and that the infrastructure supports all these actions seamlessly.

In Pulumi, integration testing is a black-box testing approach where your Pulumi program is run through the Pulumi CLI to deploy infrastructure to an ephemeral environment, a temporary setup specifically for testing. Once the test is complete, the infrastructure is automatically destroyed. Unlike unit testing, which focuses on the logic of your program in isolation, integration testing deploys real infrastructure to verify that your program runs without errors and that the deployed resources behave as expected.

Here are some important checks that integration tests make:

- They confirm that your Pulumi program runs without any errors, meaning the code is written correctly.
- They verify that your stack settings, including sensitive data such as secrets, are applied properly.
- They check that the infrastructure can be deployed to your cloud provider without problems.
- They ensure that the right resources are created with the right settings – for example, making sure a function app has the correct environment variables or that a SQL database has proper access rules.
- They test that the deployed infrastructure behaves as it should. For instance, a health-check endpoint should respond correctly, or an API should handle requests as expected.
- They validate that updates to the infrastructure can be made smoothly, such as scaling a database or adding new resources, without breaking existing setups.
- They confirm that the infrastructure can be cleaned up properly, leaving no leftover resources in your cloud environment.

Pulumi integration tests don't directly interact with your program's internal code. Instead, they use the Pulumi CLI to deploy, update, and delete infrastructure as part of the testing process. This helps you verify that your program can handle real-world deployments, including applying configurations, running resources, and cleaning them up after use. By using integration tests, you can ensure your Pulumi program is ready for production.

Writing integration tests

Let's write an integration test for our infrastructure and application. Here, we will assume that the app binaries were zip deployed to an Azure function app as part of the infrastructure deployment process when running Pulumi up. The goal is to test our social media application's chat feature, ensuring that the deployed infrastructure supports its functionality. Specifically, we want to validate the following scenarios:

- The function app is live and accessible
- Two users can authenticate with the application using the provided API
- The users can send messages to each other using the messaging API, and the messages are stored and retrieved correctly

To achieve this, we'll deploy the infrastructure with Pulumi and write integration tests to simulate these scenarios. Here is the Pulumi code for setting up the infrastructure:

1. The following code defines an Azure function app that will host the chat application, including endpoints for authentication and messaging. The application binaries are packaged and uploaded as a ZIP file to Azure Storage, from where the function app will run:

```
import * as path from "path";

const resourceGroup = new azure_native.resources.ResourceGroup(
"resourceGroup", {
    location: "eastus",
    resourceGroupName: "my-resource-group",
});

const storageAccount = new azureNative.storage.StorageAccount(
"storageAccount", {
    ...
});
const appServicePlan = new azureNative.web.AppServicePlan(
"appServicePlan", {
    kind: "FunctionApp",
    ...
});
const functionAppFolder = "./function-app-code";
const zipFile = new pulumi.asset.AssetArchive({
```

```
    ".": new pulumi.asset.FileArchive(functionAppFolder),
});
const storageContainer = new azureNative.storage.BlobContainer(
"functionapp-container", {
    accountName: storageAccount.name,
});
const codeBlob = new azureNative.storage.Blob(
"functionapp-zip", {
    ...
    type: azureNative.storage.BlobType.Block,
    source: zipFile,
});

const codeBlobUrl = pulumi.interpolate`https://${storageAccount.
name}.blob.core.windows.net/${storageContainer.name}/${codeBlob.
name}`;

const primaryStorageKey = azureNative.storage
    .listStorageAccountKeysOutput({
        resourceGroupName: resourceGroup.name,
        accountName: storageAccount.name,
    }).keys[0].value;

const functionApp = new azureNative.web.WebApp("functionApp", {
    serverFarmId: appServicePlan.id,
    kind: "FunctionApp",
    siteConfig: {
        appSettings: [
            { name: "AzureWebJobsStorage",
              value: pulumi.
interpolate`DefaultEndpointsProtocol=https;
              AccountName=${storageAccount.name};
              AccountKey=${s primaryStorageKey}` },
            { name: "WEBSITE_RUN_FROM_PACKAGE", value: codeBlobUrl
},
        ],
    },
}, { dependsOn: [codeBlob] });
```

```
export const functionAppEndpoint = pulumi.
interpolate`https://${functionApp.defaultHostName}/api/`;
```

2. Now, let's write an integration test to validate the deployed infrastructure. The test will ensure the following:

    - The function app is live.

    - Two users can authenticate successfully.

    - The users can send and retrieve messages using the API.

3. Here's the integration test code using Mocha and `node-fetch`. To start, import all the necessary modules and dependencies, including Pulumi to access the deployed infrastructure, Chai for assertions, and `node-fetch` for making HTTP requests to the function app:

```
import * as pulumi from "@pulumi/pulumi";
import { expect } from "chai";
import fetch from "node-fetch";
import * as infra from "./index"; // Import the Pulumi program
```

This setup allows you to access the function app endpoint exported from the Pulumi program (`infra.functionAppEndpoint`) and perform assertions on API responses.

4. Next, define the test suite using Mocha's `describe` function as shown in the following code snippet. Set a timeout to allow enough time for the infrastructure to be deployed and accessible:

```
describe("Integration Test: Chat App", function () {
    this.timeout(300000); // Time for resource creation
});
```

5. In the `describe` block, add a `before` hook to retrieve the function app's endpoint before running any tests. The `before` hook ensures that this information is available for all subsequent test cases. See the following code snippet:

```
let functionAppEndpoint: string;
 before(async () => {
    // Get the Function App endpoint
    functionAppEndpoint = await infra.functionAppEndpoint;
});
```

6. The first test case in the following code snippet checks whether the function app is live. The snippet sends a `GET` request to the `healthcheck` endpoint and verifies that the response status is `200` and that the body includes the message **App is running**. This confirms that the function app is operational.

```
it("should validate that the Function App is live", async () => {
    // Send a request to the health-check endpoint
    const response = await fetch(`${functionAppEndpoint}
healthcheck`);
    const responseBody = await response.text();
    // Validate that the Function App is live
    expect(response.status).to.equal(200);
    expect(responseBody).to.include("App is running");
});
```

7. Next, the following snippet adds a test case to validate user authentication. Two `POST` requests are sent to the `auth/login` endpoint with credentials for two users. The responses are checked to ensure that both users receive valid authentication tokens.

```
it("should allow two users to authenticate", async () => {
    // User 1 authentication
    const user1AuthResponse = await fetch(`${functionAppEndpoint}
auth/login`, {
        method: "POST",
        headers: { "Content-Type": "application/json" },
        body: JSON.
stringify({ username: "user1", password: "password1" }),
    });
    const user1AuthBody = await user1AuthResponse.json();
    expect(user1AuthResponse.status).to.equal(200);
    expect(user1AuthBody.token).to.exist;
    // User 2 authentication
    const user2AuthResponse = await fetch(`${functionAppEndpoint}
auth/login`, {
        method: "POST",
        headers: { "Content-Type": "application/json" },
        body: JSON.
stringify({ username: "user2", password: "password2" }),
    });
```

```
            const user2AuthBody = await user2AuthResponse.json();
            expect(user2AuthResponse.status).to.equal(200);
            expect(user2AuthBody.token).to.exist;
    });
```

8. The following snippet adds the final test case to validate messaging functionality. User 1 sends a message to User 2 using the `messages/send` endpoint, and User 2 retrieves it using the `messages/inbox` endpoint. The test confirms that the message is successfully sent and retrieved.

```
    it("should allow users to send and retrieve messages", async () => {
        // User 1 sends a message to User 2
        const messageResponse = await fetch(`${functionAppEndpoint}
    messages/send`, {
            method: "POST",
            headers: { "Content-Type": "application/json" },
            body: JSON.stringify({
                from: "user1",
                to: "user2",
                message: "Hello, User 2!",
            }),
        });
        const messageBody = await messageResponse.json();
        expect(messageResponse.status).to.equal(200);
        expect(messageBody.status).to.equal("Message sent");
        // User 2 retrieves messages
        const inboxResponse = await fetch(`${functionAppEndpoint}
    messages/inbox?username=user2`);
        const inboxBody = await inboxResponse.json();
        expect(inboxResponse.status).to.equal(200);
        expect(inboxBody.messages).to.be.an("array").that.deep.
    includes({ from: "user1", message: "Hello, User 2!" });
    });
```

These integration tests simulate real-world usage of the function app and validate its health, authentication, and messaging functionality. By running these tests after deploying the infrastructure, you can confirm that the application behaves as expected and is ready for production use.

Testing deployments without Pulumi integration tests

Teams might opt out of mocked integration tests and instead deploy straight into a cloud sandbox because spinning up and maintaining realistic test doubles is often more work than it's worth, especially for complex services such as IAM policies, networking, or managed databases that don't behave the same under emulation because their existing CI/CD pipelines, monitoring, and manual QA processes are already geared toward real environments, because compliance or security requirements sometimes demand proof against actual resources, because smaller teams or tight deadlines can't afford the overhead of building and updating a full suite of stubs and mocks, and because the cost of ephemeral test deployments is outweighed by the confidence gained from exercising the real stack end to end. As a result, some teams prefer to deploy infrastructure into a real cloud environment and test it directly using their existing processes. This means actually standing up the infrastructure and running tests against it as if it were a production system, allowing you to see how it behaves in a live environment. This approach can be especially helpful for teams that already have a well-defined way of testing their applications and want to extend that process to include infrastructure validation.

To do this, you would deploy your infrastructure to a specific test environment, such as a staging subscription or a separate resource group. Once the deployment is complete, the testing process begins by interacting directly with the live environment. For example, you could make requests to the APIs your application exposes, simulate user workflows, or validate that all components are working as expected. This hands-on method allows you to test not only the individual resources but also how they interact with each other in a real-world setup.

This process often involves creating temporary environments that mirror production as closely as possible. After the tests are completed, the environment can be torn down to avoid unnecessary costs or resource clutter. Automating the creation and destruction of these environments is key to ensuring this approach doesn't become time-consuming or error-prone.

Testing in a live environment provides an opportunity to catch issues that might not show up during local testing or in mocked scenarios. It helps validate that your infrastructure works as intended and supports the application effectively. While this method requires more manual setup and monitoring, it aligns well with workflows that prioritize real-world validation over pre-deployment checks, and it gives you confidence that everything works as expected when it matters most.

Common challenges in integration testing

Integration testing can be very useful, but it also comes with challenges that teams often face. One common issue is handling network delays or timeouts, especially when working with cloud environments. Since integration tests interact with live infrastructure, network latency or temporary outages can cause tests to fail even when the infrastructure is working correctly. This can make it hard to tell whether a failure is due to the system being tested or an external issue. Another challenge is running tests in shared environments, where conflicts might occur if multiple tests try to access the same resources or make changes at the same time.

To deal with flaky tests caused by network issues, a simple solution is to use retries. For example, if a test fails because a resource wasn't ready or a network delay occurred, retrying the test a few seconds later can often solve the problem. You can implement retries with a simple loop or a utility function. Here's an example of how to retry a request:

```
async function fetchWithRetries(url: string, retries: number
= 3, delay: number = 2000): Promise<Response> {
    for (let attempt = 1; attempt <= retries; attempt++) {
        try {
            const response = await fetch(url);
            if (response.ok) return response;
        } catch (error) {
            if (attempt === retries) throw error;
            await new Promise((resolve) => setTimeout(resolve, delay));
        }
    }
    throw new Error("Request failed after retries");
}
```

For shared environments, conflicts can be avoided by isolating resources for each test. One way to do this is by giving resources unique names based on the test or the time it runs. For instance, appending a timestamp or a random ID to resource names ensures that each test uses its own set of resources, avoiding overlap with other tests. Here's an example of dynamically generating unique resource names:

```
const uniqueId = new Date().getTime();
const resourceName = `test-resource-${uniqueId}`;
```

Another option is to create entirely separate environments for each test, such as using different resource groups or accounts. This ensures tests don't interfere with one another. You can automate the creation of isolated environments in your Pulumi program like this:

```
const resourceGroup = new azureNative.resources.ResourceGroup(`test-rg-
${uniqueId}`);
```

These small adjustments help you avoid common pitfalls, so that you are able to focus on finding meaningful issues in the system rather than dealing with test failures caused by external factors. The next section will cover automating tests in your CI/CD pipelines.

Automating tests in CI/CD pipelines

In a typical CI/CD pipeline, the Pulumi test step fits between the build and deployment stages. Its purpose is to validate your infrastructure code to ensure that any issues are caught before the deployment step. By running the tests *after* the code is built but *before* any resources are provisioned, you can confirm that your infrastructure logic is correct and ready for deployment.

Imagine your CI/CD pipeline starts with a **build step** that compiles your application code and packages it for deployment. Once the build is successful, the pipeline moves to the **test step**, where Pulumi tests are run. This step checks for issues in your infrastructure code, such as incorrect configurations or missing dependencies. If the tests pass, the pipeline continues to the **deployment step**, where the infrastructure and application are deployed to the cloud.

```
name: CI/CD Pipeline
on: push
jobs:
  test:
    runs-on: ubuntu-latest
    steps:
      - name: Check out code
        uses: actions/checkout@v3
      - name: Install dependencies
        run: npm install
      - name: Run Pulumi tests
        run: npm test
  deploy:
    runs-on: ubuntu-latest
```

```
        needs: test
      steps:
        - name: Deploy to cloud
          run: pulumi up -y
```

In the preceding code snippet, the test step runs Pulumi tests right after the dependencies are installed, validating your infrastructure code. The deploy step only runs if the test step passes, preventing faulty code from being deployed. This approach tests the infrastructure thoroughly while keeping the pipeline configuration concise and easy to maintain.

For a pipeline that involves deploying to a staging environment and using external tools or mechanisms to test, the CI/CD pipeline includes a step to deploy the infrastructure and application to a temporary staging environment. Once deployed, other testing tools or automated workflows interact with the environment to validate functionality, performance, and reliability.

This type of pipeline often follows a structure like this:

1. **Build step**: The pipeline begins by building the application and packaging it for deployment.

2. **Deploy to test stack**: The pipeline deploys the infrastructure and application to a test stack (or staging environment). This environment is a temporary setup that mimics production as closely as possible. Pulumi's `pulumi up` command can be used here to automate the deployment.

3. **External testing**: After the deployment, external tools or scripts run tests against the live staging environment. For example, API endpoints can be tested for expected responses, user workflows can be simulated, and system behavior under load can be validated.

4. **Teardown**: Once the tests are complete, the staging environment is destroyed to save costs and clean up resources.

Here's an example of such a pipeline using GitHub Actions:

```
name: Staging Test Pipeline
on: push
jobs:
  deploy-and-test:
    runs-on: ubuntu-latest
    steps:
      - name: Check out code
```

```
    uses: actions/checkout@v3
  - name: Install Pulumi CLI
    uses: pulumi/actions@v3
  - name: Deploy to staging
    run: pulumi up -y --stack staging

  - name: Run external tests
    run: ./run-tests.sh
  - name: Teardown staging environment
    if: success() || failure() # Always run teardown
    run: pulumi destroy -y --stack staging
```

In this pipeline, the deployment step uses Pulumi to set up the staging environment with the infrastructure and application. The testing step runs external scripts, such as run-tests.sh, to check that the APIs and workflows work as expected. Finally, the teardown step removes the staging environment to avoid leaving any resources running. This method lets teams test real infrastructure in a flexible way without needing Pulumi integration tests. Now that you know the different ways to run tests, the next section will cover debugging Pulumi programs.

Debugging Pulumi Programs

When something goes wrong during a deployment, it can be caused by anything from a simple typo in the configuration to more complex issues such as misconfigured resources or missing dependencies. Here, you'll see some methods for troubleshooting and debugging Pulumi deployments, helping you identify and fix problems efficiently. Let's list them:

- **Using the Pulumi CLI**: The Pulumi CLI gives you detailed output during deployments that can help you identify issues. When running pulumi up, any errors encountered during the deployment process are displayed in the console, often with specific details about the failing resource and the associated issue. For example, if a required configuration value is missing or a resource property is invalid, the CLI will point to the problem. Reviewing the output carefully is one of the first steps in debugging Pulumi deployments.

- **Debugging resource definitions**: Many errors stem from incorrect resource definitions. For example, missing required properties, invalid values, or incorrect dependencies between resources can all cause failures. Breaking down complex resource configurations into simpler parts can help isolate issues. For instance, if you're deploying an Azure function app, check whether all required app settings are defined, such as the WEBSITE_RUN_FROM_PACKAGE setting for deploying code.

- **Adding debugging output:** You can add `console.log` statements or use Pulumi's `pulumi.log.info` to output debug information during the execution of your program. For example, you can log the value of dynamically generated resource names or check whether a configuration value is being read correctly. This helps track the flow of your program and identify where things might be going wrong. See the following code snippet for an example:

```
const storageAccount = new azureNative.storage.
StorageAccount("storageAccount", {
    resourceGroupName: resourceGroup.name,
    sku: {
        name: azureNative.storage.SkuName.Standard_LRS,
    },
    kind: azureNative.storage.Kind.StorageV2,
});

pulumi.log.info(`Storage Account Name: ${storageAccount.name}`);
```

- **Testing resources in isolation:** Sometimes, issues occur because of interactions between multiple resources in your stack. Deploying resources in isolation can help narrow down the problem. For example, if an Azure SQL database fails to connect with a function app, try deploying each resource separately to verify they are independently functional before testing their integration.

- **Using cloud provider tools:** For runtime issues or resource-specific errors, using the tools provided by your cloud provider can be helpful. In Azure, you can use the Azure portal to view logs, check resource health, or inspect metrics. For an Azure function app, the Log Stream feature or Kudu in the Azure portal are good places that can help identify errors in your application.

Testing and debugging are key to creating a solid infrastructure with Pulumi. They help catch problems early and confirm everything works as expected. This process improves the quality of infrastructure code and keeps it reliable for real-world applications.

Summary

In this chapter, we covered how testing and debugging play an important role in creating reliable Pulumi **Infrastructure as Code (IaC)** projects. We explored various testing methods, including unit testing for validating logic without deploying resources and integration testing to confirm infrastructure behaves as expected in real-world environments.

We also looked at how to automate tests in CI/CD pipelines and effectively debug Pulumi programs by using tools such as the Pulumi CLI and cloud provider diagnostics.

In the next chapter, we will cover policy as code.

Questions

1. What is the purpose of testing in Pulumi **Infrastructure as Code (IaC)** projects?

2. How does unit testing differ from integration testing in Pulumi?

3. What is the role of mocking in Pulumi unit tests, and why is it important?

4. What are some common challenges in writing unit tests for Pulumi programs?

5. Describe how to run Pulumi integration tests using a staging environment.

6. What is the advantage of using retries in integration tests?

14

Implementing Policy as Code

In modern infrastructure management, ensuring that systems are secure, efficient, and compliant with organizational standards is essential. This is where **property testing** plays a critical role. Property testing is a method for checking whether certain rules or **properties** are true about a system, such as making sure a server is configured securely or a network is set up to prevent unauthorized access.

Policy as code (**PaC**) takes this concept further by turning these rules into automated, programmable policies. Using Pulumi's policy framework, you can define and enforce these rules directly within your infrastructure code. Instead of manually reviewing configurations, policies written in code allow for quick, consistent checks during every deployment. This helps teams catch issues early, improve security, and align infrastructure with best practices automatically.

This chapter will guide you through the process of implementing PaC with Pulumi. You'll learn how to define policies using familiar programming languages, apply them to your infrastructure, and integrate these checks into your CI/CD pipelines. By the end of this chapter, you'll have the skills to automate governance and compliance, making your infrastructure deployments more reliable and secure.

In this chapter, we're going to cover the following main topics:

- Introduction to PaC
- Writing and defining policies
- Applying policies to infrastructure

Technical requirements

If you would like to follow along with the examples in this chapter, you will require the following:

- The Pulumi CLI is required for executing commands. You can download it from here: `https://www.pulumi.com/docs/iac/download-install/`.

- Pulumi supports multiple programming languages, but for this chapter, we'll be using JavaScript/TypeScript, which requires Node.js. You can download and install it from the Node.js official site here: `https://nodejs.org/`.

Introduction to PaC

Beyond defining application infrastructure, you can use code to set rules and enforce standards for how that infrastructure is built and managed. This approach, known as PaC, allows organizations to encode compliance, security, and operational requirements directly into their infrastructure code base. Instead of relying on manual checks or external audits, PaC ensures these rules are applied consistently and automatically during every deployment.

In the context of cloud infrastructure, PaC acts as a property testing method. Property testing is about verifying whether a system adheres to specific rules or properties, such as ensuring all storage accounts are encrypted, network traffic is restricted to secure channels, or compute instances are appropriately sized for workloads. By adding these checks as policies in your infrastructure code, you can spot problems early, even before your systems go live.

With the pace and scale at which we interact with cloud environments today, it's easy for things to go wrong. Teams often manage hundreds or thousands of resources across different environments, which can lead to different kinds of mistakes. PaC helps solve these problems by automating the process of checking and enforcing standards.

Using PaC has many important benefits. One of the biggest is that it lets you automate compliance and governance checks. Instead of having people manually check whether resources follow organization rules, you can write these rules as code. This means every deployment is automatically checked against the policies you've created. For example, you can make sure all storage accounts have encryption turned on or that virtual machines are only deployed in approved regions, without needing to check each one yourself.

Another great benefit is that it helps keep things consistent across different environments. Whether you're deploying to development, testing, or production, the same rules are applied every time. This consistency reduces the chance of mistakes that could cause problems later. It also helps ensure that your systems work as expected, no matter where they are deployed.

PaC also saves time by reducing the need for manual work. Manually reviewing and fixing configurations can take a lot of effort, especially if you're managing a large number of resources. Automated policy checks handle this for you, so your team can spend more time focusing on improving your infrastructure instead of fixing mistakes. This is especially helpful for organizations with hundreds or thousands of resources to manage.

PaC also makes your systems more secure and reliable. Best practices, such as using encryption, limiting public access, or sticking to approved configurations, are automatically enforced. This lowers the risk of mistakes or vulnerabilities that could cause security issues. It also ensures that resources are deployed in a stable, predictable way.

How PaC works in Pulumi

Pulumi's policy framework is central to CrossGuard, a product that enables PaC by providing a framework to define, enforce, and manage infrastructure governance directly in your Pulumi projects. It allows policies to be written as code using popular programming languages such as TypeScript, JavaScript, and Python, the same way you can create IaC declarations using regular programming languages. These policies can validate resources in a Pulumi stack and enforce rules during the deployment process (`pulumi preview` and `pulumi up`). For example, a policy might prevent deploying publicly readable storage buckets or require that virtual machines include specific security configurations.

This automation ensures that non-compliant resources are flagged or remediated before they are created or updated.

During `pulumi preview` or `pulumi up`, the engine checks resource inputs against resource policies before any changes are made. If a violation is detected, it either flags the issue, halts the deployment, or applies a remediation to fix the resource.

Policies in Pulumi are written as **validation functions**. These functions are evaluated against resources in a stack and determine whether they meet specific rules. If a resource violates a policy, the `reportViolation` method flags it. Policies can also include **remediations**, which automatically adjust the resource's properties to bring it into compliance:

- A validation function might ensure that storage buckets are not publicly accessible
- A remediation can automatically change the bucket's access control settings to `private` if a violation is detected

When organizing these policies, Pulumi uses a **policy pack**. A policy pack is a collection of related policies grouped together for better management and enforcement. For example, an organization might create a policy pack for security best practices, another for cost management, or separate packs for AWS and Kubernetes policies. Each policy pack includes a name for easy identification, a list of policies it enforces, and an enforcement level for each policy, such as the following:

- **Advisory**: Logs warnings for policy violations but allows the deployment to continue
- **Mandatory**: Stops the deployment if a violation is detected
- **Remediate**: Fixes violations automatically where possible
- **Disabled**: Disables the policy entirely

There are two types of policies in Pulumi:

- **Resource policies**: These validate individual resources before they are created or updated. For example, you might use a resource policy to ensure that all Azure function apps use Linux. Resource policies can also include remediations to fix issues automatically.
- **Stack policies**: These validate all resources in a stack after they have been created or updated. Stack policies are useful for checks involving multiple resources, such as ensuring that a load balancer is configured to route traffic to specific instances. However, they cannot remediate issues and only flag violations.

Now that you have an insight into the different types of policies and how PaC works, let's look at some use cases and how we can apply them.

Use cases for PaC

Here are some use cases that illustrate how PaC improves infrastructure management and helps teams maintain control.

Enforcing security standards

This is one of the ways PaC makes a difference in cloud infrastructure. Let's say you have a storage account; you can write a policy that checks whether encryption is enabled. If it's not, the policy can either stop the deployment or fix it by turning encryption on. You can also use policies to secure your network by ensuring only approved IP addresses can access certain resources or that firewalls are properly set up. These kinds of automated checks make it easier to protect sensitive data and avoid security gaps.

Validating resource configurations

Validating resource configurations is another important use of PAC. For example, in Azure, you can use policies to check whether App Service Plans are set to the right pricing tier. You might require all non-production plans to use the B1 tier to keep costs low. A policy can also check whether important tags such as Environment or Owner are added to the App Service Plans to make it easier to track and manage resources. If something doesn't match the rules, the policy can either flag the issue or automatically fix it, such as switching the pricing tier or adding the missing tags. This helps keep infrastructure organized and cost-effective without relying only on checks such as PR reviews.

Auditing infrastructure for regulatory compliance

Auditing infrastructure for regulatory compliance is another powerful use of PaC, especially in industries such as finance, healthcare, or government, where compliance is non-negotiable. With PaC, you can automate certain compliance checks, such as ensuring that databases have encryption at rest enabled, access logs configured, and backups scheduled. A policy might also validate that resources are deployed only in approved Azure regions to meet data residency rules.

While PaC helps with compliance, it's important to remember that it's only one part of the solution. Compliance involves more than just checking infrastructure. It includes things such as proper data handling, audits, and documentation. Take GDPR as an example. PaC can enforce technical rules, such as ensuring that resources are deployed in EU regions or making sure encryption is enabled for databases. But meeting GDPR requirements also means managing how personal data is collected, processed, and deleted. PaC handles the technical side of compliance efficiently, but achieving full compliance requires addressing both technical and operational aspects.

Preventing misconfigurations

Misconfigurations are a major cause of security problems, performance issues, and even outages in cloud environments. PaC can help catch these issues early, during deployment. For example, imagine you're building an application that uses an Azure function app to process user requests and an Azure SQL database to store the data. A misconfiguration, such as failing to assign the correct managed identity role for the function app to access the database, could prevent the app from working properly or open up security risks if overly permissive roles are used.

With PaC, you can write a policy to check that the function app is assigned the correct db_datareader or db_datawriter roles in the database, ensuring it has just enough access to perform its tasks.

Another policy could validate that the database is deployed with geo-redundant backups enabled to protect against data loss. When you catch these configuration issues during deployment, PaC helps make sure your app runs securely and efficiently. It reduces the risk of downtime caused by misconfigurations and helps prevent vulnerabilities that could expose sensitive data or disrupt your application.

You've seen that PaC can help catch misconfigurations, enforce security, and maintain compliance in your infrastructure, but to make it truly effective, you need to know how to write and define the policies that enforce these rules. In the next section, we'll explore how to create these policies using code and customize them to fit your organization's specific needs.

Writing and defining policies

To start writing policies in Pulumi using TypeScript, it's important to understand the structure of a policy and how it's defined. Policies in Pulumi are written as validation functions, and their primary role is to check whether resources meet specific requirements. A policy typically includes key components such as a name, description, enforcement level, and the validation logic that checks resource configurations against your rules.

Here's a simple example to demonstrate these components. Imagine you want to ensure that all Azure storage accounts in your stack have encryption enabled. The policy would need to validate the properties of each storage account to confirm that encryption is configured correctly.

The structure of such a policy looks like this:

```
const ensureStorageEncryption: ResourceValidationPolicy = {
    name: "ensure-storage-encryption",
    description: "Ensures that all Azure storage accounts have
encryption                      enabled.",
    enforcementLevel: "mandatory", // Stops deployment if the policy is
                                   // violated
    validateResource: validateResourceOfType(azure.storage.
StorageAccount,    (storageAccount, args, reportViolation) => {
        // Check if encryption is enabled for blob services
        if (
        !storageAccount.encryption || storageAccount.encryption.
services?.        blob?.enabled !== true
        ) {
            reportViolation("Encryption must be enabled for all Azure
                    storage accounts.");
```

```
            }
    }),
};
```

In this example, `name` identifies the policy, making it easier to manage within a policy pack. `description` explains what the policy enforces. `enforcementLevel` is set to "mandatory", which means the deployment will stop if the policy is violated. Finally, the validation logic uses the `validateResource` function to inspect each resource in the stack. If the resource is an Azure storage account and encryption is not enabled, the `reportViolation` function flags the resource as non-compliant.

To get started with writing a policy to validate Azure resources using Pulumi, the first step is to scaffold a new policy pack project. You can do this using Pulumi's command-line tools. Begin by running the following command:

```
pulumi policy new azure-typescript
```

This initializes a new policy pack project using TypeScript with a template geared toward Azure resources. The project will include the necessary dependencies and a basic structure for defining policies. Once the project is created, navigate into the project directory and open the `index.ts` file, which is where your policies will be defined.

Let's walk through creating a policy that ensures Azure function apps are configured with the correct pricing tier. This is critical to avoid unnecessary costs in non-production environments or to enforce scalability requirements in production. For this example, we will validate that function apps use the `Consumption` or `Premium` tier, depending on the environment:

1. First, update the `index.ts` file to define the policy:

```
import * as azure from "@pulumi/azure-native";
import { ResourceValidationPolicy, validateResourceOfType,
PolicyPack } from "@pulumi/policy";

const functionAppPricingPolicy: ResourceValidationPolicy = {
    name: "validate-function-app-pricing",
    description: "Ensures Azure Function Apps use the correct
pricing tier based on the environment.",
    enforcementLevel: "mandatory", // Halts deployment if the policy
is violated
    validateResource: validateResourceOfType(azure.web.
AppServicePlan, (appServicePlan, args, reportViolation) => {
```

```
            // Determine the deployment environment from the stack tags
            const environment = args.stack.tags?.Environment
|| "unknown";


            // Define allowed pricing tiers for each environment
            const allowedTiersByEnvironment: { [key: string]: string[] }
= {
                production: ["Premium"], // Production environments must
use Premium
                staging: ["Consumption", "Premium"], // Staging
environments can use Consumption or Premium
                development: ["Consumption"], // Development
environments must use Consumption
            };


            // Get the allowed tiers for the current environment
            const allowedTiers = allowedTiersByEnvironment[environment.
toLowerCase()] || [];


            // Check if the App Service Plan's pricing tier is valid for
the environment
            if (!allowedTiers.includes(appServicePlan.sku?.tier
|| "")) {
                reportViolation(
                    `Invalid pricing tier '${appServicePlan.
sku?.tier}' for Azure Function App in
'${environment}' environment. Allowed tiers are: ${allowedTiers.
join(", ")}.`
                );
            }
        }),
    };
```

In this policy, the validateResourceOfType function is used to focus specifically on resources of the AppServicePlan type, which defines the pricing tier for Azure function
apps. The appServicePlan.sku.tier property is validated against an array of allowed
tiers. If the pricing tier doesn't match the allowed options for the environment, the policy
uses reportViolation to flag the issue with a clear message indicating what is wrong
and what is expected.

2. Next, add this policy to the policy pack so it can be applied during deployment. Modify the index.ts file to include the policy in a policy pack:

```
new PolicyPack("azure-function-app-policies", {
    enforcementLevel: "mandatory",
    policies: [functionAppPricingPolicy],
});
```

This groups functionAppPricingPolicy into a named policy pack called azure-function-app-policies. A policy pack is a way to manage and enforce multiple policies together, making it easier to apply a set of governance rules across your Azure infrastructure. For example, alongside functionAppPricingPolicy, you could add a policy to ensure that all Azure storage accounts have secure transfer enabled. This allows you to define and enforce multiple rules within the same pack.

Here's how you can add another policy to the same policy pack:

```
const secureStoragePolicy: ResourceValidationPolicy = {
    name: "secure-storage-account",
    description: "Ensures that secure transfer is enabled for all
Azure Storage Accounts.",
    enforcementLevel: "mandatory",
    validateResource: validateResourceOfType(azure.storage.
StorageAccount, (storageAccount, args, reportViolation) => {
        // Check if secure transfer is enabled
        if (!storageAccount.enableHttpsTrafficOnly) {
            reportViolation("Secure transfer (HTTPS only) must be
enabled for all Azure Storage Accounts.");
        }
    }),
};

// Group the policies in a Policy Pack
new PolicyPack("azure-function-app-policies", {
    enforcementLevel: "mandatory",
    policies: [functionAppPricingPolicy, secureStoragePolicy],
});
```

Now, the policy pack contains both functionAppPricingPolicy and secureStoragePolicy. This structure allows you to manage policies for different resources, such as function apps and storage accounts, in a centralized and reusable way.

3. Once the policy is defined, you can test it. Run the following command in your project directory:

```
pulumi preview --policy-pack .
```

If you are not in the project directory, run the following command:

```
pulumi preview --policy-pack <path-to-directory>
```

This applies the policy pack to the stack and checks resources against the defined policies. If a function app is deployed with a pricing tier outside the allowed options, the reportViolation function halts the deployment and displays an error message, as in this example:

```
Policy Violation: validate-function-app-pricing
Invalid pricing tier 'Basic' for Azure Function App. Allowed tiers
are: Consumption, Premium.
```

When you follow these steps, you'd create a custom policy to validate individual Azure function apps and Azure storage configurations. Now that you know how to define these policies, let's see how to automate policy checks for our infrastructure projects.

Applying policies to infrastructure

In a production environment, you won't be able to run pulumi preview manually, and you'd need to automate the policy checks because that's where the critical deployments happen. To automate policy checks, you integrate Pulumi's policy packs directly into your pipeline workflow. For example, if you are using GitHub Actions, you can configure a pipeline that runs Pulumi commands with policy enforcement during each deployment. Here's how the workflow might look:

```
name: Production Deployment
on:
  push:
    branches:
      - release
jobs:
  deploy:
```

```
runs-on: ubuntu-latest
steps:
  - name: Checkout code
    uses: actions/checkout@v3
  - name: Set up Node.js
    uses: actions/setup-node@v3
    with:
      node-version: '18.x'
  - name: Install Pulumi CLI
    uses: pulumi/actions-install-pulumi-cli@v1
   - name: Install dependencies
   run: npm install
  - name: Deploy with Pulumi
    env:
      PULUMI_ACCESS_TOKEN: ${{ secrets.PULUMI_ACCESS_TOKEN }}
    run: pulumi up --policy-pack ./path-to-policy-pack --yes
```

In this example, the workflow is triggered on a push to the release branch, which may represent a production deployment. After checking out the repository and setting up the required environment, the pipeline runs pulumi up with the --policy-pack flag to enforce the policies defined in your policy pack. If a policy violation is detected, the deployment will fail, and the issue will be reported in the pipeline logs, preventing non-compliant resources from being deployed.

This is something you can do with other CI/CD tools such as Azure Pipelines, CircleCI, GitLab CI, and more. By integrating Pulumi policy packs into these pipelines, you can automate policy checks as part of your **infrastructure as code** (IaC) deployments, regardless of the tools your team uses. This ensures every deployment is validated against organizational standards before reaching production, no matter the platform.

For teams with dedicated security engineers, this approach becomes even more powerful. Security engineers can take the lead in defining critical policies that enforce compliance, security, and best practices. They can create policy packs tailored to the organization's requirements, ensuring that all deployments adhere to these rules automatically. Developers can then focus on building infrastructure while the policies act as guardrails that catch issues like misconfigurations or non-compliance before they become problems.

Summary

In this chapter, we covered the foundational concepts of PaC and its implementation using Pulumi. From understanding how policies enforce compliance and security to writing effective policies in TypeScript and automating their application in CI/CD pipelines, you've gained the skills to integrate governance into your infrastructure deployments. When you apply these principles, you can make sure that your systems are secure, compliant, and aligned with organizational standards, all while minimizing manual oversight.

In the next chapter, we will cover how to migrate from other tools to Pulumi.

Questions

1.   What is PaC, and how does it relate to IaC?

2.   What are the different enforcement levels available for Pulumi policies, and what do they do?

3.   How does Pulumi handle a policy violation during a deployment?

4.   What is a policy pack, and how is it used in Pulumi?

5.   What is the difference between a resource policy and a stack policy in Pulumi?

6.   How can policy packs be integrated into CI/CD pipelines for automated validation?

7.   How do you define and test a policy locally before integrating it into a pipeline?

15

Migrating from Other Tools to Pulumi

You may already be familiar with other kinds of IaC tools, and you might be looking to switch to Pulumi. Making the switch requires more than simply rewriting code; it involves understanding the fundamental differences in how Pulumi operates compared to other frameworks. This chapter is designed to guide you through the migration process, highlighting key considerations and providing practical steps for transitioning from tools such as Terraform, AWS CloudFormation, Azure Resource Manager, Kubernetes YAML, or Helm.

As you explore this chapter, you'll learn how to translate your existing configurations into Pulumi code. Each section will focus on specific tools, demonstrating how to coexist with or migrate away from them, ensuring minimal disruption to your current systems. By the end, you'll be equipped with strategies for minimizing downtime, managing gradual migrations, and adopting Pulumi at scale within your organization, making the transition as smooth as possible.

In this chapter, we're going to cover the following main topics:

- Introduction to migration
- Migrating from Terraform to Pulumi
- Migrating from AWS CloudFormation to Pulumi
- Migrating from Azure Resource Manager or Azure Bicep to Pulumi
- Migrating from Kubernetes YAML or Helm to Pulumi
- Migrating from any other cloud to Pulumi
- Best practices for minimizing downtime during migration

Technical requirements

If you would like to follow along with the examples in this chapter, you will require the following:

- The **Pulumi CLI** is required for executing commands. You can download it from here: `https://www.pulumi.com/docs/iac/download-install/`.

- Pulumi supports multiple programming languages, but for this chapter, we'll be using JavaScript/TypeScript, which requires Node.js. You can download and install it from the Node.js official site here: `https://nodejs.org/`.

Introduction to migration

Migrating requires moving your existing infrastructure setup from one tool to another, which can affect everything from how resources are provisioned to how they are managed long-term. This shift involves more than just rewriting configurations; it requires careful planning and consideration to avoid unnecessary disruptions. As a result, it's crucial to carry out informed decision-making to determine whether migrating to Pulumi aligns with your current and future infrastructure needs. This process starts with understanding the key differences between Pulumi and the tools you currently use, as well as the unique advantages Pulumi offers.

Pulumi stands out because of its programming model, which allows you to use familiar languages such as TypeScript, Python, Go, and C#. This means you can apply standard programming practices, such as loops, conditionals, and reusable modules, to define and manage your infrastructure. Additionally, Pulumi's multi-language support makes it flexible for teams with diverse skill sets, enabling collaboration without requiring a single tool or language expertise. Beyond its programming capabilities, Pulumi simplifies state management and supports resource importing, making it easier to transition from existing setups without losing track of your infrastructure's history.

When considering migration, it's essential to evaluate whether Pulumi can address the challenges you face with your current tools. For instance, if you've struggled with the limitations of declarative approaches, Pulumi's imperative style might be a better fit. Similarly, if your team has been using Azure Bicep for their Azure infrastructure and now wants to go multicloud, and as a result, they need a unified approach for managing cloud resources across multiple providers, Pulumi could be a good solution.

In addition to assessing Pulumi's features, you must analyze your current infrastructure. What does your existing setup look like? Are your configurations straightforward, or do they include complex interdependencies that could complicate migration? Is your infrastructure relatively static, or do you frequently need to update and scale resources? Answering these questions will help you gauge whether Pulumi can meet your needs and how much effort will be required to make the transition.

Finally, the decision to migrate should take into account the long-term benefits versus the short-term effort. Migration can simplify how you manage infrastructure, improve maintainability, and open doors to features that weren't available in your current tool. However, it also requires a commitment of time and resources to plan, test, and implement. By the end of this chapter, you'll have a clear understanding of how to migrate to Pulumi from other tools, and you'll also learn about migration best practices.

Migrating from Terraform to Pulumi

Migrating from Terraform to Pulumi can be done in several ways, including coexisting with existing Terraform workspaces, converting HCL configurations to Pulumi code, and integrating Pulumi into your current Terraform-based workflows.

Coexisting with existing Terraform workspaces

If you have infrastructure already managed by Terraform, an immediate full migration to Pulumi might not be feasible. Fortunately, Pulumi allows you to coexist with your existing Terraform workflows by referencing Terraform state files (`.tfstate`). Pulumi's `RemoteStateReference` resource lets you seamlessly access outputs from Terraform-managed infrastructure and integrate them into Pulumi programs.

For example, if your Terraform state file contains outputs such as AWS VPC IDs or subnet IDs, you can use these directly in Pulumi.

Install Pulumi's Terraform plugin through your CLI using the following command:

```
npm install @pulumi/terraform
```

Reference the Terraform state in your Pulumi program, similar to the following code snippet:

```
import * as pulumi from "@pulumi/pulumi";
import * as aws from "@pulumi/aws";
import * as tf from "@pulumi/terraform";
```

```
// Reference the Terraform state file
const tfState = new tf.state.RemoteStateReference("tfstate", {
    backendType: "local",
    path: "terraform.tfstate",
});

// Access outputs from the Terraform state
const vpcId = tfState.getOutput("vpc_id");
const subnetIds = tfState.getOutput("subnet_ids");

// Use the outputs in Pulumi
const server = new aws.ec2.Instance("server", {
    instanceType: "t2.micro",
    ami: "ami-0c55b159cbfafe1f0",
    subnetId: subnetIds[0],
    vpcSecurityGroupIds: [vpcId],
});
```

This approach enables you to manage new resources with Pulumi while continuing to rely on Terraform for existing infrastructure. This coexistence reduces the risk of disruptions and provides flexibility to adopt Pulumi incrementally.

Converting HCL configurations to Pulumi code

One of the most significant hurdles in migration is translating your existing Terraform configurations into Pulumi's programming model. Pulumi simplifies this with a conversion tool that automatically transforms Terraform HCL code into Pulumi programs written in TypeScript, Python, Go, or C#.

To perform a conversion, navigate to your Terraform project directory and run the Pulumi conversion command:

```
pulumi convert --from terraform --language typescript
```

This command generates a Pulumi program that replicates your Terraform configuration in the language of your choice. For example, let's say you had Terraform code that looked like the following snippet:

```
resource "aws_s3_bucket" "example" {
  bucket = "my-example-bucket"
```

```
    acl    = "private"
}
```

After conversion, it will look similar to the following TypeScript code:

```typescript
import * as aws from "@pulumi/aws";

const example = new aws.s3.Bucket("example", {
    bucket: "my-example-bucket",
    acl: "private",
});
```

After the conversion, you can refine the generated code to align with Pulumi's best practices, such as modularizing infrastructure or taking advantage of loops and functions.

Integrating Pulumi into Terraform-based workflows

Migrating from Terraform to Pulumi doesn't have to happen all at once. You can *gradually introduce* Pulumi into your current workflows while continuing to use Terraform for parts of your infrastructure.

You can start by managing new resources with Pulumi while keeping your existing infrastructure under Terraform. For instance, if Terraform already manages your network (such as VPCs or subnets), you can use Pulumi to handle other resources, such as servers, storage, or Kubernetes clusters.

You can also decide to move things gradually. Instead of switching everything at once, you can move parts of your infrastructure to Pulumi step by step. Start with simpler resources such as storage buckets or IAM roles, and move to more complex resources such as databases or networks later. This lets you test each part and make sure everything works before moving on.

Pulumi has a feature called **resource importing**, which makes it easier to bring existing resources under Pulumi's control. For example, if you already have an S3 bucket managed by Terraform, you can import it into Pulumi with this command:

```
pulumi import aws:s3/bucket:Bucket my-bucket my-storage-bucket
```

Once imported, you can manage the bucket using Pulumi without losing the existing setup. This gives you a clue on how to move your Terraform declarations to Pulumi. Let's look at how to also do this for AWS CloudFormation.

Migrating from AWS CloudFormation to Pulumi

You may want to migrate from CloudFormation to Pulumi to take advantage of multi-cloud support, allowing you to manage resources beyond AWS in one place. To do this, you can start by keeping your current CloudFormation stacks, then gradually move to Pulumi by importing resources or rewriting your templates. This way, you can make the transition without disrupting your existing infrastructure.

Working with CloudFormation and Pulumi together

You don't have to stop using CloudFormation right away. Pulumi lets you work with your existing CloudFormation stacks while you begin using it for new resources. For example, if CloudFormation is already managing your network, such as VPCs or subnets, you can use Pulumi to deploy things such as servers or storage in that network.

Here's an example of referencing a CloudFormation stack from Pulumi:

```
import * as aws from "@pulumi/aws";

// Reference the CloudFormation stack
const networkStack = aws.cloudformation.getStackOutput({
    name: "my-network",
});

// Use a subnet ID from the CloudFormation stack
const subnetId = networkStack.outputs["SubnetId"];

// Deploy a new EC2 instance using Pulumi
const instance = new aws.ec2.Instance("exampleInstance", {
    instanceType: "t2.micro",
    ami: "ami-0c55b159cbfafe1f0",
    subnetId: subnetId,
});
```

This allows you to build new things with Pulumi while keeping the resources managed by Cloud-Formation untouched.

Importing resources into Pulumi

If you want Pulumi to take over managing specific resources, you can import them. This is helpful for gradually moving away from CloudFormation without deleting or recreating resources. Before importing, ensure the CloudFormation stack won't delete your resource. For example, add this to its template definition:

```
DeletionPolicy: Retain
```

You can also remove the resource from the template altogether so that future stack updates won't destroy it. Then, import it into Pulumi like this:

```
const bucket = new aws.s3.Bucket("myBucket", {}, { import: "my-example-
bucket" });
```

Now, Pulumi manages the S3 bucket. You can update it using Pulumi while keeping the existing setup.

Converting CloudFormation templates to Pulumi code

Instead of moving everything at once, you can convert CloudFormation templates into Pulumi code piece by piece. Start with smaller resources, then move on to more complex ones.

For example, take this CloudFormation YAML:

```
Resources:
  MyBucket:
    Type: "AWS::S3::Bucket"
    Properties:
      BucketName: "my-example-bucket"
```

This can be rewritten in Pulumi like this:

```
const myBucket = new aws.s3.Bucket("myBucket", {
    bucket: "my-example-bucket",
});
```

This gradual approach makes it easier to test and ensures that everything works correctly before moving to the next resource.

Migrating from Azure Resource Manager or Azure Bicep to Pulumi

If you're currently using **Azure Resource Manager (ARM)** or Bicep templates, moving to Pulumi can be done gradually without disrupting your existing infrastructure. This process involves using Pulumi alongside your ARM or Bicep templates, converting ARM or Bicep templates to Pulumi code, and importing existing resources into Pulumi as needed.

Working with ARM or Bicep and Pulumi together

You can reference resources managed by ARM templates or Azure Bicep without making immediate changes to them. You can use deployment outputs from Azure in your Pulumi programs, and it makes the integration smooth.

For instance, let's say your team has deployed a key vault using ARM, and you need to reference its name in Pulumi. Instead of hardcoding the name, you can dynamically fetch it from the ARM deployment.

The following code snippet shows an example of how to do this:

```
const deployment = azure.resources.Deployment.get("myKeyVaultDeployment",
"/subscriptions/<YOUR-SUBSCRIPTION-ID>/resourceGroups/myrg/providers/
Microsoft.Resources/deployments/myKeyVaultDeployment");
const keyVaultName = deployment.properties.outputs["keyVaultName"].value;
// Use the Key Vault name in Pulumi to add a new secret
const secret = new azure.keyvault.Secret("mySecret", {
    resourceGroupName: "myrg",
    vaultName: keyVaultName,
    properties: {
        value: "my-secret-value",
    },
});
```

In this approach, Pulumi queries the ARM deployment to read its output values, such as keyVaultName. These outputs are treated as reference data, meaning Pulumi doesn't alter the original deployment or its resources.

The resources provisioned by ARM remain under ARM's control, while Pulumi focuses on creating new resources, such as the secret, that depend on the ARM-managed key vault. This ensures a clean separation between resources managed by ARM and those managed by Pulumi.

Importing existing resources into Pulumi

To manage ARM or Bicep resources fully with Pulumi, you can import them into Pulumi's state. This allows you to bring existing resources under Pulumi's control without recreating them. Pulumi uses the resource's Azure ID to adopt it into its state, so that you can do future updates and lifecycle management directly through Pulumi. For instance, you can import an existing Azure key vault by retrieving its resource ID and specifying it in your Pulumi program using the import option.

The following code snippet shows an example of how to do this:

```
const keyVault = new azure.keyvault.Vault("keyVault", {
    location: "eastus",
    resourceGroupName: "existing-rg",
    properties: {
        sku: { family: "A", name: "standard" },
        tenantId: "your-tenant-id",
    },
}, {
    import: "/subscriptions/<YOUR-SUBSCRIPTION-ID>/resourceGroups
            /existing-rg/providers/Microsoft.KeyVault/vaults
            /existingKeyVault"
});
```

After importing a resource, Pulumi treats it as though it were created by your program and will track its live state going forward. Azure often injects system-generated values (such as unique IDs, hostnames, timestamps, or default configuration settings) that you don't declare in your Pulumi code. When Pulumi compares your program to the actual resource, it will see these differences and propose to "fix" them on every update, even though you never intended to manage them. To suppress those spurious diffs, add an ignoreChanges array in the resource options listing the exact property paths of the auto-generated fields you want Pulumi to skip. This tells Pulumi not to include those fields in its diff or update plan, avoiding unnecessary update operations and having no negative impact on your migration. If you later decide you do want to manage any of those values, simply remove them from ignoreChanges, and Pulumi will resume tracking them.

Converting ARM templates to Pulumi code

For a full migration, you can convert ARM templates into Pulumi programs using the arm2pulumi tool. This tool simplifies the process by taking an ARM template and generating equivalent Pulumi code. It preserves the structure and configuration of your resources while enabling you to begin managing them within Pulumi. By converting templates into Pulumi programs, you can transition from declarative templates to programmatic infrastructure management while maintaining consistency with your existing setup.

The conversion process is simple. You copy and paste your ARM template into the arm2pulumi tool, available at https://www.pulumi.com/arm2pulumi/. Select the language you want to generate the code in, and click the **Convert** button. The tool generates Pulumi code that mirrors your ARM configuration, which you can then integrate into your Pulumi projects. After conversion, you can further refine the generated program, such as adding dynamic parameters or handling resource dependencies.

Migrating from Kubernetes YAML or Helm to Pulumi

You can also migrate your current Kubernetes manifests or Helm charts to Pulumi. This approach allows you to keep using your existing configurations while moving to Pulumi gradually. You can deploy YAML files and Helm charts without rewriting them, use them alongside Pulumi-managed resources, or convert them into Pulumi programs.

Reusing Kubernetes YAML files in Pulumi

Pulumi supports deploying Kubernetes YAML files using the ConfigFile resource for single files or the ConfigGroup resource for collections of files. This enables you to integrate existing YAML configurations with Pulumi workflows without changes.

Suppose you have a YAML file that defines a deployment and service. You can use Pulumi to deploy these resources as follows:

```
import * as k8s from "@pulumi/kubernetes";

// Deploy resources from a single YAML file
const appResources = new k8s.yaml.ConfigFile("appResources", {
    file: "app-resources.yaml",
});

// Export the name of the deployed service
```

```
const service = appResources.getResource("v1/Service", "my-app-service");
export const serviceName = service.metadata.name;
```

If you have multiple YAML files, you can deploy them together using `ConfigGroup`:

```
import * as k8s from "@pulumi/kubernetes";

// Deploy resources from multiple YAML files
const appResources = new k8s.yaml.ConfigGroup("appResources", {
    files: ["manifests/deployment.yaml", "manifests/service.yaml"],
});

// Export the namespace of the deployed resources
export const namespace = appResources.getResource("v1/Namespace", "my-app-
namespace").metadata.name;
```

This is useful when you have a set of files defining different parts of your application that need to be deployed as a group.

Deploying Helm charts with Pulumi

Pulumi also supports deploying Helm charts, making it easy to integrate Helm-based applications into your infrastructure management. If you have a Helm chart for your application stored locally, you can deploy it using Pulumi:

```
import * as k8s from "@pulumi/kubernetes";
import * as path from "path";

// Deploy a Helm chart from a local path
const appChart = new k8s.helm.v3.Chart("myApp", {
    path: path.join("charts", "my-app"),
    values: {
        replicaCount: 2,
        service: {
            type: "LoadBalancer",
        },
    },
});

// Export the IP address of the LoadBalancer service
```

```
const service = appChart.getResource("v1/Service", "default/my-app-
service");
export const loadBalancerIp = service.status.loadBalancer.ingress[0].ip;
```

This approach lets you manage Helm charts dynamically, customize parameters, and combine them with other Pulumi-managed resources.

Converting Kubernetes YAML to Pulumi programs

For a complete transition to Pulumi, you can convert Kubernetes YAML files into Pulumi programs. This can be done using the `pulumi convert` command, which translates YAML into Pulumi code in your preferred language (a language that Pulumi supports). To convert the code base from Kubernetes to a language such as TypeScript, you can run the following command:

```
pulumi convert --from kubernetes --language typescript \
--out <output-directory>
```

After conversion, you can adjust the generated code to make it more efficient or easier to manage. For example, you can introduce loops to handle repetitive resource definitions, add conditions for environment-specific configurations, or create functions to simplify resource reuse across projects.

Migrating from any other cloud to Pulumi

Beyond Terraform, AWS CloudFormation, ARM, Azure Bicep, and Kubernetes, Pulumi can also manage resources created on other cloud platforms. No matter how your infrastructure was originally provisioned, Pulumi allows you to import existing resources and bring them under its management. This approach helps unify the way you manage your cloud infrastructure, using Pulumi as a single tool for managing resources across providers.

Pulumi uses the resource IDs provided by your cloud provider to adopt existing infrastructure. By specifying these IDs in your Pulumi program, you can link resources to Pulumi's state without recreating or disrupting them. For instance, if you have a virtual machine created on Google Cloud, you can seamlessly bring it into Pulumi's control.

Here's how you can import a virtual machine from Google Cloud into Pulumi:

```
import * as gcp from "@pulumi/gcp";

const instance = new gcp.compute.Instance("myInstance", {
    machineType: "e2-medium",
    zone: "us-central1-a",
```

```
}, {
    import: "projects/my-project/zones/us-central1-a/instances
            /my-instance",
});

export const instanceName = instance.name;
```

In this example, Pulumi's import option links the existing virtual machine to your Pulumi program. The virtual machine is adopted into Pulumi's state, allowing you to manage configurations and updates without recreating the resource. This ensures that the current setup remains operational during the transition.

Once resources are imported, you can integrate them with other Pulumi-managed infrastructure and apply consistent configurations across environments. The next section will explore migration best practices, which can provide additional guidance on how to plan and execute a successful migration to Pulumi from other providers.

Best practices for minimizing downtime during migration

Disruptions can happen in the middle of migrations, and it is good practice to learn about ways to reduce (or completely eliminate) the negative effects that they may have on customer experience:

- One effective strategy is to create a new infrastructure environment with Pulumi while maintaining the existing infrastructure. This approach allows both environments to run simultaneously, giving you the flexibility to thoroughly test the new infrastructure before gradually shifting traffic. By running the two environments in parallel, you minimize risks and ensure that any potential issues can be addressed without affecting your live systems.

- When handling data migration in such setups, you should make sure that data consistency is maintained between the old and new environments. This might involve setting up *data replication*, where changes made in the old infrastructure are mirrored in the new one during the transition. For databases, this could mean enabling read replicas or building custom tools that synchronize changes in real time. Once the new infrastructure proves stable, you can switch the primary database to the new environment with minimal disruption.

- Testing the new environment is a key step before moving traffic. You should run *integration tests* to ensure that all services interact as expected, *load tests* to verify that the new infrastructure can handle peak traffic, and *chaos testing* to see how the system behaves under failure scenarios. These tests provide confidence that the new setup is ready to handle production workloads. *Gradual traffic migration* is also recommended. Start by directing a small percentage of traffic to the new environment and monitor the system for issues before increasing the load.

In addition to setting up a parallel environment, there are other best practices that can help. First, maintain a *clear rollback plan* in case the migration introduces issues. A rollback strategy helps you quickly revert to the old infrastructure if needed. Second, *communicate effectively* with stakeholders, including internal teams and customers, about the migration timeline and any expected impact. *Transparency* helps manage expectations and reduces confusion. You can also use Pulumi's preview feature (`pulumi preview`) to understand what changes will be applied before running them. This step allows you to catch unintended changes and refine your configurations in advance.

With these practices, you can minimize downtime and make sure that your migration process is stable and reliable.

Summary

In this chapter, we looked at how to move your infrastructure from other tools such as Terraform, AWS CloudFormation, ARM, Azure Bicep, Kubernetes YAML, Helm, and even other cloud platforms into Pulumi. The chapter explained how you can start by running your current setup alongside Pulumi, import existing resources, and convert configurations into Pulumi programs. We also covered how to test the new setup before fully switching and shared tips for avoiding downtime, such as creating a parallel environment, keeping data in sync, running detailed tests, and having a rollback plan in case anything goes wrong. The next chapter will cover tests and exercises on infrastructure automation with Pulumi.

Questions

1. How does Pulumi's import option work, and why is it important during migration?

2. Explain how you can run Kubernetes YAML files in Pulumi without rewriting them.

3. What is the purpose of the `pulumi convert` tool, and how can it help during migration?

4. Why is it important to test your new Pulumi-managed infrastructure before fully switching?

5. What are the benefits of setting up a parallel environment during migration?

6. What is the role of gradual traffic migration when transitioning to Pulumi?

7. What is the difference between the `ConfigFile` and `ConfigGroup` resources in Pulumi?

8. What types of tests should you run on your new Pulumi environment before switching?

9. What is a rollback plan, and why is it essential in Pulumi migrations?

10. What best practices can help you avoid downtime during a Pulumi migration?

Unlock this book's exclusive benefits now

UNLOCK NOW

Scan this QR code or go to `packtpub.com/unlock`, then search for this book by name.

Note: *Keep your purchase invoice ready before you start.*

16

Tests and Exercises on Infrastructure Automation with Pulumi

The previous 15 chapters of this book have introduced you to the key ideas behind **Infrastructure as Code (IaC)** and Pulumi. Now, it's time to put everything you've learned into practice. This chapter focuses on hands-on exercises and real-world scenarios to help you strengthen your skills. You'll work on tasks such as writing Pulumi scripts, setting up complex projects, handling multi-cloud deployments, and using policy as code. Along the way, you'll revisit best practices and apply advanced techniques. By completing these exercises, you'll be better prepared to automate and manage infrastructure confidently in real-world environments.

In this chapter, we're going to cover the following main topics:

- Getting started with Pulumi IaC scripts
- Building and testing complex Pulumi projects
- Simulating multi-cloud deployments
- Implementing policy as code
- Best practices and advanced techniques

Technical requirements

If you would like to follow along with the examples in this chapter, you will require the following:

- The Pulumi CLI is required for executing commands. You can download it from here: `https://www.pulumi.com/docs/iac/download-install/`.

- Pulumi supports multiple programming languages, but for this chapter, we'll be using JavaScript/TypeScript, which requires Node.js. You can download and install it from the official Node.js site here: `https://nodejs.org/`.

- You'll need an Azure account. You can sign up for a free account or use your existing Azure account. For more details, visit the Azure website here: `https://azure.microsoft.com/en-us/pricing/purchase-options/azure-account`.

- The Azure CLI is required to interact with Azure resources from your local machine. You can install the Azure CLI by following the instructions here: `https://learn.microsoft.com/en-us/cli/azure/install-azure-cli`.

- You'll need an AWS account. You can sign up for a free account or use your existing AWS account. For more details, visit `https://aws.amazon.com/`.

- The AWS CLI is required to interact with AWS resources from your local machine. You can install the AWS CLI by following the instructions here: `https://aws.amazon.com/cli/`.

- You may also need a Google Cloud account. You can sign up for a free account or use your existing Google Cloud account. For more details, visit `https://cloud.google.com/free/`.

- The gcloud CLI is required to interact with Google Cloud resources from your local machine. You can install the gcloud CLI by following the instructions here: `https://cloud.google.com/sdk/docs/install`.

- You'll need a GitHub account so that you can create a GitHub Actions workflow. You can create an account here: `https://github.com/`.

Getting started with Pulumi IaC scripts

In this section, you'll work on writing simple **Pulumi scripts** to practice the basics of IaC. The exercises will help you define resources, manage configurations, and understand how Pulumi works. By completing these tasks, you'll build a solid foundation for creating infrastructure with Pulumi, starting with straightforward setups. While Pulumi supports a variety of cloud providers, these exercises will use popular platforms such as Azure, AWS, and GCP.

Exercise 1: Creating a storage bucket

Objective: Create a simple storage bucket on GCP to practice basic resource creation and configuration.

To create the storage bucket, use the following code snippet. Note that it contains placeholders for your input:

```
import * as gcp from "@pulumi/gcp";
const bucket = new gcp.storage.Bucket("myBucket", {
    // YOUR CODE HERE: Add bucket properties
});
```

> 🔍 **Quick tip**: Need to see a high-resolution version of this image? Open this book in the next-gen Packt Reader or view it in the PDF/ePub copy.
>
> 📖 **The next-gen Packt Reader** is included for free with the purchase of this book. Scan the QR code OR go to packtpub.com/unlock, then use the search bar to find this book by name. Double-check the edition shown to make sure you get the right one.

Your tasks are as follows:

- Add properties such as `location` (e.g., `US`) and `storageClass` (e.g., `STANDARD`).
- Deploy the stack using `pulumi up`, and verify the bucket in the GCP console.
- Add a property to enable versioning for the bucket.

Exercise 2: Setting up multiple resources using a loop

Objective: Use a loop to dynamically create multiple resources, such as buckets, to streamline repetitive tasks.

To create multiple buckets, modify the following snippet to include your configuration:

```
import * as aws from "@pulumi/aws";
const bucketNames = ["bucket1", "bucket2", "bucket3"];


// Loop to create multiple buckets
const buckets = bucketNames.map((name) => {
    return new aws.s3.Bucket(name, {
        // YOUR CODE HERE: Add bucket properties, such as ACL or tags
    });
});
```

Your tasks are as follows:

- Replace YOUR CODE HERE with properties such as acl and optional tags for each bucket.

- Deploy the stack and verify that all buckets are created in AWS.

- Experiment by adding and removing more bucket names to the array and redeploying.

Exercise 3: Using conditionals to control resource creation

Objective: Learn how to use conditional logic to decide whether resources should be created based on specific flags or criteria.

Use the following snippet to create a resource only when a condition is met:

```
import * as azure from "@pulumi/azure-native/network";


// Define a flag to control resource creation
const createNetwork = true; // Change this to false to skip resource
creation


// Conditional virtual network creation
const vnet = createNetwork
    ? new azure.VirtualNetwork("myVNet", {
```

```
              // YOUR CODE HERE: Add required properties, such as address
    space and location
         })
      : undefined;

    // Export the virtual network ID if created
    export const vnetId = vnet ? vnet.id : "No network created";
```

Your tasks are as follows:

- Add properties such as addressSpace (e.g., ["10.0.0.0/16"]) and location (e.g., "eastus") to the virtual network.
- Test the conditional logic by toggling the createNetwork flag and deploying the stack.
- Modify the code to add a default subnet if the network is created.

Exercise 4: Using outputs as inputs for dependencies

Objective: Understand how to create dependent resources by using outputs from one resource as inputs for another.

The following snippet demonstrates how to use the output of a VPC to create a dependent subnet:

```
import * as aws from "@pulumi/aws";
const vpc = new aws.ec2.Vpc("myVpc", {
    // YOUR CODE HERE: Add required properties, such as CIDR block
});
const subnet = new aws.ec2.Subnet("mySubnet", {
    vpcId: vpc.id, // Use the VPC ID as an input
    // YOUR CODE HERE: Add required properties
});
```

Your tasks are as follows:

- Add properties such as cidrBlock for both the VPC and subnet.
- Deploy the stack and verify that the subnet is correctly created within the VPC.
- Add additional subnets by creating an array of configurations and iterating over them.

Exercise 5: Dynamically configuring resources with stacks

Objective: Learn how to use Pulumi stacks to dynamically configure resource properties based on the deployment environment.

The following snippet shows how to create environment-specific resources using Pulumi stacks:

```
import * as aws from "@pulumi/aws";
import * as pulumi from "@pulumi/pulumi";

const stack = pulumi.getStack();
const bucketName = stack === "prod" ? "my-prod-bucket" : "my-dev-bucket";
const bucket = new aws.s3.Bucket(bucketName, {
    // YOUR CODE HERE
});
```

Your tasks are as follows:

- Replace YOUR CODE HERE with bucket properties.
- Create separate stacks for dev and prod using the Pulumi CLI (pulumi stack init).
- Deploy the stack in both environments and observe how the bucket name changes based on the stack.

Once you have a clear understanding of the concepts in these exercises, you are ready to take on more complex challenges with Pulumi. Now that you've practiced creating resources, using loops, applying conditionals, and working with dependencies, you can start working on bigger and more detailed projects.

Building and testing complex Pulumi projects

In this section, you'll work on creating more advanced Pulumi projects that involve multiple resources, complex dependencies, and additional features. You'll also learn how to write unit and integration tests to verify that your infrastructure code works as intended. These exercises will help you build the skills needed to design, implement, and test more sophisticated setups.

Exercise 1: Dynamically managing environments with stacks

Objective: Use Pulumi stacks to define and manage separate environments, such as development and production, with environment-specific configurations.

Here's a snippet to configure resources dynamically based on the current stack:

```
import * as pulumi from "@pulumi/pulumi";
import * as aws from "@pulumi/aws";
const stack = pulumi.getStack();
const instanceType = stack === "prod" ? "t3.large" : "t3.micro";
const bucketName = stack === "prod" ? "prod-bucket" : "dev-bucket";
const bucket = new aws.s3.Bucket(bucketName, {
    // YOUR CODE HERE
});
const instance = new aws.ec2.Instance("myInstance", {
    instanceType,
    ami: "ami-12345678", // YOUR CODE HERE: Replace with a valid AMI ID
                         // Other properties as needed
});
```

Your tasks are as follows:

- Set up separate stacks for dev and prod using the Pulumi CLI.
- Deploy the stack in each environment and verify that the configurations differ (e.g., instanceType and bucket names).
- Extend the logic to handle additional environments or resource types.

Exercise 2: Using stack references to share data between projects

Objective: Use Pulumi stack references to pass outputs from one stack to another.

Here are snippets to use outputs from a networking stack in an application stack.

Networking Stack (networking/index.ts): The following code snippet illustrates how a Networking Stack is used:

```
import * as aws from "@pulumi/aws";
const vpc = new aws.ec2.Vpc("myVpc", {
    // YOUR CODE HERE: Add VPC properties
});
export const vpcId = vpc.id;
```

Application Stack (`application/index.ts`): The following code snippet illustrates how an Application Stack is used:

```typescript
import * as pulumi from "@pulumi/pulumi";
import * as aws from "@pulumi/aws";

// Reference the networking stack
const networkingStack = new pulumi.StackReference("your-org/networking/
dev");

// Get the VPC ID from the networking stack
const vpcId = networkingStack.getOutput("vpcId");

// Use the VPC ID to create a security group
const securityGroup = new aws.ec2.SecurityGroup("appSecurityGroup", {
    vpcId: vpcId.apply(id => id), // YOUR CODE HERE: Add rules
});

// Export the security group ID
export const securityGroupId = securityGroup.id;
```

Your tasks are as follows:

- Create two separate stacks: `networking` and `application`.
- Deploy the `networking` stack first and ensure its outputs are available to the `application` stack, then deploy the `application` stack next.
- Add logic to verify that the correct resources are linked.

Exercise 3: Securing resources with Pulumi secrets

Objective: Use Pulumi's secrets management feature to securely store and reference sensitive data.

Here's a snippet for securely managing database credentials:

```typescript
import * as pulumi from "@pulumi/pulumi";
import * as aws from "@pulumi/aws";
const config = new pulumi.Config();
const dbPassword = // YOUR CODE HERE: retrieve the password as a secret
const database = new aws.rds.Instance("myDatabase", {
    username: "admin",
    password: dbPassword, // Securely pass the password
```

```
        engine: "mysql",
        instanceClass: "db.t3.micro",
        // YOUR CODE HERE: Add other properties like allocated storage
});
```

Your tasks are as follows:

- Use the Pulumi CLI to set dbPassword as a secret: pulumi config set --secret dbPassword mySecurePassword.

- Retrieve the password in your code base

- Deploy the stack and confirm that the secret is encrypted.

- Experiment with referencing secrets in other parts of your infrastructure.

Exercise 4: Implementing cross-region infrastructure

Objective: Deploy resources in multiple regions and link them together.

Here's a snippet to create resources in two regions:

```
import * as aws from "@pulumi/aws";
const primaryBucket = new aws.s3.Bucket("primaryBucket", {
    region: "us-east-1",
    // YOUR CODE HERE: Add bucket properties
});
const secondaryBucket = new aws.s3.Bucket("secondaryBucket", {
    region: "us-west-1",
    // YOUR CODE HERE: Add bucket properties
});
const replicationConfig = new aws.
s3.BucketReplicationConfig("replicationConfig", {
    role: "YOUR CODE HERE", // IAM role for replication
    rules: [{
        id: "replicationRule",
        destination: {
            bucket: secondaryBucket.arn,
        },
        // YOUR CODE HERE: Add replication rules
    }],
    bucket: primaryBucket.id,
});
```

Your tasks are as follows:

- Add properties for both buckets, including versioning and replication rules.

- Set up the IAM role required for S3 replication.

- Deploy and verify that objects in the primary bucket replicate to the secondary bucket.

Exercise 5: Writing unit tests with Pulumi's testing framework

Objective: Write unit tests to validate resource configurations using Pulumi's testing library for Azure.

Use the following snippet to test a storage account configuration:

```
import * as pulumi from "@pulumi/pulumi";
import * as azure from "@pulumi/azure-native/storage";
import * as assert from "assert";
const storageAccount = new azure.StorageAccount("myStorageAccount", {
    // YOUR CODE HERE
});


// Unit test to validate the storage account configuration
pulumi.runtime.invoke("pulumi:pulumi:test:unit", {}, (args) => {
    assert.strictEqual(storageAccount.kind, "StorageV2", "Storage account
                      kind should be StorageV2");
    assert.strictEqual(storageAccount.sku.name, "Standard_LRS",
                      "SKU should be Standard_LRS");
    // YOUR CODE HERE: Add additional assertions for tags, encryption, or
    // other properties
});
```

Your tasks are as follows:

- Replace YOUR CODE HERE with the appropriate configurations.

- Add assertions to validate the properties of the storage account, such as encryption settings, tags, or replication.

- Run the unit tests to ensure the configuration matches the expected requirements.

Exercise 6: Writing integration tests to validate deployed infrastructure

Objective: Use integration tests to validate that deployed Azure resources behave as expected in the cloud.

Here's a snippet for testing an Azure SQL Database connection:

```
const sqlServer = new azure.Server("mySqlServer", {
    // YOUR CODE HERE
});


const database = new azure.Database("myDatabase", {
    // YOUR CODE HERE
});


// Integration test: Verify the database connection
const testDatabaseConnection = async () => {
    const connectionString =
        pulumi.interpolate`Server=${sqlServer.fullyQualifiedDomainName};
        Database=${database.name};
        User Id=adminUser;Password=YOUR_CODE_HERE`;
    // YOUR CODE HERE
};
```

Your tasks are as follows:

- Replace YOUR CODE HERE with the Azure infrastructure and testing logic.
- Deploy the stack and use a Node.js SQL library (e.g., mssql or tedious) to test the connection to Azure SQL Database.
- Automate the test to run after deployment and verify that the database is accessible and operational.

Once you understand the concepts in these exercises, you are ready to take on even more challenges with Pulumi. Now that you've practiced building and testing complex projects, managing dependencies, and ensuring your infrastructure is reliable through testing, it's time to expand your scope to multi-cloud deployments.

Simulating multi-cloud deployments

In this section, you will deploy infrastructure across multiple cloud providers to understand the complexities of a multi-cloud environment. These exercises will give you hands-on experience in building and managing resilient systems that operate across diverse cloud ecosystems.

Exercise 1: Load balancing AWS Lambda and Azure Functions with Azure Traffic Manager

Objective: Use Azure Traffic Manager to distribute requests between an AWS Lambda function and an Azure function for better availability and performance in a multi-cloud environment.

Here's a sample code snippet:

```
import * as aws from "@pulumi/aws";
import * as azure from "@pulumi/azure-native/network";
import * as azureFunctions from "@pulumi/azure-native/web";
const awsLambda = new aws.lambda.Function("awsLambda", {
    // YOUR CODE HERE
});
const azureFunctionApp = new azureFunctions.
FunctionApp("azureFunctionApp", {
    // YOUR CODE HERE
});
const trafficManager = new azure.TrafficManagerProfile("trafficManager", {
    // YOUR CODE HERE"
});

// Add AWS Lambda and Azure Function endpoints to Traffic Manager
new azure.TrafficManagerEndpoint("awsEndpoint", {
    profileName: trafficManager.name,
    resourceGroupName: "YOUR CODE HERE",
    target: "YOUR CODE HERE"
});

new azure.TrafficManagerEndpoint("azureEndpoint", {
    profileName: trafficManager.name,
    resourceGroupName: "YOUR CODE HERE",
    target: "YOUR CODE HERE"
});
```

Your tasks are as follows:

- Replace YOUR CODE HERE with appropriate settings for Azure resources and configure the AWS Lambda and Azure Functions apps.

- Write a health check endpoint for both AWS Lambda and Azure Functions to monitor their status.

- Test the Traffic Manager URL to verify requests are routed to both AWS Lambda and Azure Functions based on latency.

Exercise 2: Accessing an AWS database from an Azure Web App

Objective: Configure an Azure Web App to access an AWS RDS database securely.

Here's a sample code snippet:

```
import * as aws from "@pulumi/aws";
import * as azure from "@pulumi/azure-native/web";
import * as pulumi from "@pulumi/pulumi";
const awsDb = new aws.rds.Instance("awsDb", {
    // YOUR CODE HERE: Create an AWS RDS Database
});


const appServicePlan = new azure.AppServicePlan("myAppServicePlan", {
    // YOUR CODE HERE: Create an Azure Web App
});
const webApp = new azure.WebApp("myWebApp", {
    resourceGroupName: appServicePlan.resourceGroupName,
    location: appServicePlan.location,
    serverFarmId: appServicePlan.id,
    siteConfig: {
        appSettings: [
            { name: "DB_HOST", value: awsDb.endpoint },
            { name: "DB_USER", value: " YOUR CODE HERE " },
            { name: "DB_PASSWORD", value: "YOUR CODE HERE" },
        ],
    },
});
```

Your tasks are as follows:

- Replace YOUR CODE HERE with appropriate settings for the AWS RDS database, Azure App Service plan, and App Settings (Database Config).
- Write and deploy a basic CRUD API that reads and writes to the database, and ensure that the API behaves correctly.

Exercise 3: Implementing a multi-cloud backup solution

Objective: Configure a backup solution where Azure Blob Storage acts as a failover for data stored in AWS S3.

Here's a sample code snippet:

```
import * as aws from "@pulumi/aws";
import * as azure from "@pulumi/azure-native/storage";
const awsBucket = new aws.s3.Bucket("awsBucket", {
    // YOUR CODE HERE
});
const azureStorageAccount = new azure.
StorageAccount("azureStorageAccount", {
    // YOUR CODE HERE
});


const azureBlobContainer = new azure.BlobContainer("azureBlobContainer", {
    // YOUR CODE HERE
});


// Set up a backup job to sync data
const backupJob = new aws.s3.BucketPolicy("backupPolicy", {
    bucket: awsBucket.bucket,
    policy: // YOUR CODE HERE
});
```

Your tasks are as follows:

- Replace YOUR CODE HERE with appropriate infrastructure details.
- Use AWS DataSync or a custom script to sync data from S3 to the Azure Blob container.
- Test the backup by adding files to the S3 bucket and verifying their presence in Azure Blob Storage.

Demonstrating a clear understanding of the concepts in these exercises means that you're ready to take on even more challenges with Pulumi. Now that you've practiced deploying and managing multi-cloud infrastructure, it's time to shift your focus to governance and compliance.

Implementing policy as code

In this section, you will learn how to create and enforce rules in your Pulumi projects to keep your infrastructure secure and well managed. You'll see how to write policies that automatically check your deployments to make sure they follow important standards and best practices.

Exercise 1: Enforcing resource tags across deployments

Objective: Write a policy to ensure that all resources created in a Pulumi project include specific tags for better organization and cost tracking.

Here's a sample code snippet:

```
import * as pulumi from "@pulumi/pulumi";
import * as pulumipolicy from "@pulumi/policy";

const policy = new pulumipolicy.PolicyPack("tagPolicy", {
    policies: [
        {
            name: "enforce-resource-tags",
            description: "Ensures that all resources have required tags",
            enforcementLevel: "mandatory", // Policy must be followed
            validateResource: (args, reportViolation) => {
                const tags = args.props?.tags || {};
                if (!tags["environment"] || !tags["owner"]) {
                    reportViolation("All resources must include
                                    'environment' and 'owner' tags.");
                }
                // YOUR CODE HERE
            },
        },
    ],
});
```

Your tasks are as follows:

- Add logic to check for additional required tags, such as `project` or `costCenter`.
- Write the infrastructure that complies with this policy.
- Test the policy by deploying resources without the required tags and observing the violation.
- Modify the policy to make it `advisory` instead of `mandatory` and compare the behavior.

Exercise 2: Restricting public access to storage buckets

Objective: Write a policy to prevent the creation of storage buckets that allow public access.

Here's a sample code snippet:

```
const policy = new pulumipolicy.PolicyPack("bucketPolicy", {
    policies: [
        {
            name: "restrict-public-buckets",
            description: "Disallows storage buckets with public access",
            enforcementLevel: "mandatory",
            validateResource: (args, reportViolation) => {
                // YOUR CODE HERE
            },
        },
    ],
});
```

Your tasks are as follows:

- Write the policy to prevent the creation of storage buckets that allow public access.
- Add support for other cloud providers such as AWS, Azure, and GCP to enforce the same restriction.
- Test the policy by creating a public bucket and verifying that the policy prevents it.
- Extend the policy to allow public access only for specific projects by checking tags or resource names.

Exercise 3: Limiting resource creation to specific regions

Objective: Write a policy to restrict the deployment of resources to approved regions for compliance.

Here's a sample code snippet:

```
const policy = new pulumipolicy.PolicyPack("regionPolicy", {
    policies: [
        {
            name: "limit-regions",
            description: "Restricts resources to specific regions",
            enforcementLevel: "mandatory",
            validateResource: (args, reportViolation) => {
                // Add allowed regions here
                const allowedRegions = ["us-east-1", "eastus"];
                // YOUR CODE HERE
    // Add logic to restrict the deployment of resources to approved regions
            },
        },
    ],
});
```

Once you have a clear understanding of the concepts in these exercises, you are ready to take on even more challenges with Pulumi. Now that you've practiced creating and enforcing policies to ensure compliance and governance, it's time to focus on refining your workflows and mastering advanced techniques.

Best practices and advanced techniques

In this section, you will focus on best practices and advanced techniques to enhance how you manage infrastructure with Pulumi.

Exercise 1: Implementing CI/CD for deploying to dev, staging, and prod environments

Objective: Set up a CI/CD pipeline to deploy Pulumi stacks to development, staging, and production environments using a popular CI/CD tool such as GitHub Actions.

Your tasks are as follows:

- Configure secrets for AWS and Azure credentials in your GitHub repository settings.

- Set up separate Pulumi stacks for dev, staging, and prod and ensure they use appropriate configurations.

- Set up the deployments in the pipeline after the code is merged to main, so that it deploys to dev first, then staging, before production. The entire pipeline should halt if one deployment step fails.

- Verify that the correct environments are deployed.

Exercise 2: Using the Pulumi Automation API for programmatic deployment

Objective: Use Pulumi's Automation API to programmatically manage deployments from a Node.js application.

Here's a sample code snippet:

```
async function deployInfrastructure() {
    const stack = await pulumi.automation.createOrSelectStack({
        stackName: "dev",
        projectName: "my-automation-project",
        program: async () => {
            const bucket = new aws.s3.Bucket("myBucket", {
                acl: "private",
            });
            // YOUR CODE HERE
            return { bucketName: bucket.bucket };
        },
    });

    console.log("Setting up config...");
    await stack.setConfig("aws:region", { value: "us-east-1" });

    console.log("Updating stack...");
    const upResult = await stack.up();
    console.log(
```

```
            `Deployment finished: ${upResult.outputs.bucketName.value}
    );
}
deployInfrastructure().catch(err => console.error(err));
```

Your tasks are as follows:

- Modify the script to deploy additional resources, such as a Functions app and databases in Azure.

- Test the script by running it and verifying the infrastructure.

- Extend the program to support multiple environments by parameterizing the stack name and region.

Exercise 3: Implementing resource modularization for code reuse

Objective: Refactor your Pulumi project to follow modular design principles by organizing resources into reusable components.

Here's a sample code snippet that creates a `networking.ts` module for network resources:

```
import * as azure from "@pulumi/azure-native/network";
export function createVirtualNetwork(resourceGroupName: string,
location: string) {
    const vnet = new azure.VirtualNetwork("vnet", {
        resourceGroupName,
        location,
        addressSpace: { addressPrefixes: ["10.0.0.0/16"] },
    });

    const subnet = new azure.Subnet("subnet", {
        resourceGroupName,
        virtualNetworkName: vnet.name,
        addressPrefix: "10.0.1.0/24",
    });

    return { vnet, subnet };
}
```

Here's a sample code snippet that uses the module in your main Pulumi project:

```
import { createVirtualNetwork } from "./networking";

const resourceGroupName = "my-resource-group";
const location = "eastus";
const networkResources = createVirtualNetwork(
    resourceGroupName, location
);
```

Your tasks are as follows:

- Create additional modules for common resource types, such as storage or compute, and refactor your project to use them.
- Deploy the refactored project and verify that the resources are created as expected.
- Extend the modules to support parameterization so that it is more flexible. Some of the parametrized settings/parameters can be CIDR ranges, resource tags, or resource base names.

Exercise 4: Building a custom resource component with validation logic

Objective: Create a reusable custom resource component that validates its inputs to ensure correctness and applies default values for optional properties.

Here's a sample code snippet:

```
export class ValidatedBucket extends pulumi.ComponentResource {
    public readonly bucketName: pulumi.Output<string>;
    constructor(name: string, args: ValidatedBucketArgs,
    opts?: pulumi.ComponentResourceOptions) {
        super("custom:resource:ValidatedBucket", name, {}, opts);

        if (!args.environment || !["dev", "staging", "prod"]
        .includes(args.environment)) {
            throw new Error("Environment must be 'dev', 'staging', or
                            'prod'");
        }
        Const bucketName =
            args.bucketName ?? `${name}-${args.environment}-bucket`;
```

```
        const bucket = new aws.s3.Bucket(name, {
            bucket: bucketName,
            tags: {
                Environment: args.environment,
                Owner: args.owner || "unknown",
            },
            acl: "private",
        });

        this.bucketName = bucket.bucket;

        this.registerOutputs({
            bucketName: this.bucketName,
        });
    }
}
export interface ValidatedBucketArgs {
    environment: string;
    bucketName?: string;
    owner?: string;
}
```

Your tasks are as follows:

- Use the `ValidatedBucket` component in a Pulumi project. It will look similar to the following code snippet:

```
const devBucket = new
ValidatedBucket("myDevBucket", { environment: "dev" });
export const devBucketName = devBucket.bucketName;
```

- Deploy the stack and test the validation logic by providing invalid values for environment or omitting required properties.

- Extend the component to include additional validations, such as enforcing specific naming conventions for the bucket.

- Write unit tests to verify that the component behaves correctly under various input scenarios.

Once you have a clear understanding of the concepts in these exercises, you can create infrastructure that can go all the way to production with Pulumi. By using techniques such as modular design, custom components, validation, and testing, you can write cleaner, more reliable code. These best practices will help you keep your projects organized and easy to manage, even as they grow larger and more complex.

Summary

You have officially come to the end of the exercises and the end of the book, and I am truly proud of you. Throughout this journey, you've learned how to use Pulumi and IaC to design, deploy, and manage your systems. Starting with the basics and moving to more advanced features and real-world examples, you've built the skills needed to handle infrastructure across different cloud providers and environments.

Now, you should feel confident in creating and managing systems that are reliable, easy to maintain, and scalable. You've seen how Pulumi works with CI/CD pipelines, supports policy as code, and helps manage multi-cloud setups. These tools and ideas will help you solve challenges and build better solutions.

This book wasn't just about teaching Pulumi. It was about helping you think clearly about automating infrastructure in a way that saves time and makes your work easier. Keep learning, experimenting, and trying out new features as you grow your skills.

Thank you for letting me guide you on this journey. I hope this book inspires you to use what you've learned to build systems that make a real difference. Now it's your turn to take these tools and ideas and create something great. Good luck!

‹packt›

packtpub.com

Subscribe to our online digital library for full access to over 7,000 books and videos, as well as industry leading tools to help you plan your personal development and advance your career. For more information, please visit our website.

Why subscribe?

- Spend less time learning and more time coding with practical eBooks and Videos from over 4,000 industry professionals
- Improve your learning with Skill Plans built especially for you
- Get a free eBook or video every month
- Fully searchable for easy access to vital information
- Copy and paste, print, and bookmark content

At www.packtpub.com, you can also read a collection of free technical articles, sign up for a range of free newsletters, and receive exclusive discounts and offers on Packt books and eBooks.

Other Books You May Enjoy

If you enjoyed this book, you may be interested in these other books by Packt:

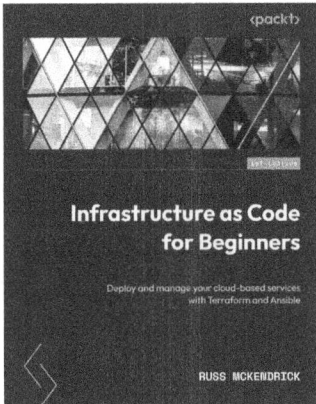

Infrastructure as Code for Beginners

Russ McKendrick

ISBN: 978-1-83763-163-6

- Determine the right time to implement Infrastructure as Code for your workload
- Select the appropriate approach for Infrastructure-as-Code deployment
- Get hands-on experience with Ansible and Terraform and understand their use cases
- Plan and deploy a workload to Azure and AWS clouds using Infrastructure as Code
- Leverage CI/CD in the cloud to deploy your infrastructure using your code
- Discover troubleshooting tips and tricks to avoid pitfalls during deployment

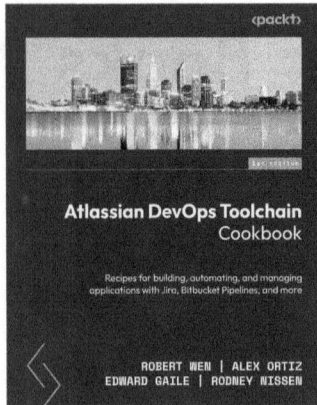

Atlassian DevOps Toolchain Cookbook

Robert Wen, Alex Ortiz, Edward Gaile, Rodney Nissen

ISBN: 978-1-83546-378-9

- Extend reporting capabilities in Jira using Open DevOps

- Integrate Jira with popular tools for tracking the build and deployment status

- Track the progress of product ideas with Jira Product Discovery

- Document and report projects using Confluence

- Create and deploy CI/CD pipelines in Bitbucket and perform testing in SonarQube

- Integrate security scanning into your CI/CD pipeline using Snyk

- Create an observability portal in Compass

- Use Opsgenie to collaborate with other teams when incidents occur

Packt is searching for authors like you

If you're interested in becoming an author for Packt, please visit authors.packtpub.com and apply today. We have worked with thousands of developers and tech professionals, just like you, to help them share their insight with the global tech community. You can make a general application, apply for a specific hot topic that we are recruiting an author for, or submit your own idea.

Share your thoughts

Now you've finished *Infrastructure as Code with Pulumi*, we'd love to hear your thoughts! Scan the QR code below to go straight to the Amazon review page for this book and share your feedback or leave a review on the site that you purchased it from.

https://packt.link/r/1835467520

Your review is important to us and the tech community and will help us make sure we're delivering excellent quality content.

Index

www.ingramcontent.com/pod-product-compliance
Lightning Source LLC
Chambersburg PA
CBHW081044220326
41598CB00038B/6975